A Memoir - in 1985 a 27 year old gay man came to London to start a new life with his partner - oblivious to the AIDS epidemic that had already begun. This is just one of the thousands of untold stories of the time.

CW00552874

The Fighting Temeraire

By

Rob Lewis

Copyright © 2012 by Rob Lewis

Cover design by dreamingdesign.co.uk
Book design by dreamingdesign.co.uk

All rights reserved.

No part of this book may be reproduced in any form or by any
electronic or mechanical means including information storage
and retrieval systems, without permission in writing from the
author. The only exception is by a reviewer, who may quote
short excerpts in a review.

Rob Lewis
Visit my website at www.roblewis-publishing.com

Printed in the United States

First Printing: December 2012

Published by Rob Lewis Publishing

ISBN: 978-0-9574766-0-8

In loving memory of my partner
Tim Tyrrel 1951 - 1990

Dedicated to

Mrs. Gillian (Gil) Parker
Psychoanalyst

&

Mrs. Shirley Lunn
the inspiration for this book without whom
it wouldn't have been written

Acknowledgments

Mark Stogdon
Lennox Thomas
Veronica Moss
Geoff Warburton
William Davidson
Max Balestra
Maria Popowicz
Frank Romany
Stéphane Masetto
Suzanne Murphy
Jenny Lord
Julia Carson Sims
Peter Watson
Vicky Gilbart
Ruby Milton
Barbara Stuart
Jeremy Sutcliffe
Ian Weaver
Menna Davies
Stevie Holland
Glen & Andy Mc William
Kristen & Francis O'Connor
Kate & Mark Terrell
Melanie Terrell
Didier & Sylvie Bodin
Patrik Ling
John-David Ridge
Peter Bussell
John Copley & John Healey
Hywel David
Mary Meldrum
Pasha

Gil Parker
Psychoanalyst

Tim was referred to me as suffering from overwhelming anxiety, underneath a courageous front. He was HIV positive, and was unwell. We met in the 14th Century tower of All Hallows Staining, and our long talks included going back in to the past, the importance of the present and finally how all the future had to be held in every year, month and day that remained. Though Tim had love and respect for his parents, he determined that he would not lay his feelings of worry, anger and injustice on them, nor on his friends or work associates. Now it was at this point that Tim suggested that Rob also should come on a regular basis. They never came together, occasionally swapped appointments. They had that kind of love and trust for each other that allowed them to know that each could talk freely about the problems within their relationship. Rob had the weighty responsibility that Tim wanted no one to know that he was HIV positive and had become ill. Rob had to forgo a natural openness, after much heart searching, to fit in with Tim's decision on this matter. During the years I came to understand more about the devotion of these two to each other and to Tim's work, and saw that inspite of the experience of pain, they each found in the other growth, courage and creativeness in the face of an uncertain future.

Shirley Lunn
Former Senior Counsellor at Mildmay Mission Hospital

In my role as counsellor at Mildmay I have been privileged to share in the bereavement of many gay men as they mourn their partners. Many have expressed their feelings of isolation and separation. I feel that Rob's book gives focus and value to their emotions and relationships. Many professionals in the caring service will be helped by this book. The differences and the similarities between gay and heterosexual bereavement have to my knowledge not been covered in such a deeply personal and sensitive way. The author's courage in allowing his innermost thoughts and feelings to be open in this way deserves the widest possible audience.

Dr William Davidson
General Practitioner MB. BS

Rob was a patient of mine throughout the period of his partner's illness and it is only now after reading this deeply personal story that I can appreciate the true extent of their anguish.

Little has been published to enlighten G.P's of the complex family dynamics that are clearly present during the experience of living, dying, and grieving in the context of HIV. This book aims to do just that to a profession that all too comfortably confines its attention to the academic understanding of disease rather than face hitherto taboo issues affecting society and as such their patients.

The Queen's Head, Chelsea
Autumn 1988

The Retro, The Strand
Autumn 2008

৵৽

I am 31. It is raining. I find an opening in the continuous roll of mainstream traffic and dash between the cars in The King's Road. I separate and turn into pretty Tryon Street with its short row of painted houses that lead to the local gay pub. The road is empty. Though lights sprinkle into the night from every window the road seems uninhabited. I run for refuge from the gathering storm. Abba is playing. I order a pint of Foster's. I wait. He's late.

I am 51. It is raining. I run down the two short flights of steps from the bustle of The Strand to The Retro Bar in the narrow alleyway of St. Georges Court. Reaching the protection of the large canopies outside this popular gay bar, I plough headlong into a noisy crowd of revellers who have spilled outside. They are oblivious to the downpour. I go in. Abba is playing. 'Pint of Kronenbourg?' the barman asks me with his usual presumptuous familiarity. I wait for Ben.

৵৽

What's happening? Edward, Riccardo, Colin, David, Jean-Paul, Graham and Tom have died. Keith and Paul are dying. Mickey and Geoff are ill. Tim is HIV +ve. Maybe I am. 'Voulez-

It's the Tuesday night quiz - 70's music. A young lad in his early twenties turns to me and asks if I know the name of the song. Of course I do. 'It's Abba - 'Head Over Heels''. 'Thanks mate', he says and

Vous', blares from the jukebox. Someone has sentenced us to a medley of Abba, but I don't mind, I like Abba. Where is he?

turns back to his friends. He reminds me of Andrew - the Joe 90 glasses, the I-know-I'm-good-looking-but-I-have-no-confidence demeanour.

❧

It's getting late. He's coming from a charity dinner. I hope he won't be drunk again - that's how he deals with 'it', that's how everyone does, myself included. I wish he didn't drink so much. Everyone comes or goes to and from hospitals, bedsides, funerals and the endless round of fundraising events. Friends become too ill to work, partners become carers, carers become single again. We live in the now, there is no past before AIDS, there is no future. I am impatient for him.

The quiz moves into the 1980's. When I last saw Andrew twenty years ago this young lad next to me was just a boy playing with his Tonka toys. Riccardo, Colin, David, Jean-Paul, Graham, Tom, Keith, Paul, Mickey, Geoff, Tim, Andrew and Sean died in their beautiful youth. There is absolutely nothing here to say 'it' ever happened. To be forgotten one has to have been remembered - they might have never existed.

❧

The collection pots on the bar for The Terence Higgins Trust, Frontliners and Crusaid are testimony to this escalating crisis. The windowless walls and solid

The glass - panelled door is propped open. Through the wide expanse of window, friends gesture to friends, subtle pick-up contacts are made. Individuals and pub door segregate us from the world beyond. Princess Diana has elected herself as Warrior Queen of the afflicted. 'The Princess of Sodom' someone called her in the papers. Her compassion and the visibility she gives us provoke reactions from those who would gladly see us all dead - they are getting their way. Where are you Sean?

groups walk by - gay and straight - some come in for a drink - others make their way with the general current of youth to the footbridge that connects to the Southbank. The Mamma Mia film poster between the windows reminds us of feeling good - despite the miserable wet summer we've had. Ben texts me. He is late but he is on his way. Its ok, I'm not in any rush.

❧

Andrew comes in with his new lover and bursts into tears, 'Paul died this afternoon at The Chelsea and Westminster (Hospital)'. I give him a hug while his friend goes to the clumsy pay phone on the back wall of the pub that increasingly distributes HIV/AIDS statistics.

Joe 90 picks up my book from the bar - Bruno Bettelheim's, 'The Uses of Enchantment - The Meaning and Importance of Fairy Tales'. I use Gil's 'Order of Service' as my bookmark - she died this Summer. 'Is it a funny book?' he asks.

❧

Andrew starts to get drunk. Abba is unrelenting. 'Gimme! Gimme! Gimme!' takes on a meaning Abba couldn't have imagined.

I shake my head musingly. He looks at Gil's funeral service sheet - I could feel annoyed or intruded upon, but I don't. 'She's important isn't she? ', he states nervously. I nod. We're both in quite deep now. He doesn't have the repertoire to get out of this. I have to rescue him. Where is Ben?

అనిని

At last Sean comes in. I find my only respite when I am with him. He swallows me up in his big bear hug - in that moment 'it' could not be happening. 'Paul died', I mumble incoherently. 'You've had too much to drink', he says chastisingly but forgives me by the end of the sentence. We lose ourselves in each other and a lager overload. We walk out of the smoky pub into the deluge. S.O.S.

How can I describe Gil in a few sentences between quiz questions? I can't. I'm saved by the 90's music round. Joe turns back to his friends. Last night I didn't want to go to bed - for some strange reason I wanted to sleep on the sofa. I've puzzled over it all day. Now I remember. In the week before Tim died I could no longer sleep in my bedroom. On the second floor, it was too far from the world. That week Gil rang me every night to say goodnight and every morning to start the day.

అనిని

Passionate love affairs like ours flourish in our brazen attempts to challenge, deny and escape death in an increasingly comfortless world. We walk along Beaufort Street hand-in-hand. Sean is so big no-one would dare challenge

I'd always dreaded Gil's death - she who helped me through so many dyings, deaths and bereavements - she who helped me sort out a lot of my baggage - she who inadvertently put me on the road to train as a psychotherapist - an evolutionary step. The us, but as the rain gets heavier we tighten our grip. I notice that hundreds of bulbs have gone out on the brightly lit Albert Bridge ahead.

irrational fear was her death would rob me of all she'd given me. It didn't. All she gave me remained as part of my legitimate life - but Gil's legacy in trust to me for my life and to pass on to others.

৵৽

I fumble for my keys. A piece of crumpled paper falls out of my pocket. It has the appointment time and address for the first therapy session I had today with Mrs. Gil Parker. Although warm and kindly, I've been wondering how talking to a posh woman a bit younger than my grandmother could make any difference. What could she know? Tim wanted me to go to see her. I went for him. What can she do? She can't bring back the dead or save those of us who are going to die.

Custodial sentences in Pentonville may have given way to Civil Partnerships, openly gay ministers fill cabinet posts and the gay scene now more overlaps with the mainstream. Retroviral drugs have changed the map of AIDS and Joe 90 isn't going to lose all the friends he is with tonight. Ben's here! He's drunk again - I wish he didn't drink so much. I understand why he does. He's been like this since he came out to his parents and they kicked him out. He's a bit of a mess now but he'll sort himself out and be ok. He leaves. I'm on my own again but its fine. I get a text. Mark will be along in a while. He's been swimming. I had a run earlier. It's good to feel fit and well.

৵৽

I expected to pay for the session but it was free. I am still shuddering at her stark words, 'I don't charge for murder, rape or AIDS'.

There is still too much alcohol in flow. The rain is torrential. I am not going yet. Abba plays on and on and on. I will stay a while.

December 17th 1990

With a sense of foreboding I picked up the Christmas mail from the doormat. My partner Tim was dying in hospital. I felt quite blinkered about the Christmas hype going on all around me but I was glad for the cards. I saw them not as the usual greeting cards but as 'love cards' - Tim had been so private until this day about his illness that few people knew he was HIV, least of all that he had only thirteen days to live. But because Christmas and his dying coincided it allowed for him through the cards to receive thoughts and love from people he had held at a distance. On arrival at The Mildmay Mission I slit the envelopes as Tim was too weak to open them himself. Though his eyes would occasionally mist with tears he received each card as a loving touch, reading the names aloud with the voice of a child. But one card was not in fact a Christmas card but from a colleague in Belgium thanking Tim for his assistance at work a month earlier; and quite unaware of Tim's plight. The card carried a picture of Turner's haunting painting of 'The Fighting Temeraire', companion to Nelson's 'Victory' at Trafalgar, now being towed with sails furled, powerless, to the breakers yard. The pathos of Turner's brushwork, more eloquent than any words, he grasped the card as he grasped the truth, his truth.

His voice changed. Speaking with a firm realisation he said, 'That's me' pointing to The Temeraire. Touching the tug towing the great fighter ship he said, 'That's you'. If ever there was a moment when Tim faced and accepted his destiny; a fate he had denied with earth shattering anger for four long years, this was it. As much as I had encouraged him to live with AIDS I realised he now needed me to help him die from AIDS. 'Yes', I said resolutely, the metaphor was true - I had nursed him along to The Mildmay his last resting place; he was magnificent still. He smiled. I had said the right thing. I would have failed him in his moment of truth if I had said crass things; and together we shared an absolute sense of love and harmony. With that momentous breakthrough Tim allowed people into his reality; his mother and sister who had known but had to pretend otherwise; friends similarly and those who had not known or suspected. He wanted to talk about AIDS, to tell people, he lost his shame. He wanted to raise money and help other people with AIDS, but it was too late for that. However Tim proved it wasn't too late to make peace with his family and friends; and more importantly with himself. He may have made the breakthrough anyway but I thank 'The Fighting Temeraire'. When I returned home that day I wasn't so strong alone. In my diary I wrote three words, 'The Fighting Temeraire'. With that dedication I too faced Tim's approaching death unblinkered, and with a sense of solitariness, and of that to come. It seemed meaningless to contemplate writing anymore in my diary after that. The next day December 18th, I managed three more words, 'My Fighting Temeraire', the following day just one word, 'Tim'- then nothing until the early hours of New Years Eve when with the time of Tim's last heartbeat I wrote '10.50', and with his death my years of diary writing ended. A few months later Shirley Lunn, the Senior Counsellor at The Mildmay proposed to me the idea of writing my bereavement story. She validated that bereavement is a profound experience and if I put pen to paper it could prove cathartic in the aftermath of Tim's death. Without doubt my diaries had allowed for me to unload, express my feelings and work things through during the four long years of pre-bereavement. I could not contemplate keeping a diary again but the idea of writing again appealed. Still I wasn't sure. Before making a decision she asked me to read a book, 'The Long Road Home', by Wendy Green. The only book I read that first year, it is the story of a young widow's bereavement experience. In a period when one has lost so many points of reference it proved both reassuring and comforting to identify with similar aspects of her bereavement. Yet her book unequivocally exposed the difference between heterosexual and homosexual bereavement. There was no point when Wendy Green was denied her rightful role of partner, either asked or expected to play role of 'just a good friend', or displaced altogether, as I was from Tim's obituary for example, something that hurt bitterly. I decided to write my story of gay/AIDS bereavement. The only brief Shirley gave me was to be honest; it's tempting to round off the rough edges. I knew the title immediately - Tim had given it to me. When I told Shirley she said, 'That's strange, I have the oak bookcases at home taken from the master's cabin of 'The Fighting Temeraire'!

The Fighting Temeraire

By

Rob Lewis

CHAPTER 1

10.50pm December 30th 1990

Many of the themes and phases of bereavement have no clear beginnings or endings. I do not know whether bereavement gradually diminishes, or is only snuffed out with ones own death, or in fact has a defined conclusion; but I do know my bereavement began precisely at 10.50pm on December 30th 1990. I was with my parents at home in the sitting room killing time until midnight when I was to ring the Elizabeth Ward. They would tell me of Tim's chances of getting through the night, and whether I should return to The Mildmay. Though he could die at any moment, equally he could live a few days longer. You may wonder why I wasn't there already: Tim's condition had been grave for three weeks. In that time I learned that it is virtually impossible to spend twenty four hours a day with ones partner; at least this was so for Tim and me. More so Tim had always needed space in living, no less in dying. The phone interrupted the waiting game. It was Kate. I gave her an update of the situation. As I put the phone down it rang again. It was Debbie, one of Tim's nurses. 'He's just gone', she said. I told her I would be there as quickly as I could. I didn't think in terms of pre-bereavement and bereavement, but the latter had begun.

It felt as if my brain had been numbed with a strong measure of vodka. Immediately I rang Kate. Because we had been speaking at the moment of his death it seemed right she should be the first to know Tim had died. Conveniently Tim and I lived very near The Mildmay; it was only a ten minute drive at this time of night. As I sped past stragglers leaving 'The Falcon & Firkin' I was amazed life could carry on without Tim. In Hackney Road party-goers were queuing to enter a disco pub. How dare they! The night porter had opened the hospital gates and admitted me to the hospice. I raced up to the Elizabeth Ward and was immediately embraced by Debbie, Helen and Bernie the night staff. Surprisingly, not surprisingly the ward was warm and cosy, the fish in the aquarium still swimming aimlessly around - I found this thread of continuity extremely comforting. Debbie led me to the day room where Bernie made a big pot of tea. My parents arrived soon after. Tim's parents were with him. My parents were with me. We waited, I wasn't sure for what.

Helen told me the circumstances of Tim's death. At 10.50pm she had asked Tim if he wanted some morphine to help relieve his cough. His breathing suddenly changed, he breathed three times more and died with his mother beside him. Tim's father, asleep in a room nearby was called. Debbie had been assigned to other patients that night but because a special friendship had developed between us she had asked Helen's permission to telephone me, to be the one to break the news of his death. Tim had been such an independent character it wouldn't have been wrong for him to die alone; but that he had kept his family out of his reality for so long it seemed right his mother should have the moment of his death; and likewise for his sister who had the privilege of sharing his last morning at home. We didn't have to wait very long before Tim's parents came in, his father clearly numb with shock, his mother had an expression of the most profound grief I have ever witnessed. What was the protocol? The fathers' who had not met before shook hands with a stiff awkwardness. The mothers' embraced. Tim's mother said, 'You will excuse us if we are not sociable'. There were no words of condolence from me to them or from them to me. It would be wrong to say we ignored one another; it would be wrong to say we were unaware of one another. Simply they were dealing with the enormity of their loss, I with mine. Yet we were vulnerable to one another's grief.

Helen led me to Tim's room. There seemed to be a format to follow. Walking along that familiar corridor I was in her hands, malleable, I had lost all reference points but for Helen, I had no mind of my own and would do whatever she told me. I had cried tears of anticipatory grief for this moment on December 20th 1986 when Tim told me he was HIV; and nearly every day for the first six months of 1987 knowing in my heart I would lose him. I had wept when we separated on August 31st 1988, Tim needing total space to contemplate his destiny. I had cried in early 1989 when he became ill and again when we were reunited shortly after. These previous three weeks confronting Tim's imminent death I had cried more than I'd thought it possible. Now I had no tears, I had cried them all. Approaching the door of his room I was scared, I'd never seen a dead body before. I asked Helen to come in with me. I corrected my thoughts before even opening the door - how could I ever be frightened of Tim, especially he now so vulnerable. Maybe I had only imagined death bed scenes in terms of clinical mortuaries. I don't know why I was surprised the room was the same as when I'd left at 9.30pm - the bedside lamp casting a soft light, his clock and radio on the bedside cabinet, my Christmas card to him on the bookshelf next to the one from Veronica Moss, the medical director, the little Christmas bear he'd given me the year before, the Christmas bauble from Barbara, the flowers, his slippers and dressing gown - but I was surprised; it was all so normal, familiar and comforting. Tim was lying peacefully, his arms outside the sheets, his head nestling in the supporting pillows. I was startled that his mouth was wide open. He had died gasping for breath to hold onto the life he had cherished and relinquished so reluctantly - but it didn't matter. We sat down on stools next to the bed. I wasn't quite sure what to do. I spontaneously took out a number of photographs I had been carrying of Tim from happier days to show Helen. She said it helped her to see such photographs because often patients have changed irrevocably by the time they are referred to

The Mildmay for respite or terminal care. She thought it a good idea we spend some time alone and said she would be nearby if I wanted her; also that it was best if we said our final goodbyes. And she left us. I couldn't fathom or comprehend this as our last time together. It just didn't register. Couldn't I see Tim again, I wondered? Apparently it wasn't possible. I wanted to know why but I felt too frail to question the nurse's authority. I held his hand and called his name. I wanted to hold him once more so I climbed onto the bed and lay next to him, holding, cuddling, comforting, and protecting him one last time. I kissed him but the weight of my body caused fluids to gurgle within him. And then he moved! I almost fell off the bed with fright. I thought for an instant he had come back to life or that it was a nervous reaction. In fact the special water mattress sent ripples of water beneath him so gently lifting his body. It hadn't been turned off! It would have appealed to his sense of humour but did not to mine. It seemed right after that to just sit quietly by his bedside holding his hand. I said and thought different things. You are free now Tim. The virus is dead. No more pills, treatments, pain and suffering and peace at last for my dear Timmy. I was so relieved his lovely face had largely escaped the ravages of Kaposi Sarcoma. I felt I should think or say other things, or cry, or pound the floor with grief, or be melodramatic in some way, but it wasn't like that. It was very quiet. I sat perfectly still, my breathing slowed until it was almost imperceptible; my mind was empty of thought. One minute passed, maybe twenty, probably just a few. No-one called me; it just seemed the right moment to go. I held his hand tightly, the two T's[1] (Tim and Tony) as Barbara always called us, together for the last time. I wished him 'God Bless, Sleep Tight', as I'd said a thousand times before. I kissed him and left the room as quietly as I could trying not to disturb the stillness.

Practical necessities dominated - Debbie and Helen were going to shave, wash and dress Tim - but in what? I didn't want him in a

---

[1] Some old friends knew me by the diminutive Tony of my middle name Anthony

shroud or funeral clothes. I nominated his smart navy blue pyjamas. I knew he liked them and they suited his dark colouring. Luckily I'd brought them to The Mildmay earlier that day so he would have a spare pair with no idea of their ultimate purpose. I suspected he may have left funeral instructions attached to his will. I told the nurses that if when I returned home and discovered he wished to be laid out in a particular motorbike T-shirt for example then I would ring and return with the specified item(s). They asked me to return anyway the next morning at 10.00am. I couldn't think why. I didn't ask. I said I would. I next remember being in the car alone driving home. I was horrified that people were still queuing to enter the same disco pub I had passed two hours before.

It was the early hours of New Years Eve, December 31st. It was hard to grasp the fact Tim had been left behind on December 30th - he'd already died 'yesterday'; harder still the prospect that within 24 hours I would be cast into 1991, alone. Death had separated us. My parents arrived home soon after me. I poured three large gins and tonic but they were left untouched. My mother made tea. I rang my sister. Earlier that evening she had arrived at The Mildmay to give me some moral support. She and Tim had never been close - until the end, when as his last visitor Diana and he shared the reality of what was his leave-taking of this earthly life. She had offered to stay the night but it was possible he might live days more yet. There was nothing she could do so I said she might as well go home. My mother had reached her on the car phone to tell her of Tim's death. She had been so upset her boyfriend had to stop the car on the motorway to comfort her. Now she seemed relieved and reassured to know I was calm and controlled - I was on the outside; but extraordinary things stirred deep. I said goodnight to my parents who seemed to have a stoical acceptance of what had occurred since their arrival in London eight hours before. I was reassured by their presence.

I went to my bedroom shutting the door on the world. I wanted to be alone. Tim had made his will only ten days before at The Mildmay and given it to me to take home for safekeeping. I took it from my bedside cabinet and opened it. Glancing through the many pages I was surprised how detailed it was; but I found no funeral instructions at all. This surprised and worried me, but that problem would have to wait until tomorrow. I was glad I didn't have to return to The Mildmay. I undressed and climbed into bed quite content with the knowledge Tim was in good hands; that he unknowingly had bought his own funeral clothes with his purchase of those blue pyjamas from Marks & Spencer's. Unexpectedly I was overtaken by an extraordinary sense of liberation for both Tim and myself. It was as if I had been locked away behind a thousand prison doors and every few minutes another door opened. Already this unfettering had released me from my two year sexual torpor since our reconciliation; I was quite unprepared for this reawakening. I couldn't explain or understand it at the time, I felt ashamed I should even have such thoughts; but the truth was I felt very in touch with my sexuality - my homosexuality. If one of my hero film stars had materialised in bed next to me........but profound exhaustion took over. For the first time in four years since Tim's HIV diagnosis I had regained some certainty in my life again; no more weeks and months of helpless looking on; no more wondering what hells each new day would bring; no more nights of fitful sleep half listening for Tim to call, or waiting for the phone to ring. I knew where I was. I switched off the light and amazingly had the best night's sleep I'd had for years.

CHAPTER 2

New Years Eve

During the first year cycle following the loss of ones partner there are many emotional hurdles, anniversaries, birthdays and festivals to negotiate. New Years Eve was to be my first complete day of bereavement, my first complete day of life that Tim would not be part of. I woke to discover the sense of liberation on which I had gone to sleep had mutated to euphoria during my deep dreamless sleep; but it was tempered by an underlying numbness and an overlying feeling of disorientation. Everything looked the same as it had the morning before - the house, the car, the road to The Mildmay; but nothing felt the same or was the same anymore; and never would be again. I was given a warm welcome by the day staff of The Elizabeth Ward. I had to stop myself asking, 'How is Tim, how did he sleep?' I couldn't help but glance along the corridor that led to Room 5. Contrary to my usual habit of saying hullo to Tim I now headed for the day room at the opposite end of the ward. I spied Tim's parents in the adjacent conservatory, they had stayed overnight at the hospital. They reminded me of a photograph of Titanic survivors on board the rescue ship Carpathia; as I probably looked too; trying to take stock of the unimaginable. Again as the night before there could be no words between us; but the silence was overwhelmingly eloquent.

It was Vera, the mother of one of the lads on the ward who embraced me; yet I comforted her too. 'I've just been told', she said with tears in her eyes, 'remember the good things.' She had never met Tim for he had been too ill to leave his room unlike her son who hadn't lost his mobility; but Tim's death was acutely painful for her, a rehearsal of the imminent loss of her much loved son; and the bereaved mother she would shortly be too.

All cultures have their gestures of palliative countermeasure. The British make tea. I held the mug the nurse gave me as if she had given me a draught of some strange elixir that would make everything feel OK that wasn't so. A consequence of too many powerful and diverse emotions had left me emotionally hungover. Mrs Shirley Lunn, the Senior Counsellor stepped into my bewilderment. She introduced herself to me and gently explained that when I was ready we would join with Tim's parents in the ward counselling room to discuss the funeral arrangements - this was the reason I had been asked to return. The blend of emotions left me extremely impressionable; I can still remember the flower motif on the mug I held, Shirleys attractive olive green outfit, Vera's pale blue blouse, indelibly recorded on memory. Not twenty four hours before Tim had come out of a deep sleep and said, 'you've got to do something (to make me live).' I could do nothing except love him. It showed just how much Tim and I had lived with his dying; my mind always boomeranging back to the living side of HIV every time my thoughts had dared to venture beyond the ending of Tim's life. I wasn't ready or prepared for this discussion. Shirley immediately became my strongest orientating factor. She was in command. I followed willingly. I had never had a serious sit down discussion with Tim's parents about anything; it seemed bizarre to be doing so now, and doubly bizarre that the subject was Tim. His father was still in deep shock but His mother had reined in her emotions and was very much in control. Tim's life had kept us deferentially apart; his death now thrust us rudely together. I was feeling very proprietary about my partner; she of her son. Having been Tim's prime carer all along, this role still accorded to me (by policy) of the staff who took over terminal nursing responsibilities; I found it hard now to share any responsibility, even posthumously. I volunteered that Tim had left no formal funeral instructions in or attached to his will; that we should pool our knowledge to follow Tim's wishes through as we best believed he would have wanted. Casting her eyes down to avoid mine Tim's mother declared, 'a small private family funeral'. There was no negotiation. Maybe this had been Tim's wish, she did not say so if it was; I was left with the feeling it was her wish; that having been excluded for so long, she would now claim him and exclude everyone else, me included if she had been able to. It just seemed so sad that following Tim's triumphant breakthrough of December 17th after which he admitted family and friends she now closed it all up again. Tim didn't belong just to his blood family and 'little family' (as he called me and Pasha, our dog); he had given himself to many people. I knew Tim wanted to be cremated for he had said on a number of occasions, 'I'll just be a pile of ash and all you'll have left of me will be a pile of photographs.' Tim's mother stated the spot in Epping Forest where he wanted his ashes scattered that Tim had confided to his mother. Though I was the only one who could find the picnic spot Tim had nominated, I was jealous that even one detail he could share with anyone but me; to be excluded by Tim from anything was agonizing; it gave me some measure and understanding of the store of pain his mother carried at her near four year exclusion, and the jealousy and envy she had not been able to conceal from me the last days of his life. We all want to be included interpreting inclusion for the validation of how much the departing/departed loved one values us; but sometimes exclusion is a sign of protection. Though Tim never gave his family a chance to prove themselves during the long course of his illness believing they didn't have the strength to cope collectively as a family unit with the realism of AIDS; he was never short of gestures of love for them that strangely he would communicate to me and not to them; the first time he met his mother following his HIV diagnosis he came home and cried volumes of tears on my shoulder for his love for her; her unawareness protecting her from the veiled prebereavement she was experiencing; Tim crying her tears of anticipatory grief; his own too; she allowed for this that he couldn't. One of the nurses told me many months later that similarly Tim doubted my coping ability to survive without him. Knowing how much I loved him and depended on him he feared I would take my own life; that he just could not discuss aspects of his funeral with me. I asked Shirley if I could see Tim again. She said, 'there has to be a parting and maybe its best not to disturb the memory of your goodbye.' I pushed the point. I put her in the difficult position of having to confront me with DHSS rulings that state that a person dying from a communicable disease must be sealed on death in a body bag. I was aghast. An image of Tim being sealed in a black rubbish sack flashed into my mind. I started to get very anxious for Tim; I couldn't bear the thought of him being humiliated in any way. To relinquish the caring role to a mortician who as I saw it was going to degrade Tim to nothing better than refuse was unthinkable. Tim's mother said, 'Don't (cause a fuss)', under her breath. How could she allow it either? Shirley said, 'There is a way around it. Come and see me this afternoon when you come back to collect Rob's things.' I backed down. Shirley was the first but not the last to unknowingly interchange my name with Tim's following his death. It was interesting to hear my name being used in the past tense and Tim's in the present; I imagined my parents here with Tim discussing arrangements for my funeral with Shirley; it could have been so. Such is fate and the indiscriminate chance of life. 'I am one of the chosen', he once said. People had always mixed our names up; this thread of continuity from our life together was gently comforting. Whenever I am still called Tim I glow inside.

With Shirley's help we achieved that morning what otherwise would have taken days. She provided us with a route map to Bromley Public Hall to register Tim's death and to a sympathetic undertaker in Dalston. While we were on the road she would liaise with Golders Green Crematorium and the undertaker to arrange the funeral. It felt very strange as we set off in the car. Life hadn't deviated from the roads that linked home to The Mildmay for what seemed like time immemorial. To be on the open roads of London in unfamiliar neighbourhoods in heavy New Years Eve traffic was a brutal exposure to life again. Everything had been so focused it was like being forced to stare at the sun; it was too powerful. The world seemed very big, I felt very small. Additionally I had never driven Tim's parents anywhere before; this too was as strange for me as it must have been for them. Suddenly we were quite detached from the AIDS situation. As I sped past Mile End underground station I wondered if it had happened at all. A sense of unreality joined the other emotions in my head. Was it all just a bad dream? No, the map gave proof of our grim task. His mother summed up how we felt, 'we don't want to be doing any of this but it has to be done.'

Tim's father was incapable of entering into any of the proceedings still quite immobilized by shock. His mother and I took our places in front of The Registrar of Deaths, a kindly talkative woman. We came not as mother and partner but informants. His mother handed over the death certificate signed by Ruth Richmond one of The Mildmay doctors. This was the bureaucratic side of death; the Registrar began to enter details in a ledger. I was in the midst of learning that death is the begetter of bereavement for some; yet a source of occupation for others. She told us she held the original ledgers certifying the deaths of Jack the Rippers victims slain in the locale - I wondered who had been the informants of those unfortunate women; you don't see this side of it in the films made about the notorious murders. She then transferred the details to a separate certificate and made ten copies at Shirley's suggestion. Tim who I could still only see as a symbol of life was now bound to death; his name inextricably linked to the boxed word 'DEATH' at the top of the certificate; this was the immediate representation of what had befallen Tim, his parents and me. In the heavy rain outside it seemed the sky shed tears for Tim.

On we went to the undertaker. By bus, motorbike and car Tim and I had passed this funeral parlour a thousand times, obliviously; it having been Tim's destiny to be brought to this place. I tried to tell myself that the important thing was that Tim was looked after respectfully; but I felt overwhelmed by the impedimenta of death - the black crosses, purple drapes, the smell, the 'menu' of coffins we were shown. It was totally unreal as if being on a set of a Hammer Horror film. I couldn't wait to get out. Shirley had already arranged the funeral with Golders Green Crematorium and telephoned the undertaker with the facts. All we had to do was agree details of Tim's sojourn in the Chapel of Rest and the funeral itself. Though I would have liked the funeral to be open to all; we both agreed absolutely in the simplest form of service free from expensive needless trappings that Tim would have hated. Still we had to pay £25 for the use of a tape recorder to play a cassette that I would provide for the funeral which seemed an outrageous sum of money. This was the moneymaking side of death. The palpable manifestation of Tim's death kept mutating. It began with a phonecall, then it was Tim himself lifeless and inert, then it was a certificate, now it was ritualistic.

I felt I was a traitor to Tim, he a champion of life and living; we had just betrayed him to a keeper of death. His mother wanted to arrange for some flowers to go in the coffin with Tim from her. I walked her through the rain to an impoverished depressing flower shop nearby. There was nothing suitable so I promised to arrange this for her. Then the first hiccup followed. She created the moment to begin the public misrepresentation of Tim's demise; that Tim's obituary would state 'family flowers only, donations to 'cancer' charities.' 'We only want to respect Tim's wishes', she said betraying Tim's triumphant breakthrough of

December 17th. Whatever conversations he had had with his parents; they were not the same as the ones with me; this was her wish. Already on the truth side of four years of deceits, lies and collusion I found any tampering of the truth abhorrent. I did not have the emotional vigour to assert my legitimate viewpoint. Then glancing at Tim's father in the car I was more than a little perturbed to see an expression of anger, rage and hate takeover his features as his eyes briefly met mine. She was right; we did not want to be doing any of this. I did not want to be doing any of this. I just wanted to go home. I drove back to The Mildmay so they could collect their car. I shook his hand and kissed her goodbye. 'See you Friday', she said. I put them on the road for home.

As they were swallowed up in the compassionless New Years Eve traffic for the long drive home to Sussex I felt a deep sympathy for them; yet a vague sense of unease loomed; things were not the same between us as before Tim's death; seeds of discord had been sown both sides. It seemed strange that one could feel good about such morbid things as 'arrangements' having been completed so swiftly; euphoria returned. I gladly returned to my home to my parents. Their stalwart support against an emotional and physical backdrop where everything had altered was incredibly reassuring. I felt like a young boy again not a fellow of 33. They were so dependable for being exactly who they were - Mum and Dad. I wanted a drink. Instead my mother as mothers do insisted I sat down to have a bowl of soup and toast, my first food since Tim's death. Everything seemed so new, it could have been the first bowl of soup I ever tasted. It was going to be a busy day.

After lunch I returned to The Mildmay to collect Tim's things. The immediate hype had passed, families and friends had dispersed; it was back to how it had been prior to December 17th when The Mildmay had seemingly belonged to just Tim and me and the nurses. But now we were separated. Tim was in the mortuary awaiting collection by the undertaker. But I wasn't alone, Shirley met me. She advised me that she had arranged for the coffin to be delivered to The Mildmay; that Tim would be transferred in it; the body bag would not be used. With this last action I relinquished my caring role for Tim; it was the last thing I could do for him. I knew he would have done similarly for me. In fact The Mildmay were about to review the use of body bags. On examination of DHSS directives they discovered they were in fact guidelines and not rules. The hospital consequently dispensed with this practice; though they are still used at most acute centres. The Mildmay would only use them in certain cases of body fluid leakage. And now it is possible for family and friends to view/visit the body after death. Though this wasn't accorded to me, my adieu to Tim the night before was free from all funereal trappings, devoid of any morbidity, as natural a goodbye can be. It is a treasured memory and always close by. For the last time I trod the familiar path to Tim's room. The sheet-less bed shocked me. Where was the light blue bedding and comforting duvet? The plastic coated mattress was so final. It felt as if Tim had been abducted. The mattress became another representation of death; I could only interpret death at this early stage through symbols. All Tim's things and the few of mine had been packed by the nurses in cardboard boxes; it was astonishing that death could dislodge someone from life so easily. 'We have 40 years together', Tim had once said; I had come to the room of my partner to find death had devalued our relationship to superfluous baggage. Then I saw the beautiful bouquet of red roses delivered that morning, for Tim - too late. I read the card, 'Thinking of you all the time, lots of love Julia x x x.' Kate had been the first friend to be told of Tim's death; now it seemed Julia was the first friend to honour his good life as if she had laid the flowers at the foot of his deathbed herself. It was time to leave again. I felt very emotional, far more than the night before. It was the room where his generous life drew to a close; the room where our physical relationship had ended; where my privileged role of carer terminated. More so this room, ward and hospital had become our joint home since Tim had been admitted for terminal care. With a terrible ache in my heart it was for me to take his things quickly; as someone had died and made way for Tim; the room already belonged to the next patient. It was (and still is) the room where my bereavement began.

I unpacked everything as quickly as possible. I put Tim's clean clothes back in his wardrobe, the dirty ones in the wash basket in the utility room, his books, magazines, clock and radio by his bed, his address book back in its usual place atop mine on the kitchen window sill by the wall phone, his slippers by his bed, his dressing gown in the airing cupboard where he always kept it, the little Christmas bear he had given me back on the top of the Christmas tree from where I had taken it to The Mildmay, the travel bags back in my wardrobe, his wash bag and toiletries in the bathroom, the empty boxes in the rubbish room. This was the last time I would unpack for Tim; I had helped him many times on return from work trips abroad, holidays and more recently stays in hospital. Already I mourned the passing of my caring role; this time unpacking felt more like a solemn rite because it wasn't part of life ongoing; I put everything in its normal place because I didn't know what else to do. But by the time I finished I realised that in the whirl of speed I reinstated everything I had re-established Tim's home, my home, our home back in the modern town house in Hackney where we had lived together. It had been a shell of bricks and mortar since Tim left almost one month before. I had truly come home. I placed Julia's red roses on Tim's desk in the sitting room. My parents had been acting as switchboard giving the news of Tim's death to friends ringing in to enquire after him. Word was spreading. I was running on adrenaline and was about to begin the formidable task of working through our address books but Mum made me a cup of tea and made me sit down for a moment. I tried to take stock. I felt surprised that in fact I felt no different than if Tim was working abroad; emotional feelings for him had not been nullified with this physical departure. When he had worked in Vienna, Cardiff, or Hamburg we had been physically separated but love remained. No less now. Peter rang in tears. It was strange I should be the one to console him; but how could I miss Tim or weep if I still felt he was nearby. Ominously I grasped the fact that if he had been at work his motorbike, crash helmet and gloves wouldn't be in the garage or his jacket over the back of the kitchen chair. If he had been abroad his address book wouldn't be on top of mine, one or more travel bags would be missing from my wardrobe and clothes from his. All Tim's possessions were here, everything - but for Tim himself. EVERYTHING being here plus the large manilla envelope on the kitchen divider with its morbid papers gathered that morning from the registrar and undertaker were the tangible proof Tim was not working in London or abroad on business. Like a dragging anchor I grappled hopelessly trying to comprehend the fact, 'Tim is dead'.

When I opened Tim's address book I was nonplussed to discover that since I had last looked up a telephone number for him only a couple of days before he had carefully annotated all entries of who he wanted me to contact and not. It would have been one of if not his final tasks of life, endorsing the value with which he held his friends and colleagues; and most importantly that he did it at all, his begrudging but no less acceptance of impending death. The first person I rang was shocked and very upset; but there was also a feeling of 'how can anyone be telling me such bad news, it is New Years Eve and my guests are about to arrive'. The reality is that people do die during festivals and times of celebration, not only at anonymous times of the year. However I decided to postpone the job of informing people, it wasn't fair on them, and this could wait until tomorrow. I had been running parallel to New Years Eve but at this point my first day of bereavement amalgamated with the festive nature of the day unexpectedly giving me time-out from first bereavement responsibilities. I had a welcome hot bath. I bathed in euphoria. I felt like partying; to celebrate the end of Tim's suffering. I dressed in bright clothes. Tim's boss Jeremy arrived with a long list of foreign colleagues he and his secretary Anina had informed; this was exceptionally helpful and took the pressure off the task ahead of me. Jeremy didn't stay but other close friends congregated. Vicky, Andy and his wife Glen had cancelled formal celebrations; yet it seemed right for us to join together in meaningful union in

Tim's home. Somebody suggested we went to 'The Falcon & Firkin' for a drink. It was appropriate. My homecomings the previous weeks after the nurses' bedded Tim down for the night at 8.30 were to the shell of the house it had become. With no Tim or Pasha our dog for company, just to counteract the agonizing loneliness I would walk around the corner to the pub for last orders before going back to the house to ring the ward for an update. The bright lights, dogs, music, tinkle of fruit machines, whirling fans, laughter, even an argument I witnessed; my short nightly visits remained my only surviving reference to normal life. Now with happy people crowding into the pub 'The Falcon & Firkin' seemed to be the very source of ordinary life itself.

What I didn't understand was that already this first day, the overall definition of the year ahead had been defined. Prebereavement had been a long drawn out process, a diminishing, relinquishing, narrowing process of four years leading to that inevitable lonely walk with Helen to Tim's deathbed; bereavement has proved similarly a lengthy process, an expanding, enlarging experience where at any one moment there are a large number of responsibilities to be juggled with in tandem.

While we were jostled in the growing throng my brain crowded with thoughts; the flowers I had to organise for the Chapel of Rest and the funeral; the music I had to choose for the service; I didn't have a suit and would have to buy one; the solicitor had to be contacted; the bank also to freeze Tim's accounts; I had to talk to Tim's sister the other executor of his will; and there were so many people to inform. Suddenly there was so much to do my mind baulked. But separately I held a deeply private image like a little cloud hanging in my mind of Tim in The Chapel of Rest. My euphoria soared carrying me to Tim, bathing him in my love. At 10.50 I celebrated the fact I had survived one full day; it seemed impossible to believe that a full twenty four hours had already passed. I didn't want to join in the approaching revelry so we went home. As midnight approached all feelings of euphoria dissolved. I started to panic. To survive one day was one thing. But so suddenly at the stroke of the clock to be precipitated into another month and year was appalling. Glenys hugged me through the midnight hour. I left Tim in 1990. It was a brutal wrench as if I had been physically dragged out of his arms where I lay with him in my little cloud of private thoughts. The separation had begun.

CHAPTER 3

January

*I*t was the end. It was the beginning.

My Dear Rob,

I was so shocked by your news about Timmy that I'm afraid my response to it was quite inadequate. My thoughts are very much with you, for I know what a very great part you played in his life. I was very touched that it should have been from you that I heard the news. I loved Timmy very much. Over the years we became very close and I have so many memories of the fun we had. He was very special to many people and will be greatly missed. Please let me know what the funeral arrangements are. If it is at all possible I would like to go, but of course it may be private. If there is a service of any kind later, and you would like me to take part, I would be honoured to do so. My husband joins me in sending you our deep sympathy.

With Love

With the first post of the year came this letter from an eminent opera singer initiating the phase of 'letters' which became the dominant theme of January; ensuing deliveries adding to the growing pile of sympathy letters on Tim's desk; a one sentence card, 3/4/5-page long letters, formal, informal, no two were the same. Hywel rang me and advised me I should change the message on the answerphone. My first task exposed my feebleness. Tim had always recorded the messages. I'd always meant to ask him how to do it. My friend Kate had helped me a few weeks before but she was in Australia. I saw just how dependent I had been on Tim and others. I cursed myself - I didn't even know where Kate had put the handbook. I had to find it and learn myself.

I could not get rid of Tim's medicines quickly enough; I wanted no reminders of his suffering. There were too many dangerous drugs to dispose of safely by putting into the rubbish, and too many preparations impossible to flush away down the toilet so Glenys volunteered to return them all to the pharmacy at The Royal Free Hospital where she worked - a 'sharps' box full of used needles, hypodermics, ampoules, bags of unused injecting material, phials of 'interferon' in the fridge, boxes of AZT, pill pots of 'warfarin' to stop blood clots, 'acyclovir' - anti Herpes, all sorts of anti fungal treatments, chest and throat sprays, creams and ointments, tonics and vitamins. Altogether they catalogued Tim's illness from when it began two years before with mumps to when it ended two days before with his death. My father took all Tim's remaining 'build-up' drinks to The Mildmay. All I kept was a single pot of paracetamol; and an enduring aversion for all medical preparations. Just over four years had passed since his HIV diagnosis which had ended the life of two healthy young men living together. It was a well house again - but now there was only one of us.

Tim was popular amongst large and diverse groups of people - the opera/theatre world, in which he had worked, the motorbike fraternity, the gay world, the straight world. It was my duty as Tim's partner to begin the daunting task of informing people of his death. I began by telephoning because it was quick; but it was exhausting work, I could only manage two or three calls at a time. Reactions varied enormously from silence, shock, tears, to anger from one lady who had not been given a chance to visit Tim at The Mildmay. Did Tim think so little of her? I tried to explain that Tim had only surmounted his difficulty of being open about his HIV status after admission to The Mildmay. She did not understand. I could not cope with anger so I turned increasingly to informing people by writing short notes on blank post cards. Ultimately there is no easy painless way to break bad news. A simple and uncluttered way seemed the best course - 'I am writing to inform you of the very sad news that Tim died on December 30th at The Mildmay Mission Hospital'. In Tim's 'editing' of his address book he had overlooked one number on a piece of notepaper tucked in between the pages of his filofax - a company producing double glazed windows! Though I contacted everyone possible, my completed task remains an unfinished one; for I was unable to get an up-to-date contact number/address for a former Greek boyfriend Tim had remained on good terms with.

Tim's sister Angela nominated her family's solicitor to execute Tim's will. I made no objection; in fact it seemed sensible as he had been in the process of completing the transaction from leasehold to freehold of the property we lived in. The solicitor asked me to deliver the will personally to Angela when we met at Tim's funeral for her to deliver to him by hand; being the only copy it should not be posted. I was advised to photocopy the will and did so. Also I rang the assistant manager of Tim's bank to freeze his accounts; I was asked to do this in writing and to supply a copy of a death certificate and so wrote the first of many business letters.

With a deluge of letters of condolence and callers one is not alone in these early days. One of my first visitors was Malcolm. He generously offered to organise the flowers for The Chapel of Rest; long stemmed freesias to go in the coffin with Tim from his mother; narcissi and mimosa atop from me - and red roses for the funeral itself. If it had been left to me I would have done something very simple; what Malcolm did I knew would be magnificent; for Malcolm was both a professional artist in flowers and one of the few who had been long involved.

Music had to be chosen for the funeral. There were to be no readings, hymns or sermon; the music was to provide the procedure of the service. What music would I choose for a period of 25 minutes? I wracked my brains trying to think of something appropriate. Music the source of Tim's working life would provide the final play out of his physical being. It was a portrait of his favourite composer Berlioz in the sitting room that nudged my memory. A flash of inspiration followed - 'La mort de Cléopâtre' (The death of Cleopatra)! This would be the appropriate piece. When I'd first met Tim he had been ecstatic about this little known work of Berlioz which he had just discovered playing it endlessly on his Walkman; and ironically two days after being diagnosed HIV he went to Spitalfields Church to see a colleague perform it. Despite the shock and numbness he must have been experiencing he returned home euphoric. I found the tape and played it. It was appropriately funereal but triumphant. Twenty three minutes long - I'd found the right music for Tim's funeral.

The first Wednesday following Tim's death I reinstated my long relinquished Wednesday appointment with Gil. The clinical consulting room, the private sitting room of a therapist - these images fail to represent the unique atmosphere of 'The Little Tower' where we met. The main body of the church long gone, a strong Gothic door separated the bustle of 'City' life from the hushed peaceful atmosphere of the high ceilinged room within the surviving 14th Century tower. There for the first time, purposely or not I do not know but I remember Gil used the word 'Prebereavement' - like the word association game, it made me think of the word 'Bereavement.' Though Gil had offered us the facility of going together we never did, I always went by myself as I did now. I'd imagined a continuum just picking up from where we had left off but Tim's death had changed things irrevocably; though Gil and The Tower were reassuringly familiar. All my previous visits had been to learn to live as positively as is possible when living with the knowledge the person you love most in the world is going to die and you don't know when or how; that one had to learn to live with fears and anxieties unparalleled - to help me - so as to help Tim. I'd had my first and last prebereavement session; for an episode of my life that had a clear beginning and ending, with four long years of struggle in between. This was my first bereavement session and nothing was clear except the beginning - 10.50pm. Of that first session I hold an image of a pile of jigsaw pieces, only the outer edge completed. Of the picture within I had no notion or suspicion that the developing picture of bereavement would ultimately successfully challenge prebereavement as my most profound life experience to date.

After leaving Gil I met up with my mother who accompanied me to buy a dark suit in the City branch of Marks & Spencers. Buying clothes was the last thing I wanted to be doing. We looked around first. When I saw shelves of pyjamas I momentarily froze - we were in the very shop where Tim had selected the clothes he now lay dead in. But then it seemed right I should buy the clothes to wear to his funeral where he had unknowingly bought his funeral robes. My aversion to buying a suit faded away completely.

The first major setback came with his family's publication of Tim's obituary in 'The Daily Telegraph'. My name was not listed. I read it again sure I'd missed my name. It wasn't there. The falsification of his life continued. In their inviolate positions as father, mother and sister, Tim's parents and Angela had been rightfully credited - in my unchallengeable role of gay partner I was excluded. It was as if Pasha (our dog) and I who Tim always called 'my little family' - we did not exist. Having seen the names of gay partners included in obituaries by more generous hearted families than Tim's I had expected to be mentioned. For what Tim was for me and me for him, for our relationship to be so publically devalued was demeaning. This was the first time I felt upset. This is a very different feeling to grief. In a strange way it was refreshing to be momentarily spared the mantle of grief. How would a heterosexual partner feel to be excluded from his/her partner's obituary? That was how I felt, it's no different. Whether our union was recognised or not by others, posthumously Tim still did recognize our close bond. Amidst the stream of sympathy letters an unmarked brown envelope arrived. It contained a 'Sea Breezes' magazine about merchant ships; a long standing interest of mine. There was an invoice slip inside - Tim had taken out a year's subscription for me shortly before he died; I looked at his cheque book, sure enough one of the last cheques he had written was to 'Sea Breezes'. I felt as if Tim had reached out to me from The Chapel of Rest; that after all he wasn't dead - but of course he was.

A few days after Tim died I fell hopelessly head over heels in love with Andy. A good friend of many years and married to my friend Glenys, I had never seen him in homosexual terms; yet suddenly I was madly in love with him. But I had enough wherewithal to understand I was experiencing the phenomenon of 'transference'. Glenys who was a nurse working in the community with the terminally ill told me once that following the death of a male patient, the surviving wife immediately fell in love with her and had to be counselled out of it. I confided in Vicky who wasn't surprised; that Andy being one of the few strong males around, he provided an innocent focus for the abundance of love I held for Tim that I still needed to release. I told Glenys I had something to confess to her one day though I never did. Throwing my arms around Andy one night he handled my infatuation as a heterosexual friend would of a bereaved gay friend - sympathetically though not without a little embarrassment. However by talking it out with Vicky within a few weeks I recovered from my fixation; and was left holding unrequited love. I felt I was going a bit mad; I didn't have control of my emotions.

As bereavement unfolds one discovers that many things are connected; there are many extraordinary coincidences. Of Tim's funeral day there was another. He always transferred his work schedule to his desk diary; with details of rehearsal periods,

Sunday technical rehearsals, lighting rehearsals, dress rehearsals, performance dates and understudy rehearsals - all the work of an opera director. Months earlier he had written across the morning of January 4th his last entry 'Cap general' (Capriccio dress rehearsal). Instead of Covent Garden's gold-embroidered red velvet curtains opening for Tim to observe the final opera rehearsal; instead the sombre door of the crematorium awaited him. He could not have known this was to be his funeral day; but his last entry symbolised his last day of earthly physical being; the empty pages ahead his disembodiment. Tim's family had one another for moral support at the funeral. I needed support too. My parents had not been invited to the funeral but still they drove me there; I needed them nearby even if it was parked in a side street close by. In our too few years together Tim had never seen me in a suit; it was ludicrous that now on such a sad occasion for once I should be smartly dressed for Tim yet not to be seen by him.

Carrying Malcolm's beautiful bouquet of 60 red roses tied with a green crepe bow I entered the crematorium. I wanted to acquaint myself with the layout of the buildings before Tim's family arrived. Having familiarised myself with The Bedford Chapel where the service would take place in three quarters of an hour's time at noon I went to the caféteria for a bolstering cup of coffee and a few quiet moments of repose. Everything seemed cold - the café, the coffee, even the men's toilets - I am sure I would have felt cold if I'd been in a desert. I needed to keep going to the toilet, I was so apprehensive. I wished one of my friends Hywel, Vicky, Francis, Kirstin, Malcolm, Glenys or Andy was there to hold my hand. Instead I had only the company of a little squirrel which came up to the French windows; the only normal and comforting thing I could relate to. Always having had an abhorrence of all things funereal, this place was living up to everything I thought it would be, I loathed every brick and stone of the place. 'Are they for a friend?' asked the coffee lady pointing to Malcolm's flowers, my testimony of love for Tim lying across the formica table. 'Yes', I replied proudly. 'Was your friend young', she continued. 'He was 39', I said. 'We get a lot of young men coming here now', she said reminding me of friends and acquaintances who had already died of AIDS and made their final journey here. But this was not a funeral for a friend, but my partner Tim. She was beginning to annoy me with her inquisitive questioning. Time to go to the toilet again; I could escape. When I returned Tim's family was seated drinking coffee; his mother emanating a forced bonhomie of smiles and small talk. Her way of coping with the nightmare situation it must have been for her, it was not mine - handing over the will as requested by the solicitor I hoped they didn't notice how much I was trembling.

The waiting game was over. It was the time. We vacated the caféteria for the tiny chapel. There were as many undertakers as mourners. I could hardly bear to look at the hearse, the coffin looked enormous. I was terrified. We entered solemnly, Tim's family sat on the left side, I sat alone on the right. Sensitively and generously Angela left her parents to sit next to me. I'd written out the movements of the music on white cards for Tim's family, my family paying their observances in the car not far away, and myself. I thought it would help to give a format to the otherwise unstructured ceremony; also to give a sense of progress through the long twenty three minutes ahead of us, and to familiarise his family with a piece of music they would not have heard before.

La mort de Cléopâtre
Scène lyrique
Poème de P.A. Vieillard

Jessye Norman, soprano
Orchèstre de Paris
Daniel Barenboim, conductor

Allegro vivace con impeto
Recitativo
Lento cantabile
Recitativo
Méditation. Largo misterioso

January

Allegro assai agitato
Moderato. Recitativo misurato

As the music began we stood. The undertakers carried the coffin past us and slid it into a square hole in the facing wall. Having anticipated scenes of heart-wrenching mad grief from any one of us; there were none. From Tim's mother there had come an unspoken command, 'at all cost don't show any emotion' thus dispiriting my mourning process. Angela and I were both irritated by the crematorium worker standing at a panel in front of us for he sniffed loudly and continuously throughout the solemnity of the music. What was actually happening seemed so unreal it wasn't a funeral anymore; just macabre fringe theatre; a three row auditorium, the dead player placed in an opening in a wall, the audience of four having travelled miles to a cold North London venue for a Friday lunchtime taped recital of Jessye Norman singing 'La mort de Cléopâtre - it was just to be survived. As Cleopatra's heart beat slowed I gave a pre-arranged signal to the crematorium worker, he activated a shutter that slowly dropped across the head of the coffin. Closing with Cleopatra's last heart beat I felt Tim would have been proud of my one and only successful stage management duty. This was the end of Tim's funeral, the end of his physical earthly being - but he had not been mourned.

Outside we were led to see the flowers from his parents, me and colleagues from the Royal Opera House. One of the undertakers broke away from his group to tell me Malcolm's flowers for The Chapel of Rest, and within the coffin, were some of the most beautiful he had ever seen. Then unexpectedly came the most real moment of the day so far. Tim's mother touched my arm with the pathos of every mother who has lost a child and invited me back to the farm to see our dog Pasha. It wasn't what she said but how she said it but was one of the most heart wrenching moments of tender courtesy I have experienced. I had to decline because of my pre-arranged rendezvous with my parents' one street away. Tim's parents' driver sped them away. I hung around for a while unable to leave; I needed a private moment of thought. I didn't know how to go, how to walk away. I didn't want to leave. How could I leave? I looked across to The Bedford Chapel, the doors now closed where Tim lay dead in his coffin. The red brick wall of the crematorium separated us. He was there and I was here, just the two of us for the last time. This was to be our parting, forever. Putting one foot in front of the other I started to walk away. I glanced back once and my heart said simply and silently, and without any to-do 'Goodbye'. I turned away. I was on my own now. I didn't look back. I turned the corner and Tim passed into history.

Tim was now in the hands of Charon, ferryman of the dead who would take him across the waters to the other side. I was in the hands of my parents who took me to 'The Spaniards', a pub on Hampstead Heath. My mother was diabetic and needed food. I couldn't eat a thing. I only wanted an anaesthetizing drink. They told me of their unorthodox 'service'; probably the only one ever held in a motor car, but no less meaningful than one on consecrated ground. I asked them whether Tim was being cremated at that very moment. They did not know. My father thought it likely he would be cremated that day. I was nervous that with him being rendered to ash I would lose my image of him. I did not.

On arrival home I received the first of many flower deliveries from friends, relatives and colleagues - the largest bouquet of white flowers I have ever seen; everything being so unreal it seemed appropriately bizarre that I should spend much of the afternoon flower arranging with my father! An activity alien to us both; death had already influenced and modified parental/filial kinship. I had invited close friends to the house that evening who hadn't been able to attend the funeral service - Vicky, Andy and Glenys, Hywel and Peter, Ralph the volunteer from The Mildmay, Tony and Charlie two motorbike friends of Tim, and of course my parents. An American friend John-David who had similarly lost his partner Edward, the first person I knew to die of AIDS, had telephoned me to say it was important to have a structure to the day. This proved true; though it was also important I believed for my guests to be included in Tim's funeral day; that they had contributed so much to supporting Tim and me, I saw it as an emotional debriefing for them. The atmosphere held of a party though my black tie and Glenys' impromptu speech 'We will miss you Tim' betrayed the absent friend for whom we gathered. That I drank enough to kill a horse to no visible affect showed just how imperiled and compromised were my emotions.

I caught the bus to Covent Garden the next day to collect Tim's things from his office at The Royal Opera House. A red London Routemaster bus! The most ordinary of transports, when had I last been on public transport? Something I used to do everyday. The smallest most ordinary step in the winning back of life can feel momentous and mountainous. The bustling London life of Aldwych this bright windy January afternoon was another rude statement that life goes on unconcerned of the agony of those within it - the seeds of loneliness had begun to sprout. Quite unexpectedly I felt very emotional on entering the office he had shared with his director colleagues. Whereas there had been nothing comforting or familiar at Golders Green Crematorium; this room held a stockpile of happy, sad, familiar and comforting memories - evoking Tim. 'I am having a ball', he said to me there when he began working at The Royal Opera House; the company were away on tour in Japan and he joked he was going to organise a coup d'état; his successful revivals 'Jenufa'; his failures 'Die Frau ohne Schatten'; 'Elektra', sabotaged by a singer refusing to cooperate; his friends, antagonists - and now all I had to show for those years were a humble few plastic bags of things from his desk, a suit and black pair of shoes. I hated leaving the Royal Opera House files on the shelves above his desk in his bold unmistakable handwriting 'Siegfried', 'Fidelio'. It's not just life that goes on but work too, I could not have them, they did not belong to me.

But I do possess and hold the precious memory of Tim

working late there one night the day before an important opening night of a new production; he rang me and said he yearned for me; would I take my work there and keep him company. Raining hard outside, it was so cosy there, just he and me, coffee after coffee, sandwiches from the canteen, his relentless teasing, the present he gave me of a bow-tie that he always did before an opening night - a night that could have gone on forever; but will remain forever.

It was not just The Royal Opera House I left but the touchstone of our relationship. Known for élitism, good/bad opera productions, and outrageous seat prices; for us as Tim's HIV experience unfurled every successive opera Tim worked on represented a different phase he/we had lived through. 'Samson' = our unsuspicious last happy days; 'Lucia' = Tim's HIV diagnosis; 'Norma' = that still he could achieve things planned previous to his diagnosis; 'Ariadne' = beginning of denial phase; 'Manon' = consolidation of denial phase; 'Elektra' = ANGER phase; 'Boris Godunov' = our separation; 'Rigoletto' = our reconciliation; 'Die Fledermaus' = beginnings of illness; 'Don Carlos' = Tim's AIDS diagnosis; 'L'Italiana in Algeri' = radiation burns and beginning of gruelling chemotherapy; 'Siegfried' = Tim's masterpiece of theatre - purporting the illusion of good health to himself, the world, me included; 'Fidelio' = Tim's swan song; 'Capriccio' = his dying and death. I had no touchstone for my life ongoing without Tim; just an empty diary.

Incredibly, one whole week had passed. My parents returned to Wales - (only to discover they had been burgled). I waved them goodbye - when I was very young I saw a neighbour putting out the rubbish in her dressing gown a few days after her husband's funeral; now I was doing the same; little things of domestic routine still have to be done, rubbish will not put itself out. The hype was over; but things had changed radically since I'd last been alone only a few weeks before - Tim was dead and I had lost my caring role; The Mildmay, The Royal London Hospital, The Royal Opera House against which our joint lives had been pitted had nothing to do with my daily life anymore, the boundaries of my life two weeks into bereavement extended only as far as 'The Falcon & Firkin' pub. I'd given all I had to give and was quite spent. With these multiple losses came a yawning sense of absence and emptiness, and I was suddenly cut off from the world we had been part of. Gratefully months of lost sleep and years of anxiety enabled me to lose myself in night after night of deep exhausted dreamless sleep.

When one is in a relationship one takes on ones partner's friends and family by association; it is only after a separation, a divorce, bereavement that you learn of the ones who value you in your own right, and those who don't. Barbara, one of Tim's longest standing friends was the first to show her allegiance; offering to come and stay the third weekend. She suggested we went to Covent Garden - I never thought I could ever return there after collecting Tim's possessions from The Royal Opera House; I now knew that unless I promptly laid this ghost I never would return. It is possible to face painful memories especially with the support of a kind loving friend - one doesn't have to do it all alone. She parked in Long Acre and we walked to the environs of the Royal Opera House - that had to be confronted first. I had made my last visit to Covent Garden as the partner of a talented man who worked at the theatre; this was my first visit as a member of Joe Public who would not join the crowds entering for a performance of 'Capriccio'. The theatre was the centrestone of Covent Garden; but it was also the cafés, pubs, shops, coffee houses, galleries, restaurants, the market itself which held precious memories - these were still accessible and comfortingly unchanged. We had a couple of drinks at 'The Globe', a meal at 'The Grill' - I had won back Covent Garden extending my boundaries beyond home and 'The Falcon & Firkin' to include Central London again. More so I took home the fact that in a changed way Covent Garden belonged to me as well, still; the enduring memory of that evening with Barbara reflecting the loss of one status, the beginning of another.

The next day Barbara accompanied me to the farm for my reunion with Pasha. I had driven there dozens of times over the previous few years; only a few weeks previously to deliver Pasha; this time the straightforward hour and a half journey seemed like a major expedition; I had to drive much slower than usual to compensate for my poor concentration. Tim's parents were welcoming but there was a decidedly formal format to events to avoid the painful topic of Tim's death; etiquette forbidding the mention of the word 'AIDS' which had taken him from us. His mother had placed a photograph of Tim on the mantelpiece; I couldn't bear to look at it - I had taken it six years before in San Francisco the very place he had contracted HIV five years prior to our visit.

This was the longest I had ever been separated from Pasha - six weeks. Our reunion was very strange. An over excitable dog he sat impassively slowly lifting his head. I patted him, he wagged his tail a little - I knew the dog well and sensed he felt he had been abandoned by Tim and me. I had to win back his trust. He was changed too. I realised that in the preceding weeks after Tim's father had gone to bed, Tim's mother would habitually stay up late cooking, sewing in the company of Pasha who was allowed into the farm kitchen in the evening; animals are very sensitive to emotions, Pasha would have witnessed and been susceptible to her grief that she may even have shared with the dog.

I'd never had an opportunity to tell Tim's family the very reason for Pasha's existence; nor did this formal luncheon provide the occasion. If Tim had not been diagnosed HIV we would never have had a dog. Following his diagnosis Tim maintained his public face; but on the home front became increasingly withdrawn as he ventured deeper into his 'denial' phase. He had always talked of having a black dog; I obliged by giving him a toy black Labrador puppy dog. Tim slept with it, carried it around the house under his arm, watched T.V. with it sitting on his lap - he would not be separated from it. If that was the effect of a toy, pulling him out of his remoteness into a 'childish' phase where he was more emotionally accessible; then what effect would a real black Labrador puppy have? I determined we would have a dog. Tim was quite a dominating character; but for once I bulldozed him into getting my own way, though there wasn't much resistance. When my aunt, who had a black Labrador heard we were getting one she asked me if I knew what a commitment we were taking on; I could say nothing of the commitment I had already taken on. For three years Pasha had spent short holidays on the farm whenever we went away, or pretended we went away if Tim was in hospital or very ill at home. This facility was now withdrawn from me. How the goal posts had changed with Tim's death. This was to be Pasha's last day as a farm dog.

Just before Barbara and I readied to leave with Pasha, Tim's sister arrived. She had just returned from a skiing holiday in Austria; she flew the day after his funeral. I found two things she said disquieting. She talked readily of crying for joy at the sight of her little boy on the ski slopes - yet I hadn't seen a hint of a tear from her at the Mildmay or the funeral. And before leaving Salzburg she had taken a ride in a pony and trap, but feeling the driver had taken a shorter route than advertised and cheated her of a few minutes carriage ride, she called the police - how can one make such a petty fuss about so trivial an incident when something as momentous as the death of a sibling has just taken place? It seemed all her emotions had sidestepped laterally from where they obviously lay with her brother - there not being a mention of Tim. I would come to recognise this phenomenon of displaced grief in relation to myself.

The good lunch was survived by the making of conversation; we all found it hard; hard for them to entertain; hard for me to be entertained. I blistered at one point when Tim's mother delivered an unnecessary broadside at me regarding 'Pasha's appalling behaviour' - though it felt more like, 'Why Tim, why not Rob?' I went into the courtyard to place the dog guard in the car for Pasha. Tim's father followed. I thought he was going to help me, instead he started shouting at me; the ambling bumble bee had turned into a hornet. 'You'll have to return the car, it's not yours, I want it back, I only lent it to Tim'. How things had changed from him shaking my hand until it almost dropped off at The Mildmay for looking after Tim; that I now along with Pasha was redundant and rebuffed. It wasn't the issue of the car or his anger that upset me; but the devaluing of the relationship and love Tim and I had shared; what their son meant to me, me to Tim - they could not possibly imagine. My first experience of gay inequality I knew that if Tim had left behind a common law wife and baby rather than a boyfriend and a dog Tim's father would have made no such demand. I couldn't wait to leave.

You may think it is none of my business how I observed the grief reactions of Tim's family. Over the years I've heard many 'horror stories' of the family of a deceased gay man versus the surviving partner. I'd never consciously thought, 'how will it be with Tim's family when he is dead?' Already I had learned that things had changed irrevocably. In their various actions and words were the ripple of troubles to come. What people think, do and say and how they grieve becomes ones business when affected by it.

Suddenly Tim's mother pulled on old trousers, tucking her pretty dress into them, the addition of an old jacket and hat transforming the elegant farmer's wife into a farm hand. She took Pasha for his last walk delaying our departure.

On her return she looked as if once again, one final time she shared her grief with her son's dog. On arrival back in London Pasha would always run up and down the stairs, search out all his toys, check out his 'territories' - under Tim's desk and the half landing, spin around in the sitting room, looking for Tim - not this homecoming. He sat impassively like a statue in the sitting room.

Barbara left the next day; this was the beginning of our life together; family and friends had effectively now returned to their own lives. I had always thought of Pasha as Tim's second carer. His role had changed too; he was now my number one companion.

Still, he needed to be exercised. Though I had walked Pasha

around Victoria Park literally hundreds of times in the previous three years; this first walk after Barbara's departure had the quality of it being the first ever; all previous walks might as well have belonged to a former life. I went to the flower shop at the end of the road and bought some early daffodils. I took Pasha to the spot near The Albert Memorial where Tim had asked me to spend the rest of my life with him; the ghost of that memory had to be faced. I let Pasha off the lead so as to be free to lay the flowers on the grass, to have a quiet moment of thought; but there wasn't much time for sentiment, I had to go and rescue Pasha who was being chased by another dog.

As of habit I walked across to the canal lock gates on the south side of the park. There one could go left or right; routes Tim and I had respectively designated 'Tim's way' or 'Rob's way'; the former remains a phantom memory, I have only followed 'Rob's way' since. I was most concerned for Pasha, even in the park he was subdued. The dog was grieving also. One night a large-engined motorbike rumbled slowly past the house sending shivers down my spine - Pasha was transformed into his old self, ran to the window of the first floor sitting room overlooking the road, turned and ran downstairs 'to wait for Tim.' I had to go down and bring him upstairs. He was quite bewildered. He whimpered. He didn't understand. Only after much hugging over the weeks did he slowly start to play with his toys again. I let him sleep on my bed at night; he needed to be hugged as much as I needed to hug him. It would have been unbearable without Pasha's presence.

The park which had shared twice daily walks with Pasha, every up and down, every anxiety and happiness of Tim's HIV experience; now shared the developing sensibility of 'stillness'; none more so than during days of heavy snow. Black as coal Pasha stood starkly out against the virgin whiteness, the red orb of the low sun hung like a bright red jewel, the snow deadened all sound, and the stillness was overwhelming. I realised Tim's death had not deprived me of the ability to appreciate beauty.

I turned around suddenly. I felt his presence. I was

convinced Tim was watching us, hiding nearby in snow laden bushes. I have been asked by a doctor if I have 'seen' Tim since his death as apparently this is quite common for the bereaved person. I have not had that experience; but for a long time I frequently felt his physical presence nearby.

I like to keep all doors in the house propped open; but now I kept the door of Tim's bedroom firmly shut, I couldn't bear the quietude of his room being disturbed. Yet to begin to fulfil my duty role of executor I had to find information and papers requested by the solicitor regarding bank accounts, building society accounts, insurances, premium bond holdings, pay slips from work. I didn't know where to begin - I'd never had anything to do with the business side of Tim's life; and had no idea exactly where to look. There were papers on his desk in the sitting room - his little green account book was still where he had left it, that he had been writing in during our last shared moment at home, I couldn't yet touch it; there were shoe boxes full of papers in his wardrobe; a huge box of files in my bedroom; numerous files and papers in the loft. Even at this early stage of exploration the role of executor became muddled with that of partner/lover. Just a job for acting solicitors, their directives laid down by the law society; for me it was not so impersonal; rummaging through files I found a bundle of anniversary and Valentine cards he had kept. Seeing the first one I had given him that I had made time warped me back to our days of falling in love at the beginning of our relationship; only then I realised I had been so numbed that our anniversary of January 11th had passed unnoticed. Tim was not a sentimental man with the exceptions of his home, dog and relationship. Having begun this afternoon's task as executor I ended it as bereaved lover missing my man. Closing Tim's bedroom door I went to my bedroom and found the pop up card of primroses Tim had given me the previous year. Just seeing his strong masculine script shored me up. I placed it on the window sill of the kitchen where it remained for months before I put it away for the last time - there are no rules.

Prior to Tim's final admission to Mildmay there had only been a polite distant friendship between Tim's sister Angela and myself; if it even qualified as a friendship. She had made only one social visit to us before the last days of his illness at home when she made several visits. I had accompanied Tim on a few courtesy visits to her home; always the conversation was pleasant but innocuous - Tim's dying and death changed the balance of our interaction completely.

Tim never asked me if I wanted any form of 'relationship' with Angela; I doubted he asked her if she wanted one with me. He just said at The Mildmay shortly before he died that he wanted a link between us. Only after his death did we learn he had named Angela and I as co-executors and co-trustees of his Trust; as if he had enticed us to a clearing, got us to sign our names together; scarpered and left us to sort things out.

By mid January we had already established a three tier relationship. On the first level we were each genuinely sympathetic to one another's loss, me to her of her brother, she to me of my partner. On this level I had told her I admired her for her strength having lost both husbands and now a second sibling. She had given me very kind words the night before Tim's funeral that I would get through it; and made the comforting gesture of sitting next to me at the service.

Not one to believe in counselling she had in fact given me counsel, the benefit of her multiple grief experiences; that these early days there is little time to grieve, it is normal for life to be very busy. A real friendship seemed possible.

On the second level as co-executors and co-trustees there was never a problem between us.

It was on the third level where she as family spokeswoman and to me as spokesman for the gay partnership, where there had already been difficulties. Prior to the first visit Tim's parents made to him in hospital Angela rang and said unkindly 'You will have the decency to keep out of the way won't you' - I knew they were upset at their exclusion; but I did not need to be told how to behave. And now with the voice of a debt collector she rang me, completely throwing me off balance. 'Money always raises its ugly head, did he have any? Also there are a large number of things we will want back from the house.' This threw me into a panic; when I could only enter Tim's room with difficulty, nor touch anything, the prospect of things being physically displaced from the house was horrendous.

The evening of Tim's parents' first visit to him in hospital I arrived with a wobbling jelly Vicky had made for him. Not even letting me put it down Tim said, 'Sit down, don't fiddle and listen', he ordered me, battling with riotous emotions. 'Promise me you won't let them poison you.' 'What on earth are you talking about Tim?', I asked wondering what on earth had been said. 'PROMISE ME', he yelled, a nurse coming in to see what he was shouting about. The only way to pacify him was to promise knowing he wasn't going to tell me anything. Well now mid January I learned that the moral is that the family of the deceased gay man who may have had little or nothing to do with the boyfriend in the lifetime of the relationship unfortunately has decisive and negative influence over the surviving partner. It would take an underdog to feel no animosity.

As Tim had left me the contents of the house I could have refused to cooperate with Angela's demands. But I did not deny that certain heirlooms rightfully belonged to his family; that they had an unquestionable moral right to repossess certain items - but in my time, not theirs. They had a set of keys for the house and I feared they would plunder the house. I had no proof they would come; yet no assurance they would not. The house was my sanctuary; I could not have it debased in any way. Only with this 'threat' did I realise my extreme vulnerability; that the heightened vulnerability of grief masquerades as paranoia. Shirley offered to act a mediator and communicated to the family I should be left in peace; that time should pass before any exchange took place. I'd fought Tim's quarter many times but I couldn't fight my own. I felt weak and unable to defend myself. Increasingly I hid behind the answer phone.

In this state of fine sensibility the after blast effects of four years of lies and deceptions brought about a mid month clash of emotion. Just because Tim had released me; his death didn't automatically dismiss 48 months of conditioning. I could still mix fact with fiction without any problem; I'd been doing it for so long I was an accomplished liar; what had become second nature I couldn't abruptly stop. Only now I recognised the psychological legacy Tim had left me with. For a long time I'd turned our fact into other peoples fiction i.e. me looking after someone very sick who I presented as healthy. It was just as easy to reverse the process - fiction into fact i.e. to believe untruths were facts e.g. I will always carry a false memory I was forced to create - I dropped Tim's razor and broke it. He forbid me to buy another. I had to borrow one yet from whom; at that time only Francis had access to Tim at The Mildmay but he didn't have one. I borrowed one from Mark though told Tim it came from Francis, pulling Francis into the collusion. I have an image of Francis giving it to me - fiction. Mark gave it to me - fact; but I have no recollection because I had to create the scenario on which Tim could accept the razor - one example of many. Mid January I wrote some crazy letters including important business letters - Shirley said a lot of people describe a feeling as if going mad; that's exactly what it was like intermittently for well over a year. Always a daydreamer I had to earnestly resist the allure of unreality; anything but the TRUTH I felt could lead me ultimately into a totally make-believe world. It was the beginning of the long haul back to reality.

Then another setback; I learned the truth of Tim's last distressing transfer from The Royal London Hospital to The Mildmay for terminal care which had been kept from me. When the nurse gave the taxi driver the destination address of The Mildmay he refused to take them and ordered them out of the taxi. Tim could no longer stand or walk unaided. The nurse panicked and ran off to get help but didn't return. Tim stumbled through the doors of the hospital and collapsed. No-one came to help him. Two hours later he was found by The Mildmay transport in great distress. When I saw him that evening he was crying and broken. All he said was, 'Torture, it was absolute torture'. I assumed he was referring to his dying, not knowing at this point of the nightmare scenario of the afternoon. He couldn't be comforted. I had never witnessed such suffering.

I rang the hospital and demanded to speak to the manager - I blasted her. She was very professional and took my anger; and in fact agreed the circumstances of the transfer had been disgraceful; that I had every right to be upset. But overall I achieved nothing for Tim, for me, for the manager - least of all for those following Tim.

Gil helped me to turn my store of negative anger into creative anger. She urged me to write a letter of complaint; that the hospital authorities would be obliged to investigate and respond; nothing could help Tim now but there were many following in his footsteps with AIDS; that perhaps he did not suffer in vain. She told me of another gay bereaved man whose partner had suffered bad experiences and had written to the hospital concerned; but that the letter written was so angry it was virulent and self defeating; that I should balance the just criticisms with just praises for the things they achieved for Tim; that if the authorities felt I was reasonable and not just angry because I'd lost Tim they might take the letter more seriously. The finished letter became an exercise too for me in not losing sight of the great care and adequate care given to Tim because of one awful and regrettable incident.

Unit Management
The Royal London Hospital   *Hackney*
Whitechapel   *London*
E1 1BB   *E9*

Re: HIV Inpatient Care of Tim
Dear Sirs

Tim was a patient of Dr. X and was under her care for the last four years. He died at The Mildmay Mission Hospital on December 30th 1990. Tim's outpatient care under Dr. X was exemplary, can not be criticised, only praised. Likewise his outpatient care under Dr. Y and Dr. Z the cancer specialists were without blemish. His respite and hospice care at The Mildmay Mission Hospital was superb. Sadly his inpatient care at The Royal London Hospital for tests, investigations and treatments seemed to us appalling and at times verged on the negligent.

Last January Tim was admitted following an excellent and accurate diagnosis for blood clots on the lungs. He was given life-saving treatment for which we were both very grateful to The Royal London Hospital. Yet it seems so sad that one such aspect of excellence became diminished by the lack of proper ward support and care verging on incompetency. This resulted in a letter of complaint by Tim and I enclose a copy of your response to Tim's letter.

The Royal London Hospital's present stance towards HIV care means that the HIV patient is 'fragmented' between many departments. Tim was quite upset last January 1990 to be admitted to a ward which appeared to be out-of-bounds to Dr. X who had to visit Tim in the same capacity as any visitor. Tim was very confident in her care for she knew his condition intimately and he felt less confident in the absolute care of a doctor he had never met. Surely this can not be to the advantage of the patient's welfare. Perhaps The Royal London Hospital could look at The Royal Free Hospital's attitude to HIV inpatient care where an AIDS co-ordinator is employed to draw all parties and departments together, where the patient is looked at as a whole and not in such a fragmented way as exists at The Royal London Hospital.

Following that admission Tim said he would never go back willingly to The Royal London Hospital for inpatient care. Autumn 1990 Tim needed a bronchoscopy. Mark, the HIV nurse rang me and asked me to tell Tim to attend the next day for this procedure. Tim was very nervous about it but attended as requested. 'Where are your pyjamas?', the doctor asked. He wanted to admit Tim for two weeks for a bronchoscopy, a lung lavage, a blood transfusion, to take arterial blood, to put Tim on an antibiotic drip if needed, etc, etc. Tim was quite emotionally unprepared for all this having psyched himself up for the one bronchoscopy procedure. He was frightened off and left. It must have taken considerable effort on the part of The Royal London Hospital to set all this up. It is such a shame that the emotional impact of such procedures for Tim, his vulnerabilities well known, were not considered. Tim told me that when one is being constantly pricked and prodded ones tolerance to such procedures diminishes.

When he finally did have the bronchoscopy and was admitted overnight, it was I who found one aspect of his care quite unacceptable. When I visited him I was asked to 'gown up.' I refused and felt outraged. Having been Tim's partner for many years and chief carer for two years I was not beginning at this stage to treat him like a leper. I thought such degrading procedures had been long eliminated. He came back to my care the next day to a home where I maintain normal hygiene/household procedures. And I can assure you that during Tim's time at The Mildmay Mission Hospital, a specialist HIV unit; I never saw any such humiliating procedures employed.

Though the bronchoscopy showed no evidence of PCP Tim still suffered shortness of breath. Routinely he attended the hospital and was kept there while X-rays were taken. This was one instance where communication worked very well. Caroline, the HIV nurse, rang me and told me of Tim's delay in coming home, that X-rays were being taken, that he would be home later. I was heartened. However I became increasingly disheartened as ten days passed before Dr. A, the chest consultant was available to look at the X-rays. During this time Tim deteriorated considerably, I was up every night with him as his bouts of coughing worsened. I understood that Dr. X's boundaries fell short of Dr. A's, that she had exerted the maximum influence she had but could only wait at his convenience, 'he is rather elusive', one of them said to me - and meanwhile Tim continued to deteriorate. My anxieties for Tim and his anxieties for himself brought about a stress situation that shook the foundations of my sanity. A great friend of ours who is a specialist nurse in palliative care at a North London Hospital was aghast at this apparent complacency, that the delay was unacceptable for one so ill and worsening, least of all addressing the considerable anxieties caused to Tim and myself. Only when she intervened directly with The Mildmay Mission Home Care Team did our anxieties begin to abate.

Shortly afterwards Tim was admitted to The Mildmay Mission Hospital for a transfusion as he did not want to be transfused at The Royal London Hospital. He was then admitted again to The Mildmay in early December for respite care where his condition seemed to stabilise.

He needed an internal investigation/scan at The Royal London Hospital as an outpatient. I accompanied him from The Mildmay. Again at an outpatient level the care was excellent - the delightful nurse in charge of the unit made a harrowing experience less so, and I thanked her accordingly. Tim was very appreciative of so many consultants being in attendance to interpret the scan and for their effort involved. Perhaps our agonies about the ten day wait for the previous X-ray results had been noted.

Yet the next day he needed a transfusion and there wasn't an available bed at The Mildmay. He rightly dreaded being admitted to The Royal London Hospital as an inpatient for the transfusion. And so began his/our most harrowing experience. I accompanied him and we waited in The STD Clinic where Caroline, the HIV nurse, had kindly arranged a consultation room for Tim to rest in - he had to lie down horizontally because of painful oedema in his legs which worsened when in the sitting position. They found him a bed and I took him to the ward myself. He was very dopey due to the small dose of morphine prescribed as a cough suppressant, he couldn't really speak for himself, he was too drowsy. On reaching the ward a disinterested nurse only knew his name for the house officer hadn't been along. She did not know he had AIDS, that he was there for a transfusion, that he needed to lie down, that he had come from specialist and sensitive HIV care at The Mildmay, that he needed privacy because he could not wear pyjama bottoms because of the sensitivity of his skin due to the extensive KS affecting them, that it would be distressing for him, and others if he was semi-naked on an open ward. She directed him to a bed in an open ward. 'Take me home', he whispered. I singled out a more amicable nurse who was very sensitive to my requests/demands for Tim. To her I am very grateful for I would have taken him home if she hadn't responded so excellently and professionally. She cleared out a room, had it cleaned and he was admitted. I dread to think what would have happened if I hadn't been there to be the patient's advocate i.e. if a porter had delivered Tim to the ward.

The next day I was appalled to learn that Tim had been moved four times from ward to ward to ward, and was very distressed. One of the moves had included a stopover on The Devonshire Ward where his sister had died just before Christmas a number of years ago. His morale which had been so good, collapsed and he didn't even want to see me. If Tim had been able to speak for himself, if I had been actively involved in Tim's care programme as I was at The Mildmay, I would have prevented that move to The Devonshire Ward. Dr. B seemed as upset as I was and apologised profusely for the terrible care he was receiving.

Once settled the care seemed kind enough and perhaps an extra effort was being made following the distress of the previous 36 hours. Still the absence of specialist care was only too obvious. At The Mildmay the patient is protected. It is impossible to see a patient there without getting through a receptionist, and a nursing station. Only then is one admitted to the patient's room if the patient is willing to be visited. At The Royal London Hospital two friends turned up to visit Tim. His morale was still so low; he still didn't want to see me. Also he was semi-naked. Instead of asking Tim if he wanted visitors and making sure he was respectable she just showed them in. They were embarrassed and left. Tim was embarrassed his physical indignities having been exposed, his dignity and vulnerability not protected by the nursing staff.

When he was moved back to The Mildmay Mission a few days later, the accompanying nurse rang to say he was being transferred *that afternoon by taxi and she would accompany him. I offered to drive to The Royal London Hospital and transfer him myself. The nurse said she had ordered the taxi and that it was in hand. What should have been a swift ten minute transfer became a two hour nightmare for Tim. (He should have been moved by ambulance anyway). The taxi driver <u>refused</u> to take him when the destination, The Mildmay, was named. I recognise that the accompanying nurse is not responsible for the transport situation at The Royal London Hospital but that in no way lessens the physical and emotional distress caused to Tim. It is absolutely appalling that one so ill and vulnerable is exposed to prejudice and humiliation of that nature only days before he died. I protest in the strongest terms at this disgraceful, bungled transfer. Your own enquiries should give you the information of the distress he experienced that day. ( ) The Mildmay Mission Hospital actively involved me in Tim's care programme, communicated with me constantly, supported and reassured me, and supported me long after his death. The Royal London Hospital's considerations for me when Tim was an inpatient were non-existent. When one makes a major commitment to look after a loved one it is not easy to 'hand over' to others, less so when the care given is inadequate. The Mildmay Mission gave Tim greater care than I could give yet they still acknowledged me as Tim's chief carer. Conversely to see Tim suffer the system at The Royal London Hospital, or lack of it caused me and still causes me despair and distress - there being no facilities to be near Tim constantly to give the continuity of care I achieved at home, that The Royal London Hospital has proved it is incapable of giving.*

HIV will become an ever increasing problem and it is vital when people are so ill that they are given as a minimum dignity, comfort and security. If the East End population is to be served properly then The Royal London Hospital must address this issue. Until then perhaps The Royal London Hospital should consider referring inpatient care to centres of inpatient excellence such as St. Mary's Paddington, The Middlesex Hospital, and The Westminster Hospital which have specialist HIV wards.

I for one when I find the courage to face my own HIV status will

*under no circumstances attend The Royal London Hospital shudder
the thought of ever needing inpatient care.*

*To conclude I am left very much with the feeling that The Royal
London Hospital's inpatient care contributed greatly to Tims'
sufferings instead of helping to alleviate them.*

Yours faithfully, Rob Anthony Lewis

*P.S. None of my above mentioned criticisms apply to Dr. X, her
team, The HIV nurses, Caroline and Mark, the receptionists, etc of
The STD Clinic who all offered many kindnesses to my friend Tim.*

copies to:
Consultant in Genito-Urinary Medicine, Royal London Hospital
Director of Crusaid, National AIDS Charity
AIDS Co-ordinator for Tower Hamlets
Tim's Psychotherapist
Medical Director, The Mildmay Mission Hospital
Director of Public Health Medicine, Royal London Hospital
Consultant in Communicable Diseases, Royal London Hospital
Director of Inpatient Services, Royal London Hospital
*Senior Nurse, Quality Assurance, Central Nursing Office, Royal
London Hospital*
*Business Manager, Acute Unit Management, Royal London
Hospital*

The General Manager of The Royal Opera House invited
me out for supper. Kenneth had unknowingly provided this
reawakening, of my first meal in a restaurant - the food was
wonderful but I felt almost guilty to enjoy it for Tim had loved
Indian food. But because Tim wasn't there to enjoy it we had
come together to discuss the mounting of a memorial service
for him by his colleagues at The Royal Opera House and from
The Welsh National Opera. I tried to explain how important it
was that Tim was properly mourned; that this could only

happen if all Tim's alter egos were evoked: the classical music lover, the rough biker, the clown, the kind and generous man he had been, etc. Kenneth nominated the actors church, 'St Paul's, Covent Garden' for the venue; that the resident rector was the honorary chaplain to The Royal Opera House nearby. The service was scheduled for sometime the following month when a date could be agreed between the two opera companies and the church. The waiting game for the date had begun; that once agreed invitations could be sent out, the details of the service agreed. Living only one day at a time, February was science-fiction.

January 24th Glenys met me at Hampstead Station. We had a coffee. I was overwhelmed by the ordinariness of the café; it didn't fit the momentousness of our mission. She drove me to Golders Green Crematorium to collect Tim's ashes. Unhampered by the formality and nerves of the funeral, the place uncomfortably familiar, the gentle company of Glenys, I felt I might cry when I saw the Bedford Chapel. This was the emotion I had fully expected to feel at Tim's funeral. While waiting in the reception area my heart started to pound - I fully expected Tim to walk out from the door through which the receptionist had disappeared. Instead she returned. She handed me a repulsive cream coloured carrier bag. I took it. It contained a heavy cardboard box. Once again I had my caring role back. The emotional impact of our 'reunion' was disturbed again by the money making side of death. I had to pay £9 for the pressed aluminium urn containing Tim's remains.

Shirley had already put my mind at rest about 'crem' stories I'd heard, 'It's not the ashes of the deceased; they are all mixed up together.' I had actually wondered whether the urn would contain surgical bolts, nuts and screws that had been used to repair Tim's arm following a bad motorbike crash. Shirley laid all my fears to rest that they were Tim's ashes and would contain nothing else. Glenys drove me home. Tim had left on December 7th in body; now he returned in metamorphosis. I was glad I wasn't alone with 'Tim'.

I wasn't sure what to do. Was there a right thing to do with Tim's remains? Was there a wrong thing to do? I was glad for Glenys' direction. 'Why don't you take the box out of the bag'? I obeyed. 'Why don't you take the urn out of the box'? Again I obeyed. My rational, logical mind was compromised - I fully expected to find a little Tim in the box. Instead I picked up a bronze coloured urn. Underneath it was an official envelope; the cremation certificate necessary should Tim's ashes be interred or scattered on hallowed ground. This not being the case I put it away with the other morbid papers. Strangely the lid of the urn was very similar to the petrol filler cap of Tim's red Japanese motorbike; but whereas the machine had the word Kawasaki engraved on it, the urn had a label on it with Tim's name, date of cremation and cremation number 280254. It seemed appropriate to clear a space on one of the workbenches in the garage, to place the urn near Tim's prized motorbikes. I was glad to share this rite with Glenys; she validating it was absolutely right for Tim. We placed his crash helmet over the urn, I tied his scarf around the base and crossed his gloves on top.

Over the next two months I turned the bench into a shrine piling up things around it that had been meaningful to Tim - a photo of his father, Pasha and me, (couldn't find one of his mother and sister at that time), music scores, and treasured recordings, flowers he had collected and dried from the garden. Tim's death had taken me completely by surprise; even though I had thought I was ready and prepared, I wasn't at all when it happened. What others might see as morbid behaviour actually allowed for me to slowly relinquish my coveted caring role - in my time. I needed a shrine now and what could be more meaningful than 'Tim' himself.

For the first time I properly understood the value and importance of memorials/shrines - be it my temporary humble home made shrine, the mighty beautiful Taj Mahal of India, the grotesque sculptures in Père-Lachaise Cemetery in Paris for all the Jews who were taken to the extermination camps - 'we', those who are left behind need a physical representation to focus our wanton grieving emotions.

My very good friend Hywel came to stay during a very cold spell in January; his boiler had broken down. His visit showed just how unusable and redundant the kitchen had become. One evening when he returned from work he cooked some baked potatoes; he asked me if I wanted one, I declined - one of the last things I had cooked for Tim; a kitchen where I had prepared so many meals; now I wanted nothing from it, nor could produce anything there myself. Still unable to use Tesco's superstore nearby, I just bought dog food and milk from the local Indian corner shop; and each night I successively alternated Indian, Chinese, and Fish and Chip meals at the end of the evening following a late bout of drinking at 'The Falcon & Firkin'.

Having also abandoned the gym and exercise for the first time in my life - how could I enhance my body when Tim had no body at all - this period signalled me letting go of myself; a spiral that would take me to the fattest, unhealthiest I had ever been before I began the long haul 'fighting back.'

Though underweight at the time of Tim's death - I lost ten pounds in weight the week before he died - I had managed to keep going on both fronts of diet and exercise through all the traumas and rest holes of prebereavement; yet I fell apart within days of Tim's demise. One day I would understand the meaning of the term 'survivor guilt'.

The dominating theme of January was 'letters' that arrived every morning from which I have taken the following extracts...

'With the wisdom of hindsight I deduce that Tim already knew of his illness when he visited me here in August to spend an idyllic summer day which is my last lovely memory of Tim.'

'I am very very sorry for I have get the your very bad news in the

card about my friend Tim's death! I don't know what I must be said .... this is very bad news! We are keeping his gift little dry flowers in our home when you are getting birth of my son in hospital .... me and my wife very very sorry. He was the very good my friend.' (from a Turkish colleague)

'I was so glad when you and Tim got together. He has seemed much happier and far more secure since you have been with him. Tim could never sing your praises loud enough.' (strange to learn this for Tim was usually ultra critical with me; I was still learning new things about him)

'You'll be tempted to recall every cross word you every uttered, I speak from experience, but DON'T!! Rather remember all the fun and joy you shared.'

'It doesn't matter how long we're with someone, when it ends it seems so short, always with so much unsaid and unfinished.'

'I hope that I can stop my tears soon. This is the first time I lost a good friend.' (from a tough German biker)

'What kind of illness was it, can you tell us about this?'

'I will always remember with pleasure being able to overlook your garden.' (from former neighbour)

'I could not believe my eyes to read your letter and can still not realise that sweet darling Tim will not be there when I come to England. I loved him for his sweet disposition, kind and generous nature, and admired him for his work. I knew him when he was starting, very young but already thorough and so serious about his work. God rest his sweet soul.'

'Your lines brought up memories inevitably: the good time I had at The Royal Opera House, thanks to Tim's warmhearted, humorous and critical companionship.'

'This is the first time I had to face the death of a friend or relative. I am certainly not used to it and probably never will be. In truth, I find it very hard to bear; maybe this marks the true end of childhood when one faces this cruelty of life.'

'He was always the greatest friend through many vicissitudes and I can't imagine him not being there. I really loved him in a serious manner because he was so kind and generous. Qualities so

very rare in this business of opera, and bountiful in Timmy. We'll always be there for you whenever you want, and in whatever spirit you find yourself. There's no more to be said at the moment but that we'll miss him terribly and hope that all the love he gave us will fortify you at this time.

'We always thought Tim was looking after you, but now it would seem that we had it the wrong way round.'

'I can count on one hand the number of friends of his stature I possess and the gap he leaves will never be filled.'

'The occasion I worked closely with Tim was in 1976 when he was my assistant on a production of 'Nabucco' in Teheran. I was extremely grateful for all his prodigious help and sense of humour and moral support during that time, and told him at the time I would never have got through the experience without him. Because it was so unsafe to discuss anything political within the city, we once took a bus to the mountains and went for a walk through what turned out to be a fascinating valley because there we knew we could talk uninhibitedly, where we could not possibly be overheard.'

'Selfishly speaking, I am haunted by the memory of you and Tim leaving that pub opposite the British Museum. Worse: I am haunted by the fact that I do not have a distinct memory of the moment. Maybe this is what everyone feels when someone is suddenly gone for ever. 'How the hell didn't I know!?' 'It suddenly seems so unbelievable that such a cursory meeting and a quick goodbye really could mean goodbye.'

'I think it will be very hard to listen to any opera again without thinking about Tim. I have been playing my collection of operatic music recently. I felt very tearful and while trying to hide my emotions from the people I was with, I made a little speech for Tim in my heart and I am sure he heard me.'

'I am sure that to a lot of people you will be 'Tim's friend 'Rob' - but for me you will also be 'Rob and Tim' as well as just 'Rob'. I hope this makes sense to you. I know that some people would not understand.'

'I realise how desperately sad you must be feeling, at being separated from Tim, after so many years of close friendship. 'In the

midst of life we are in death' - but remember Rob, 'in the midst of death, we are in <u>life</u>', and you must carry on now, in the way you, and he, intended you should. 'Life' and 'death' are so inextricably mixed and linked that separation of the spirit is not possible and so Tim will remain close to you, until the pattern is complete, and everything is made clear. I believe much courage, (my favourite virtue!) has already been shown by you both, in the past. Please do not fail now, or, in the future. You have the support of family and friends, and you will come through as Tim would expect of you. I am enclosing a little card which has helped many people, written by Canon Holland of St Paul's Cathedral many years ago, and I hope when you are feeling specially low, you will look at it, and take heart.

Death is nothing at all
I am I, and you are you. Whatever we were to each other,
that we still are. Call me by my old familiar name,
speak to me in the easy way
which you always used. Put no difference in your tone,
wear no forced air of solemnity or sorrow. Laugh as we always
laughed
at the little jokes we enjoyed together
Let my name be ever the household word
that it always was,
let it be spoken without effect,
without the trace of a shadow on it. Life means all that it ever meant.
It is the same as it ever was;
There is unbroken continuity. Why should I be out of mind
because I am out of sight?
I am waiting for you,
for an interval,
somewhere very near,
just around the corner. All is well.
Canon Holland (1847 - 1918)'

(from Vicky's mother)

'The Passing of The Sea Gull. Two women sat upon the deck of an ocean liner in that sweetly satisfying silence which only true *friends can understand. One of them had recently experienced what seemed to be the supreme tragedy of her life in the passing from her sight of a loved one, and there was still an ache in her heart which her friend had been endeavouring to assuage by tender, comforting assurances regarding life and immortality. The one who had been listening sat quietly, her hands folded, trying to grasp what had just been said, and at the same time idly watching the sea gulls play about the mast as the ship plowed its way over the dancing waters. Presently she noticed that one of the gulls had left the others, circling ever higher and higher, until it was evident that it had separated itself from them altogether and was taking a course straight away from the ship. On and on it flew, steadily, surely, its strong white wings outspread, until it became but a mere speck in the sky and finally was lost sight of altogether. But has the sea gull gone anywhere? Had that beautiful activity ceased? Was it not still identified with life, and strength, and vigour, and all that it possessed when it passed from her view? Had anything stopped? What had happened in her experience was just like the passing of the sea gull beyond her range of vision: it was still going on and on, even though her limited, human sense of sight could no longer follow it. Let us ever think aright about those who have passed beyond that blue horizon. They are in reality completely identified with that divine life which knows no end because it knows no beginning. Let us never think of this as associated with anything else, but say in our hearts what the Shunammite woman of long ago said when questioned by Elisha's servant about her son, whom the world called dead; for in response to the question, 'Is it well with the child?', she answered, 'It is well'.*

Louise Wheatley Cook Hovnanian'

(from Margot - an opera singer)

People had caught up with my reality - Tim was dead, I was bereaved; the letters of sympathy were more comforting than the authors could have imagined; in fact helped make these first days of grief less painful than the initial shock days following Tim's HIV diagnosis four years before - then I had been singularly isolated, but for one friend Peter; unable to turn to anyone else for comfort, least of all Tim whom I could not show my sadness, the sense of isolation had amounted to mental solitary confinement. I had been unbearably alone in the first days of pre-bereavement; I did not feel so in these first days of bereavement.

One letter stood out from the rest by the impact of the three words with which it ended...

I am writing to thank you for your beautifully expressed letter of appreciation for our care for Tim; as well as for you Rob. We were privileged to be involved at this special time. We are so glad that the outcome for you and Tim was so positive and creative in spite of the inevitable sadness and grief. May you continue to feel comforted by the love you shared and by the good memories you have, especially after you had found that closeness and harmony again. God Bless you.

Veronica Moss

I had written a thank you letter to The Mildmay for their great care for Tim which had extended to me, Tim's family and friends. A Christian Charity they offered religious succour to those who wanted it; not forcing it on anyone who didn't. At the point of Tim's death I had reached the deepest depths of atheism; I would have unconditionally rejected any religious, spiritual, or mystic overtones from any other source. Having experienced Tim's terrible sufferings and my consequent emotional distress, I couldn't believe in anything. I had actually put great effort into dismantling the little I had once held possible.

There couldn't be a God of any face to allow such misery. With no disrespect to H.M The Queen how could the whole righteous structure of The Church of England be based on the corporal lust of Henry VIII for Anne Boleyn; just out of pique that Rome wouldn't grant him a divorce from Katherine of Aragon; that if Henry had been happy with Katherine there would be no Church of England. Modern life is based totally on the human scale as if life began 1993 years ago; there was a peopled planet before that, why didn't God/Jesus begin with the beginning of Man? What was so special about 1993 years ago? We need Planet Earth; it does not need us; in tens of hundreds of thousands of years time when Man will doubtless be extinct like the dinosaurs what will have become of God/Jesus? The corruption of the church throughout history - Cardinal's Richelieu and Mazarin of France; the hypocrisy of the gay priesthood against the teachings of Rome - I demolished the possibility of anything existing. And why do we think we are so special, self elected 'Landlords of The Earth' that we should be blessed with a God any more than any of the other higher mammalians? There is no other animal on Earth that treats its own kind as badly as Man. Do dolphins, killer whales, elephants do the despicable things to each other that we do? No. What is the name of The Dolphin God? By the time of Tim's death I was spiritually dead; a nihilist.

Yet with those three words 'God Bless You' from Dr. Veronica Moss, Medical Director of Mildmay, who had helped look after Tim began a spiritual thaw. I simply put a question mark against my non-belief - I couldn't reject anything from Mildmay. I read and read 'The Passing of The Seagull' sent to me by a friend Margot. I looked out of the kitchen window up into the blue sky thinking of the bird and Tim that had passed from view; on and on into 'infinity'; a word quite beyond my capability of understanding i.e. no end - a concept beyond the fathom of my/our limited human experience. The last line of The Lords Prayer is 'World without end. Amen'. Looking up into the blue sky; for the first time I had a measure with which to appraise Tim's death. I could not grasp the concept of infinity. I could not grasp the concept of death.

Towards the end of January I began to reply to all the

letters of condolence I had received. The Mildmay recognised the fact that 'letters' both received and sent are an important part of early bereavement and provided a selection of stationery on which to reply. A funny one didn't seem appropriate for me, though if I had died instead that is probably the card Tim would have chosen. I liked the dove card titled, 'Onward, ever Onward.' I couldn't honestly use the religious card, 'God's Tree Changes.' It was the fourth card 'Rainbow of Hope' I chose - the bright colours of the spectrum rainbow emulated the beautiful picture Francis a talented young set/costume designer had painted for Tim's room at The Mildmay; that the rainbow in the middle of Francis' painting was one of if not the last images Tim would have held before closing his eyes forever. It was my responsibility to write to those colleagues and friends Tim hadn't lived long enough to see; people I sensed from their letters needed to know how Tim valued them; they had told me in many different ways how Tim had valued me, now it was my turn to reciprocate. I was middle man.

I took stock of where I was with Gil. As a lawnmower leaves an aftermath of grass to be cleared up so The Reaper who had cut Tim down left an aftermath of post-death responsibilities for me. I wrote the following list in my notebook of consequences I had to work through in the year ahead; some already achieved or passed through; some that wouldn't be completed in either the first or second year following...

Aftermath Consequences

Tim's funeral
Our anniversary January 11th
Informing people
Replying to letters
Collecting ashes from crematorium
Finding the spot

Ceremony of scattering Tim's ashes
What to do with the urn
St. Valentine's Day
Tim's clothes
Tim's personal effects
Mildmay Mission memorial service...
for those who had died there
Mildmay Mission Partners...
Bereavement Support Group
Probate
My 34th birthday
The three motorbikes
The car
Tim's 40th birthday, what would have been
Execution of will completed
Tim's memorial service
Mementos for friends and family
Heirlooms returned to Tim's family
First anniversary of Tim's death

A pattern had emerged already. This first month like each to follow had a quality of its own; there being a dominant theme (letters), an emotional theme (numbness), sub themes of business, reawakenings, setbacks and shifts/changes in friendships/relationships.

I became a juggler beginning the year as an amateur. At any one moment there were a large number of balls up in the air; I lost some, I gained new ones as the year progressed; some remained all year; occasionally I dropped the lot. But by the end of the first year I was a professional juggler.

The month drew to a close with my return to The Royal Opera House. Glenys accompanied me to the last performance of 'Capriccio.' Recalling words from one letter of condolence, 'in the midst of life we are in death', 'in the midst of death we are in life'; here it was the Royal Opera House that had its dress rehearsal at the moment of Tim's funeral; his score of

'Capriccio' still in the garden room where he had left it. With the first bar of music I learned 'the show goes on, life goes on, I go on.' This was my second 'beautiful experience' of the month. Despite the words of the critics - the music of Strauss, the singing of Kiri Te Kanawa, the beautiful costumes of Gianni Versace my sensibilities were assaulted! My raw senses could barely cope with the stimuli - every image graphic in its high definition 'each note of music seemingly overcharged' every change in lighting highly coloured. Was this 'death' - to grasp 'life' so vividly?

CHAPTER 4

February

'Change' was the dominant theme of my second month of bereavement; the emotional theme being a shift from numbness and stillness to loneliness.

The longest Tim and I had ever been separated was one month when he had gone to Canada to direct 'Fidelio' for the Vancouver Opera. Now he was 'overdue'. Emotions are not always logical; especially so in bereavement. I was caught very much between fact and fantasy. I knew he was dead, that there would be no reunion, no homecoming, no cards, or telephone calls, no journey to Heathrow to meet him from a trip to Vienna or Hamburg or Berlin; yet if I left everything exactly as it was, as he had left things, he might materialise, we would pick up the pieces and carry on, and I would find it would all have just been a bad dream. But truth gained victory over denial. Death had claimed him but the feeling I was left with wasn't dissimilar to the end of my first gay relationship when I was jilted by my lover Carl; he walked out on me. I waited for him to come home, he never did. Part of me was still waiting for Tim to come home. He never did.

The German composer Wagner wrote an epic tetralogy of four operas known collectively as 'The Ring of Nibelung', a story based in part on Teutonic myth. Tim had been in good health in the autumn of 1988 when he had worked on the first opera in the cycle, 'The Rhinegold'. He didn't work on 'The Valkyrie', the second opera in the cycle but we attended a memorable performance with Andy, Glenys and Julia. The very last opera that Tim and I sat at together at was the third work in the cycle, 'Siegfried', and only two months before his death. This opera had seen Tim's supreme artistic effort, 'the zenith of my life', in Tim's own words as he found extraordinary hidden energies to overcome months and months of exhaustion for this final creative burst; that I believe killed him as surely as Hagen's spear killed Siegfried.

Now on February 4th Kenneth, The General Manager of the Royal Opera House kindly invited me to the opening night of the fourth opera in the cycle, 'The Twilight of The Gods'. Tim had been scheduled to work on this production and I was proud to see his name whether by accident or design still credited in the programme. Unknown to Kenneth the last present Tim had given me had been the story of 'The Ring of Nibelung' in American style comic book form so that I would understand the complexities of the story when we attended the opening night together.

But Tim died. I went alone, with Kenneth; but that I was able to even partly fulfil a projected plan of Tim's seemed to beckon him from death; he lived on through me - I looked across the auditorium to the other side of The Grand Tier fully expecting to see Tim sitting in one of the usual seats C10/C11 allocated to him. Again fantasy and fact merged the make-believe of theatre with the reality of life. At the point in the drama when the hero Siegfried was slain and lay dead on the stage, all I could see was my champion-hero lying dead on his deathbed at The Mildmay; and with the overpowering orchestration of 'Siegfried's Funeral March' it seemed the orchestra played for Tim - how one makes circumstances fit ones own experience, but how else could it have been. During one of the intervals one of Kenneth's friends asked me, 'Do you work in opera'? The answer was, 'No' - it always had been. But when you live with someone who does work in opera you live with all the ups and downs, the hype, the boredom, the excitement, the dramas and intrigues of long rehearsal periods. Tim used to say he couldn't have coped through many difficult working periods without me keeping the home fires burning. Tim wasn't a reader and struggled to read books so I used to do background reading and research for him e.g. when he worked on Massenet's 'Manon' I read Abbé Prévost's novel 'Manon Lescaut' and fed information to him. It wasn't my world but I never felt on the outside. Now I was. Maria Callas used to say an opera begins a long time before the first night and ends a long time after the last performance; that what the public see is but a fraction of the total drama. This was so for Tim as well. Whatever opera performance I saw from now on would only be from Joe Public's side of the orchestra pit. Though I still had friends who worked in opera Tim's death had effectively closed the stage door to me; I basically only had access now through the front doors of the theatre; and any opera going experience would begin with the conductor entering the orchestra pit and would end with the final applause. The sense of loss just added to the hurt.

Following the opera there was a formal reception in The Crush Bar. Suddenly the thought of meeting so many of Tim's colleagues for the first time since his death and in such circumstances of formality overwhelmed me. Moreover whenever I'd ever been to anything similar before I had always trailed along after Tim always being introduced as, 'this is Tim's boyfriend' - the theatre/opera world is top heavy with gay men, our relationship was open and accepted - but was I still Tim's boyfriend now that he was dead? I wasn't sure. I had long grown used to being an appendage of Tim's; I had no image of myself in my own right. I felt very panicky, I wanted to turn and run out of the Royal Opera House. Then quite unexpectedly it felt as if Tim stepped right into me, calming me and giving me his abounding strength and confidence. I can provide no physiological, spiritual or unconscious explanation for this extraordinary phenomenon, it just happened. With one of Tim's colleagues Annina I stepped through the doors into The Crush Bar.

Returning home late that night alone was so different to 'our' former homecomings. We had always had our own intimate mini party usually comprising a glass of wine and bacon sandwiches. There were voids and voids to fill that I kept falling into.

That night on going to my bedroom, with Pasha already asleep on the bed, I sat on the edge of my bed for ages looking at my bedside cabinet and its deadly contents - the morphine I'd appropriated from The Mildmay and the suicide letter I'd written the day I realised Tim would not be coming home again. It was only the perceptions of one of Tim's doctors, Ruth, bridging my crumbling exterior facade where I attempted to cope, who saw through to my inner despair and touched the acute loneliness one feels when realising that the death you had known all along would happen is actually imminent, is going to happen and you can do nothing to stop it. I thought I was ready and prepared. I was not. I would never be. My mind baulked and fought against the medical reality. This was grief. I cried. I cried my heart away from the depths of my soul. It was the last time I cried for him before he died; and I never did again in the same way. Just being able to hold her hand while I wept was enough to check the fatal intentions I held towards myself; but the morphine already acquired, and the letter already written remained in my bedside cabinet. That day I had wanted to die for my life to end with his. Now I didn't want to die. But I had no idea how to live - I was caught between his death and my life. Numbness was abating from the outside in; the pain was increasing all the time. When I eventually climbed into bed I rationalised that maybe hard, bad and sad feelings were better, and inevitable, than no feelings in the emotional thaw I was experiencing. I had left a life in Wales to live with Tim. Now he had gone. I was alone. I still didn't know if I had the strength to cope. I'd given up all my career plans to look after him and had no idea of how to find the path back to life, if there was one. Coward that I was, tired that I was, weak that I felt, selfish though suicide would be, I could slip away quietly if the going got too rough. I needed the bottle and letter yet; it was my insurance.

The house was virtually exactly as Tim had left it, his motorbike magazine and book by his bed, a pair of trainers under the chair by his wardrobe. His Capriccio score was still lying next to the sofa in the garden room where he'd left it close to the records of Margaret Price singing Schubert and Schumann propped against the bookcase - the last music he had played at home with his mother. Like Miss Havisham in Dickens 'Great Expectations' who had been jilted on her wedding day I had frozen the house in Tim's time. Now I knew this to be wrong; if I stopped on the outside I would stop on the inside too; Tim wouldn't want that so I broke the spell of death hanging over the house and with a mixture of difficulty, pain and guilt I replaced the score, the records and the book in the spaces on the bookshelves from where Tim had taken them. This was an acknowledgement of his death.

I wondered what would happen next. I feared that by disturbing the stillness of death hanging over the house akin to agitating a wasp's nest would bring about cataclysm and a furore of emotion within. Absolutely nothing happened. But strangely and quite unexpectedly mingling with my apprehensiveness following the simple action on my part of replacing Tim's possessions in their customary places was a sense of excitement. This allowed for me to make my very first executive decision regarding the house - Tim had once replaced a perfectly good and functional down light in the utility room with an uncomfortably bright neon light tube that never worked properly. When I once suggested replacing the old fitting his response was less than negative. As was

Tim's right in his own house he always had the last say. Now I had my first say in the house. I switched off the electricity, took down the neon tube and replaced the original light fitting. This very basic undertaking so mundane you might think it was hardly worth mentioning was in fact the very beginning of the metamorphosis of turning the house from Tim's house where Rob had lived to Rob's house where Tim had lived. One of my mother's widowed friends had taken almost manic delight in leaving the hosepipe coiled all over the garden. Her husband had been fastidious about rolling it up after use - only now I understood what I had seen at the time as strange behaviour. For the first time ever I could make absolute decisions within the boundaries of the house and garden where I lived - my house and garden.

The process of re-establishing oneself in a property one has shared with a dominant partner is the same whether for an aristocrat like Lady Clementine Churchill in her widowhood on the grand scale of a country house like Chartwell; or for a gay man like me on the modest scale of a Hackney town house. John Pearson, Churchill's most recent biographer tells the story of Lady Churchill's sentiments towards Chartwell.

'In her widowhood Chartwell's most recent valued patron proved to be Lady Churchill. Her old resentment of the house forgotten, she generously donated pictures and possessions, and supervised the *transformation* of Chartwell into the sunny, almost feminine family house one sees today. It is no longer that profoundly masculine establishment, part Oxford college, part government department, which visitors remembered before the war. But it is possibly closer to the country home Clementine had always wanted.' (John Pearson)

Only now I actually realised the materialistic impact of Tim's death. At 10.49pm on December 30th I possessed a wardrobe of clothes, a few records, books, some bedding and a few ornaments - the old family gold signet ring my grandmother had left to me worth more than the total of my worldly goods. Yet one minute later at 10.50pm with the last beat of Tim's heart, his will took effect; only now I recognised this. From that moment I had a house to live in, everything within it including Tim's motorbikes, the washing machine, garden tools, sofas, pictures, cans of oil, cook books, vases, music scores, etc. Though it all now belonged to me morally and legally I would learn during the following two years that many things I could never make mine and would be given away; some things had to be returned ultimately to his family; other things burnt or destroyed altogether.

As for Tim's wardrobe of clothes they had to be dealt with; but not yet; not for a few weeks; I still needed them as he had left them - undisturbed. His bedroom was still forbidden territory, even for me, an absolute no go area.

St. Valentines Day, February 14th, was the first major emotional hurdle of the month. Hywel had invited me to a concert at The Festival Hall, I was glad to have some distraction from the significance of the day. Yet when it came to get ready I didn't want to go. Every place, however often one has been to it before, has to be won back; all the memories of my visits with Tim surfaced…

Ironically soon after Tim had just started work at The Royal Opera House I had fallen ill and been hospitalised suffering from profound exhaustion, debilitating sweats, strange blood counts, pains in my joints etc. Because some of the symptoms emulated HIV related symptoms the doctor carried out my very first HIV test. I was terrified and convinced I would die of AIDS before the opening night of Tim's very first opera at Covent Garden 'Fidelio'. To cheer me up he took me from the hospital to The Festival Hall to see Jessye Norman singing Salome. He had been so loving and encouraging. His gentle reassurances combated the crushing depression I felt waiting for the test result. I grieved for my life I was convinced was fast running out; and I grieved for Tim that my death would separate us. Now perversely though we had been separated by death it was Tim who had died. It was I who lived on.

Following Tim's diagnosis later that year he booked for us to see Berlioz's Requiem (La Grande Messe des Morts). I hadn't thought it a good idea. Being probably the largest classical musical work ever written I was rightly concerned of Tim's emotional reaction (and mine) when the vast forces of percussions were unleased; they struck with an almost physical discharge. Tim began to weep silently, unchecked tears rolled down his cheeks. He cried for his own mortality, his own death, just four years away. There was something so eloquent and uninhibited in his tears that the woman next to him began to cry too. I could not hold back my tears adding to the deluge. Though I suspect the majority of that audience had attended a high brow, 'heavy' cultural event; in retrospect I can see that like Turner's painting of 'The Fighting Temeraire', art, music and literature is a veritable language of communication and can reach through where words, even the wisest words of counsellors, friends and lovers fail to penetrate. Berlioz pierced Tim's armour-plate of denial.

Paradoxically our last shared experience at The Festival Hall had been with Andy and Glenys attending part of the 'Music for Life' celebrations to raise money for Crusaid, The National AIDS charity - I just wasn't ready to face all these memories but I had to be ready, Hywel had the tickets, I couldn't let him down. I went with great misgiving but even as I walked across Waterloo Bridge I discovered my reservations were worse than the reality. Surprisingly I really enjoyed myself. I was grateful to Hywel for helping me further extend my boundaries to include territory of old from the time of 'Tim and Rob; now in the time of just 'Rob'.

Afterwards we went to a gay bar in Covent Garden for a few drinks. On the way there we passed countless couples celebrating, openly kissing in shadowed doorways, red roses in abundance. Similarly in 'The Attic Bar' gay couples, showing the love that also exists between man and man.

Hywel told me his boyfriend Peter always remembered St. Valentines Day - so had Tim - so had I. That night my solo status slapped me in the face and it stung. My couplet with Tim had terminated with that no-second-chance finality of death. Feeling guilty, for Hywel had been such a stalwart friend, I felt a mean and ungenerous envy for his long standing relationship with Peter. Hywel and Peter. Rob and nobody. Still the gay environment made me confront my sexual needs. Wanting to be faithful to Tim's memory I was repulsed by the thought of sex with anyone; but at the same time I was manically desperate for sex in a way I had never felt before.

This second month of bereavement had its inescapable tally of setback and failure. Though I had shopped at our local Tesco Supermarket whenever Tim had worked away or been in hospital, I couldn't now. I tried. I half filled a hand basket. But the sight of all the little things Tim liked that I would never buy for him again; even things he disliked such as vacuum packed beetroot; quite defeated me. I left empty handed. I just bought the basics - milk, dog food and bread at the Indian shop around the corner.

I attempted to go back to Crusaid, The National AIDS charity for which I had worked as a volunteer prior to Tim's final illness. I had made the No. 6 and No. 11 bus journey to Victoria countless times. Now it seemed just so far from home I just couldn't do it. The route hadn't changed. I had. My internal geography didn't match with the real world anymore. Tim not being either at home resting or at Covent Garden, near where I changed buses and often met him - the emotional distance from home to Victoria had multiplied fourfold. I still felt too vulnerable away from home. Basic office duties had kept me going during the days of prebereavement. The good company of my friend Hywel the Administrator provided distraction from Tim's illness. I was doing something useful for 'the cause'. But my volunteer days for an AIDS charity had ended and would not feature as part of bereavement.

I could not disturb the stillness still pervading the house with music. Nor could I switch on either the T.V or radio - I found the world a very threatening place. The looming Gulf War exacerbated this. Nothing could bring Tim back. So much creative effort had gone into keeping Tim well and alive for as long as possible with the certainty of his ultimate death; it now seemed appalling that perfectly healthy strong bodied men with a natural life expectancy ahead of them were going to their deaths - British, American, Allies, Iraqis' alike. Brave soldiers have to be cared for; but never before had I seen the insanity of war so clearly; that powers and finances could not be mustered in peacetime to keep hospital wards open for creative purpose and welfare; but only following the destructive violence of Man versus Man where for example closed wards at The Royal London Hospital and Royal Free Hospital amongst others were put on alert and readied for reopening. The Honour and Glory of war? All I could see was the madness and futility of war. Tim had fought his battle bravely too knowing there was only death awaiting him over the ridge. Death comes soon enough without the wretchedness of illness and Man's intoxication for warfare and bloodshed. Life is precious and to be husbanded. With this realisation I knew the bottle of morphine and suicide letter were now redundant. I didn't yet know what to do with them. I wasn't ashamed of having had those terrible thoughts. I just felt a terrible ache in my heart for two gay men I had known who hadn't been 'given' a Ruth Richmond and had taken their lives unable to bear their grief.

Until only a few days before Tim's death we had still watched our favourite T.V. programmes together - soaps like 'Coronation Street'. 'Newsnight', a late current affair programme had been regular viewing for me at home until Tim's final hospitalisation. Now I couldn't watch anything - I needed absolute peace and quiet.

The biggest and most disappointing setback was that a

date couldn't be liaised in time for Tim's memorial service to take place in February; it was postponed to May; three months away. On the day to day basis on which I lived, May was futuristic, of the time thereafter.

On Sunday February 17th with snow still on the ground Andy and I set off for Epping Forest to explore the area of 'High Beech' to find the spot where with Tim's family we would scatter his ashes a few weeks hence. We first stumbled upon a delightful small forest church nestling amongst the trees. At that point I didn't believe it was an appropriate place, Tim not having the religious convictions to be scattered or interred there. Not very far away was a muddy car park and tea caravan where all the motorbikers gathered. There was no suitable place to scatter the ashes. Though I know Tim wouldn't have objected in the least to being scattered underfoot in the mud; I knew his family would, so we continued our search. We set out to try and locate a clearing where Tim and I, Andy and Glenys, and Francis had picnicked only the summer before. The trees all being leafless the February forest bore no comparison to the same forest of the summer. But we found it - a beech tree in the centre of a woodland glade. Unexpectedly I was overtaken by a strange blend of emotion - I felt I was crying but no tears fell - and I felt angry but nothing told of this upon my face. Tim shouldn't be reposing in an urn on a bench in the garage; he should have been on one of the motorbikes drinking that disgusting tea he had drunk so many times with his biker mates; we should have been walking Pasha here like other walkers we passed with their dogs; or planning summer picnics. But we had found the absolute right place to scatter Tim's ashes - a peaceful clearing, a church nearby and motorbikes thundering in the distance.

Running equally and oppositely to the setbacks of the month were the 'awakenings'. February was the month I first went back into the garden. Nothing but birds, cats and squirrels had disturbed the stillness of the garden since Tim would have last looked at it. That Mother Nature had reawakened the garden from its deep winter slumber - green shoots pushing up though the soil; allowed for me to open the garden gate and walk up the winding gravel path to the budding magnolia in the clearing at the bottom of the garden.

As if reading my thoughts (sex being almost constantly on my mind) Shirley told me that a strong sexual resurgence is normal especially following a long period of sexual redundancy; validating that this is the case for any partner, homo/heterosexual who has nursed his/her mate through a long illness. She prepared me for the fact that there might well be a sexual encounter shortly and that I should be aware of both my vulnerability and eligibility; that I should not let anyone take advantage of me.

It was just by coincidence that Shoreditch should contain two contrasting establishments, one partly, one wholly identified with homosexuality - the haven of The Mildmay and not 100 yards away one of London's most famous gay bars 'The London Apprentice'. The close juxtaposition of one a symbol of gay death, the other of gay life they were earthly and mortal representations of the adage 'while in the midst of death we are in the midst of life, while in the midst of life we are in the midst of death'. This I could see now no more clearly than the night Tim died; while I held his dead hand, only a stones throw away the late Sunday crowd at 'The London Apprentice' were drinking, dancing, laughing, arguing, making, consolidating and breaking liaisons.

My last brief visit to the 'L.A' had been a miserable one just two months before Tim died; more allied to the dying than the living I scurried for home. During Tim's period of terminal care at The Mildmay I don't think the 'L.A' itself or the thought of going there ever crossed my mind. February was the month I went back there. Strangely, parking outside The Mildmay I felt warmed and comforted just being nearby; yet crossing the road by Shoreditch Church I felt very nervous. By the time I reached The 'L.A' I was petrified. In my old leather jacket I returned to the gay club scene.

'The London Apprentice' was unchanged, I was changed. All my previous visits had been in the time of 'Tim and Rob'. Despite the dozens and dozens of times I had been there over the years; this was the first in just the time of 'Rob'. My friend John the barman made a joke about me 'staying out after curfew', that I had always left on the dot of 11pm to get home to go to bed with Tim or to look after him. 11pm is the hour most of the clientele start to arrive and now I could stay as late as I chose; I was answerable to no-one but myself.

There is truth in the marriage vow 'till death do us part'; this applies to the most conventional married heterosexual partnership, for heterosexuals who live together unmarried, for gay partnerships - it is no different. For the very first time since I came to London to live with Tim, I was 'free range'. This new sense of liberty fed my sexual excitement; but it was tempered by my awareness of the sexual security I'd had with Tim and lost. For now I just looked; whenever men got too interested, too close I bolted for home. But I did have the feeling it wouldn't be long before I would be taking someone home with me. There was an inevitability that this would happen - I yearned for the gentle touch of a man..

Also something else stirred deep. At the age of 33 I felt I should be well acquainted with my sexual make-up regarding gay partners; and had long accepted I liked to be sexually dominant but erred on the side of passivity. I wasn't sure of anything anymore.

On Friday February 22nd at 7.30 I attended 'A Service of Remembrance' at The Mildmay Mission Hospital. Andy and Glenys, Hywel and Francis accompanied me. The chapel was too small to accommodate the partners, boyfriends, girlfriends, husbands, wives, parents, brothers, sisters, uncles, aunts, grandparents and friends of the deceased; so the interdenominational service was held in the adjacent Buxton Hall.

There were words of welcome from the hospital chaplain

Peter Clarke followed by the choir singing a Ghanaian hymn 'Jesu, Jesu'. There were prayers, readings and an address. Then in alphabetical order the names of those who had died in the last three months were read aloud. I recognised those from the partner's group. The roll call of death reached Tim's name. This wasn't a school assembly giving awards or a university distributing degrees. His name was read out. Tim. This was the most singularly important and serious collective experience of my life. It was an uncompromisingly non-negotiable statement of death, his death and at the same time of all he had been in life - and the part of his life I had shared. I was still creating my own concept of what death was. It's an event and a word but how it translates to the personal human experience is another thing altogether. As someone said, 'A well made cappuccino isn't awesome - death is'. In baby stages I was slowly 'coming to terms with his death' and what it meant. I could now see that to be dead one has to have lived. I had flickers of memory of him alive again. Death had taken his life but not our life which memory held inviolate. In the silence that followed as we all stood silently the ceremony of The Lighting of The Remembrance Candle was performed. En route to The Black Forest we had stopped for a break in Reims. Tim suggested we light a candle in the cathedral for our dying friend Jeff. Now a candle was being lit for Tim. My agnosticism and atheism was comfortless. I was glad for the religious structure, I didn't have one. It provided a safety net for my baulking, tumultuous and unformed thoughts to fall into. The service ended with the benediction and the choir singing the Canticle of 'Nunc Dimittis', giving permission to those to be willing to depart from life. (*Luke 2:29 now lettest thou depart*)

Shirley had told me these regular services held every few months were very important and helpful to the nursing staff, doctors and counsellors. So I attended out of respect for Shirley and of course for Tim. I hadn't expected to benefit at all and was very surprised how much I had been helped by it.

I was so very grateful to those three words from Dr Veronica Moss, 'God Bless You', for without those January words from her I might not have gone. Afterwards tea, biscuits and cakes were served at the back of the hall - all the usual social inhibitions that restrict our interactions with others had been lost; people mingled and interacted in the most unprecedented manner - men in black leather jackets talking to little old ladies in funny hats as if they had known each other for years. I was quite dumbfounded when a man who seemed familiar introduced himself to me - his parents lived in the same road as my parents! I remembered him from school. I was so surprised I just stared at him; he walked away probably thinking me very rude. When I recovered from the surprise I tried to find him but regrettably he had gone. It was a very small world - I wasn't the only Welsh man from a small town by the sea affected by HIV; but whether he had lost a partner or a friend I do not know to this day.

We were asked to check the name and spelling of our loved ones on a board at the front of the hall ready to be inscribed in 'The Book of Remembrance'. After a brief discussion with my friends, I asked for Tim's name to be changed to Timothy out of deference to his mother who hadn't attended.

I couldn't help but feel angry that none of Tim's family had attended the service embracing their son while looking at all the other partners and friends and family members some of whom had travelled from as far as Ireland and Germany. Did he not deserve family representation? I would have liked them there for me too. I wished they had wanted to join with me as well. But it wasn't to be. When I told her of the name change we had made out of respect for her, she couldn't hide her horror that Tim's name was in any way permanently and irrefutably linked to that of an AIDS hospice. 'We all have our own way of grieving', Tim's mother said to me. This did not include joining with a predominantly homosexual congregation facing the AIDS epidemic with love and honesty. If there was ever a place that militated against ignorance and prejudice it was the Mildmay Mission Hospital.

The Hospital Chaplain the Rev. Peter Clarke took me aside. What he said came as quite a revelation. He wanted to tell me that he had visited Tim quite late in the evening two nights before he died. Tim had asked for a structure, a framework (in which to die). Together they recited the 23rd psalm 'The Lord is my Shepherd'. Tim found some spiritual comfort from this to face his imminent death. I was glad to know this.

Peter said he would have had no qualms about holding a Christian service for Tim if he had been asked to do so. If I had known this before I might well have asked for Tim's body to rest at The Mildmay, for the funeral service to take place in the chapel there before Tim's cremation at Golders Green Crematorium. Though it was too late for that it wasn't too late to create Tim's memorial service at St. Pauls around a Christian format. Reclaiming ones religious culture is very different to religious conversion which didn't extend to Tim or me. Though Tim never entered the Mildmay's chapel either alive or dead; I would. As I left The Mildmay that night and walked past the chapel I knew that though I still couldn't/ and wouldn't pray; that the sanctuary and peace of the holy space had been given to me for the first time ever. This was a true awakening. I would return to sit there and contemplate - the etched doves in the round glass panes of the chapel doors a symbol of something I'd known little of these last years - peace - and maybe there in quiet moments of thought I might begin to find a little. And so the most extraordinary of evenings ended.

Now the bottle of morphine and suicide letter was an impediment to the survival instinct and feeling of life that flashed through the weariness pervading my mind, body and soul. I could have just flushed the opiate down the toilet and torn up the letter; but I needed to symbolically retrieve the life I had symbolically relinquished with the writing of the letter and pilfering of the drug. This I could only do by taking them back to the day, the place from where they originated. So one morning when getting ready to go to see Shirley for a routine once-every-three-week counselling session I spontaneously opened the drawer, lifted them out, put them in a bag and took them with me to The Mildmay.

Totally compartmentalising the fundamental issue I wished to discuss, with no idea of how to introduce it I talked of the ups, the downs, the business matters of the month, my visits to 'The London Apprentice', etc. Shirley then motioned to the package I had placed on the edge of her desk and asked me if I wanted to tell her about it. Immediately all my superficial control evaporated; I cried for the first time since Tim died and relived Friday December 14th 1990.

'Tim had been taken from The Mildmay to The Royal London Hospital for tests that could not be performed at the hospice. After changing his bed, buying some flowers for his bedroom, doing a massive shop at Tesco's superstore at Bow I joined him at the Royal London Hospital. I would accompany him back to The Mildmay and pack his things up, from where we would go home. Instead he was admitted to The Royal London Hospital. I was told he would be transferred to The Mildmay for terminal care once a bed became available. Tim wasn't going to come home again.

I was shocked and unprepared for the speed of Tim's decline. The rest of the day passed blurred, time sequences back to front. I was on the 253 bus from The Royal London Hospital to Cambridge Heath. I meant to change to a 55 bus to take me to The Mildmay to collect Tim's things. Instead I was in the car driving. I didn't know where I was. The only right place where I wanted to be was at home with Tim. No place felt right. Suddenly I was at home instead writing a suicide letter. Tim didn't need me anymore, he was too sleepy most of the time to know whether I was there or not, I would pull the curtains, get into my pyjamas, drink the bottle of morphine I had appropriated from The Mildmay and slip away to wait for Tim. Now I was on the 55 bus. It was crowded with Friday night commuters. A pretty young woman sitting in front of me was showing her friend her new disco dress and couldn't wait to get home to try it on.. Of course it was Friday night. School had finished and the weekend was starting for other people. My life had ended. I was in Tim's room at The Mildmay packing. I was at home again just standing in the doorway of Tim's bedroom - never had a room seemed so empty; it was as if Tim had died already. I had to go to Tim. I put the letter and bottle of morphine in my bedside cabinet. He was very distressed and angry that he couldn't come home. Mercifully he fell asleep. The distress was unbearable. I left the hospital. It was early evening again. I felt completely out-of-control for the first time since Tim's HIV diagnosis four years before. I went to The Mildmay, I don't know why. Dr. Ruth Richmond a beautiful young doctor who had helped look after Tim saw my anguish. She led me to Tim's room and held my hand while I cried it all away; and that's what I did, I cried it all away and I was able to survive and keep going. Retrospectively I can see that some aspects of grief are self-limiting and self-extinguishing. It is not physically possible to maintain that force of crying, the body has its limit. She tried to ring my G.P. but he was unavailable. She made me promise that although Tim still didn't want people to know he was ill, that she was going to overrule him; he had no right to expect me to carry such a situation alone any longer; that I could only be of any help to him if I had the help of friends and family; that I had an unqualified right to have; that I could only go home if I promised to get some help. I promised. Whatever I did would be wrong. To tell people would be to break Tim's confidence. To not tell was a burden too great to carry any longer. But I still had the letter and bottle - that was the only thing that felt right for me.

When Shirley read the letter she said surprisingly, 'I don't feel I am reading a suicide letter but a survival letter.' By taking it there I left any further suicidal thoughts outside the compass of what would be my bereavement experience. 'You can tear it up, I can tear it up, we can burn it, you can take it home or leave it with me for now while you decide', she said giving me the different options open to me. I elected the latter option. I thought of burning it but when I began to write this book I brought it home for this is where it belongs:

I love life, I love Tim, I love you all. I have never felt so much love since Dr. Ruth gave me some last Friday at The Mildmay Mission - since then its been flooding in and I've been able to give Tim that love to make him better.

I am not weak; I have proved beyond all doubt to myself that I have great strengths despite my own image and the image of others of me not being so. (I am sure it was Dr. Jean Smith who said most people fire on four cylinders but I fire on six one of which doesn't work at all). I've picked myself up three times; after the breakdown, the problems of being honest with both myself and others about not being attracted to women as I am to my own gender, and addiction to a prescribed drug Lorazepam/Ativan.

The teenage breakdown - I fell in love with a friend and couldn't deal with the reality of being gay so I tried to stop it all. Immediately I was sucked into the psychiatric system, labelled manic-depressive, drugs for four years - it was easier to be bowled along in that system than to 'come out' - the strengths for which I did not possess then. After drug therapy was exchanged for psychotherapy (Autumn 79, and one must remember there was a heavy preponderance to the use of drugs then and not counselling as there is now) I got in touch with myself again. Not once in that group did I mention or hint at my orientation but the group gave me a mirror of what I was. At last I was in touch with my reality. I was a gay man. I was homosexual.

I had to be honest about what/who I was for there was no other reality - see 'Fifth Night Out' - its all in there. My 'coming out' and all its problems introduced me to Ativan when I didn't know the difference between a tranquillizer, an antibiotic or an aspirin. The problems of Ativan made all other problems nothing more than minutiae.

When I felt everyone including myself had given up on me I met Tim via Anthony Peattie because he invited me to supper to look at the very embryonic version of 'The Singer and The Storm' I had written. Göran was the first guest, I the second, Tim after that - and now they are both gone - and the irony of Antwerp/Ariadne last year when Tim who was supposed to assist Göran took over on Göran's death - and now a year later Tim's gone (I know Katrin Hysing will be upset, the designer of Ariadne, Tim liked her very much).

Tim gave me the structure, environment and love I needed to be able to exorcise that awful drug. Later December '86 I was falling free from Ativans grasp - moments of my own self and strength knocked holes in Ativans armour plating which had so encapsulated me. Forty years we have together Timmy said. There was a beginning. December 16th 1986 Tim was told he was HIV positive. He told Peter Day the next day, Thursday. Friday we met Julia in The Strand - already Tim knew, I had false happiness. Late that afternoon I was walking through Covent Garden Piazza and 'paid thanks' for my delivery (from Ativan) and Tim's (from HIV). I said to the market's sky - give me five good years and I can ask for no more. That night I was at home by myself - Tim 'Lucia' rehearsals. I watched the T.V. dramatisation of Vita Sackville West's novel, the name of which escapes me, not knowing it was not the beginning but in fact the end. We had four years, not five, not fourty. Saturday December 19th 1986 Tim told me 'they have found antibodies in my blood' - our shiny metallic bathroom was where this began for me, three days after it began for Tim at The Royal London Hospital - always thinking of others he didn't want to tell me to protect me, the one time I should have been able to comfort him.

Because I could not turn to anyone amongst my family or friends the only way I could make it possible to go on was by making a *contract with myself in May/June '87 - that as long as Tim lives, I shall live and we shall live - but when he dies I die too - we were too bound together - the day he told me we were like two faces of polished marble touching - there was nothing between us. Then came Tim's denial, then his anger, my sidestepping to Chelsea, my efforts to fall out of love with Tim, I couldn't - I tried - I tried - I couldn't. Why? I don't know. He gave me a hundred reasons to do so but we were destined to meet, to love, to not be parted. 'Please come home', he said. We were reunited. I made my commitment to look after Tim as he had done to me.*

He is working away now just like Antwerp, Cardiff, Vancouver. It is not I am weak or particularly suicidal or self destructive but when I fell in love with Tim, I fell wholly in love with him - I remember the moment - he was planting a begonia in the garden and broke the sporting shoot - he didn't see me watching him - he held it in his hand like a wounded bird - such was his distress at accidentally hurting it - from then - I loved him.

All along I understood Tim's responses to his status - the denial and anger - he needed his denial and anger - no-one knows better than Hywel who observed our interactions. From the moment Tim rang me (in Chelsea when he first fell ill) to say S.O.S. his anger towards me lifted but for many isolated instances when it boiled out of him - finally during his last illness, full circle, he returned to the Timmy I had known before it began - no anger, gentle Timmy. When I kissed and hugged him goodbye in the early hour of New Years Eve he took some of my life, I some of his death. Peaceful - we'd given each other peace.

Having come through this phase of reflection and contemplation upon my own death whether intentional, premature or naturally when its meant to be; I now had to face the fact I was still mortal and that my life might yet be foreshortened by accident or more likely HIV. I had shelved the question of my unknown HIV status from the moment Tim became unwell; I couldn't have looked to his needs if I'd had to look to my own and worry about myself too. Yet from the moment of his death the question of my HIV status supplanted itself from my unconscious to my conscious. Friends - Glenys, Vicky and Shirley voiced delay; that I had enough on my plate; that a positive result would be an added burden at this very stressful time; that it was best to wait if I could have a reasonable quality of existence not knowing until gentler days ahead; that I should only have it done if the anxiety of not knowing undermined my health. One thing was for sure; whatever I was could not and would not change - positive or negative.

But now that I had an enumerated amount of money to come from Tim's estate, a house to live in, its entire contents, a dog, it seemed the responsible thing to do was draw up a will of my own. Considering how verbally aggressive Tim's father had been regarding the car, I shuddered to think how Tim's family would have treated me regarding the house worth fifty times the value of the car, had Tim not protected me with a signed will. I didn't want people fighting over my inheritance; I would decide the inheritors. And just as importantly if not more so I didn't want to put any member of my family or friend(s) in the position Tim had left me in the night he died regarding laying out/funeral instructions; there would be grief enough. Unexpectedly the attached letter of funeral instructions I found harder to draw up than the actual legal document of 'the last will and testament of -' where I basically had to name only executor and beneficiaries. The final words of the solicitor who drew up my will were most helpful - 'friends change, they come and go, it is advisable to frequently return to one's will to make amendments and changes.' One thing was for sure; whether by suicide, murder, accident, illness, disease or old age, death would come one day; but most strangely once I had collected my will and filed it away I felt I had somehow taken charge of my life.

Shirley rightly validated that a will is much more than a

legal document; it is a public statement (for once probate is granted a will becomes a public document for anyone to examine who so wishes) validating the life that has gone before the death especially of those people one loves and holds dear. Tim's will must have been a slap in the face for his family's maximum recognition of me as 'special friend'; the partnership we had shared never being openly acknowledged or accepted. Though they had deliberately counted me out of being mentioned in Tim's obituary they couldn't have failed to see that his naming of me as co-executor, co-trustee, and principal beneficiary was his written testimony of love for me.

The following extracts show the varying flavours of business matters that had to be managed in unison with the emotional aspects of bereavement.

From me to solicitor: *Following a conversation with RAC Recovery it would appear the money owed to Tim can not be recovered (£200-£300). Tim had been advised he would have to sue to pursue the claim alleging a subcontracted recovery firm further damaged his motorbike following an accident. The subcontracted firm denies liability.*

I enclose a returned cheque. I guess that Alison didn't pay it into her account until after Tim's account had been closed. She had bought two expensive opera books for Tim to send to a colleague in Germany. He dispatched them from hospital. I wrote the cheque for him (as he was so weak) and he signed it and I sent it to Tim's colleague Annina who gave it to Alison. I hope it is correct for me to send this to you for her to be reimbursed for these books.

From solicitor to me: *Thank you for your letter of 29th instant enclosing the Income Tax demand. I am in touch with Timothy's accountants about this; and we will look after the situation.*

I also confirm safe receipt of the Equitable Life (insurance) Policy signed and witnessed, for which I was much obliged, and which has now been dispatched to Equitable Life.

I now enclose Tim's Income Tax demand signed by Tim's sister. I should be glad as one of Timothy's executors if you would sign it on the reverse alongside his sister's signature, and then return it to me. In due course we shall have to ask his accountants to complete a return for the year ended 5th April 1990, and then a further return to the date of death.

I have just heard from The Royal Opera House with a cheque to deal with Timothy's accrued holiday pay less usual deductions, and I am only waiting to hear now from Equitable Life about the amount of the refunds to pension payments, and I will then be in a position to think about preparing the papers to be lodged with the Probate Court.

Thank you for your letter of the 22nd instant enclosing the cheque in favour of Alison - value of £65 drawn by Timothy prior to his death but unpaid to the Bank because of his death. It was quite correct to send it to me. It can be included as a debt from the Estate in the probate papers, but I will not be able to draw a replacement cheque until probate has been obtained and we are in funds.

Tim's death and his naming of me as co-executor and co-trustee thrust me into the legal arena of solicitors. This was an unknown quantity for me. When I first introduced myself to the solicitor by telephone I didn't even know what probate meant - the official proving of a will. To fulfil the aftermath responsibility of my executorship I had to learn as I went along; luckily my father well versed in legal matters was able to advise me along with Shirley and her welfare officer - its not just emotions that take months and years to sort out after bereavement; but business and legal matters as well. As there are hiccups and setbacks with emotional recovery; so there are with business - it was difficult enough having to send a letter and death certificate to the municipal offices to have Tim's name removed from the electoral register thereby annulling demands for his payment of Poll Tax Community

Charge without a writ being immediately issued for non payment necessitating further time consuming letters and phone calls to resolve the matter. I received a formal document from Belgium in Flemish of which I could not understand a word. I had no choice than to approach Tim's multi-lingual colleagues for help.

From Tim's secretary: *I enlisted the help of Dirk - in Antwerp regarding the translation of this document, and his colleague Marc - phoned me yesterday. Basically the form is a routine tax letter, stating how much Tim earned and paid in tax when he worked there, and asking how much he earned overall in that financial year so that they can be sure he paid enough tax. Marc ~ advice is to send a copy of Tim's death certificate and he has volunteered to look after the matter for you if you would like to send the stuff to him at the following address.*

From me to Marc: *Thank you for volunteering to look after this matter for me. I enclose a copy of a death certificate as requested plus the letter sent to my address from the Ministerie Van Financien.*

Now I understood why Shirley had recommended we obtain as many as ten copies of the death certificate the morning after Tim died when his mother and I registered his death - there are problems to sort out one could not have imagined prior to the death.

Finances were a stress of gathering momentum. When I had accepted Tim's invite to share my life with him, to live together; we sat down in the kitchen with a pot of tea, toast and jam and discussed the practicalities, responsibilities and financial boundaries of living together; of what I could expect from him, what he could expect from me, what we could expect from each other. Tim being a fiercely independent and dominant character determined he would pay for virtually everything; that I would contribute towards the phone bill and food; that he would in effect maintain me as long as I helped maintain the home and garden being quite practical by nature. From that afternoon we never had any problems living together from the practical and financial standpoint.

10.50pm December 30th our understanding and agreement became redundant; and as the solicitor would keep telling me I was responsible for virtually everything - and with no financial resources of my own. Though Tim had bequeathed a block of money to me it would be seven months before I received a penny. The utility services - water, gas, electricity and telephone wouldn't wait seven months for payment. I had given up conventional employment to look after Tim; if I could even find a full time job I knew the sort of income I could expect to receive wouldn't cover the outgoings of the house. Urgent repair works to the gutters at the back of the house, and completion of the redecoration of the kitchen following Tim's wrecking of it in a fit of anger had to be deferred. I wrote to the solicitor for advice but received none. With so many things going on I just 'switched off' and let the bills mount.

Our capricious central heating system had already broken down twice this long winter but luckily the insurance policy covered the second breakdown by two days before it lapsed. Without any cover for it I knew that if it broke down again I would have no heating or hot water. Then in swift succession I received a writ from British Gas for non payment of a bill, then a disconnection notice from London Electricity. Pasha needed his annual booster vaccination and check up - I couldn't afford the veterinary fees. I started to worry and sleep badly.

Eventually I had no option but to take out a huge overdraft against the will. I was lucky and grateful that Tim had looked after me but the shortfall between the death and probate being granted leaves the one left behind in dire straits I would not wish upon anyone. The transition from living within tiny financial boundaries to the new arrangements was alarming. I liked it the way it was before, up until the moment of his death - Tim the director of our relationship, me the co-worker. His death swept him out of the picture. I was forced into the presiding role; whether I liked it or not I had no choice; it was not negotiable. With frequent letters from my bank manager regarding my rising overdraft the pressure perpetuated; I was beginning to understand why bereavement is at the top of every stress table.

Already not two complete months into bereavement there had been a dramatic change in the configuration of people around me. I'd heard bereaved people say, 'everyone's abandoned me.' Now I was saying it too. Basically, following the departure of my parents, Barbara and Hywel - Pasha and I were in effect by ourselves. Friends had rightfully returned to their own lives, loves, problems and social lives - one can not be continuously shepherded. Tim had also kept most friends at a distance, even those with the open knowledge of his condition; I did feel that though they had moved into the arena of action at the height of the drama they had now moved back to their former positions. With the best intentions in the world one can only see friends infrequently in London due to each and everyone's individual work patterns, the problems of travel, the great distance at which many friends lived from me, etc. Now I realised just how much in health and sickness Tim had fulfilled my life. Additionally my friends lived in the real world of the living, non-bereaved, non-bereaving; while I existed in the substratum of the underworld of bereavement. Following an emotional crisis of identity in my late teenage years regarding my sexual identity I had discovered that one only finds out who ones true friends are when the chips are down; some remain loyal and faithful, some abandon you, and new people come into view. I wasn't surprised to discover this was the same 15 years on at the age of 33. But this time instead of feeling hurt I just felt increasingly cynical.

The pattern of change was established. My mother, sister

and Kate continued to keep in contact by telephone and letter. I'd always met Tim's boss irregularly for a drink at 'The Globe' in Covent Garden; this custom continued. But of my main block of London friends they all seemed increasingly remote - but it was I who parted company - in the old days people talked of the mar of death; in February 1991 similarly I was beginning to experience deaths effect and its consequence of separateness and divorce from those not touched by death. This feeling was exacerbated by those 'friends' who did abandon me - one young friend who could not cope with death on any level; another friend was aghast that I had so successfully maintained the cover-up he felt I had deceived him - on that count I needed Shirley and Gil desperately, weekly, to decontaminate me from fiction-making. Other people proved their prime allegiance had been to Tim in his lifetime; and not to me in mine. But then there were new sporting friendships with Julia, Patrik, Ruby and Stella - people affiliated very much to the world of opera who I had not known well, if at all, who out of devotion to Tim now strengthened and sustained me with messages of love; not frightened of confronting death and bereavement head on for which I was very grateful as seen by the following extracts:

'ONE DAY AT A TIME, ROB'

'I hope that things are working out for you. When you feel alone and the days are long and empty - let time pass and one day you will wake up and feel stronger. Don't rush, time is one of our best friends!'

'I'll try to call you when I arrive in London but I don't want you to feel that you have to see me if you feel vulnerable and want to be by yourself. I'll respect that but I will call.'

'I hope you are calm and not tortured by too many problems and sadness.'

I had a dream which I know was a symbol of metaphorical reference to the momentous changes taking place in my life. I was a spider in the centre of a symmetrical cobweb. Some threads of the web snapped, some sagged, some tightened, some remained unaltered and new ones appeared.

Towards the end of February I began the most difficult and harrowing of all aftermath responsibilities - the question of what to do with all Tim's clothes. I believed that for Tim's spirit to rest, roam, hover, return, fly free or not even to be, I had to break all earthly ties holding him to the life he'd left. I washed his remaining clothes which had been at the bottom of the laundry basket, and his cherished collection of jumpers. This was a chore I had done hundreds of times; but now it had a ceremonial feel to it. With all his clothes returned to his wardrobe I began the task. I had already made his big black leather jacket 'mine' the day I had worn it home from The Mildmay when I had collected his effects the day after he died. I derived great solace from wearing it, feeling safe in the volume he had occupied. A few of our clothes had been interchangeable so I took those I had been accustomed to wearing to my wardrobe. I then selected a few T-shirts, shirts, a belt, a leather jacket I had always admired and a few ties. Though the majority of Tim's remaining clothes fitted me they could not ever be mine; either they were not my style or too indelibly linked to Tim - T-shirts, shirts, jeans, trousers, cardigans, jumpers, socks, underwear, thermal underwear, leather jackets, leather trousers, suits, jackets, a dress suit, pyjamas, swimming trunks, sportswear, casual wear, shoes, trainers, etc.

Nearby was a rehabilitation hostel for young homeless people many of whom were HIV. I knew Tim would have applauded my decision to take a proportion of his clothes there at Gil's suggestion. Folding each item, whether a pair of jeans, a T-shirt, a shirt I bid it farewell, memories behind every article. When it came to Tim's one designer piece, an Yves St. Laurent rugby shirt I took it out again; I couldn't part with it yet, I would never wear it, nor did I want to memorialise it; I just needed it a little longer - I remembered clearly Tim wearing it at the dress rehearsal of 'Rigoletto' when I knew we were to be reconciled after our separation. Strangely as I folded and bagged the clothes I felt as if I was laying Tim out in his funeral clothes; a job in fact Debbie and Helen had done. After delivering the first three bags I took Pasha for a walk. I was breathless and thought I was going to have a panic attack I felt so affected by my afternoon's labours. Then an incredible hurricane force wind blew up and Pasha got frightened - the weather's 'special affects' couldn't have been staged more effectively to mirror the internal unrest. Remembering the Great Storm's devastation a few years prior - mature sturdy plane trees ripped out of the ground and flung afar - with the new danger of falling trees I cut our walk short. The void in Tim's wardrobe was to date the most telling tale of Tim's death.

Similarly the Mildmay needed clothes too. Shirley told me some patients arrive wearing all they possess in the world. So there I took Tim's pyjamas, thermals, casual and sportswear, and jumpers - warm and loose easy-to-wear clothes are important for patients debilitated by fevers and shivers. It was a wonderful feeling to take his khaki trousers and 'Rowing Challenge' jumper back to The Mildmay - the last clothes he had worn the day of his final admission to The Mildmay. To make the task easier I added a lot of my clothes too; following the emotional impact of taking his clothes to the hostel. I thought I might get through the job more comfortably if I took the stance I was boosting The Mildmay's stores of clothing rather than disposing of Tim's clothes; the emotional ruse worked.

Still in his wardrobe there remained an overcoat, a dress suit, a dinner suit, silk and summer suits, two dressing gowns, trainers, shoes, gloves, socks and underwear, leather jackets, a pair of leather trousers, belts, ties, new unworn slippers from my mother. I gave the overcoat to Ralph the volunteer assigned to me and Tim from The Mildmay, one of the black suits to Andy and belts to friends as mementos. Tim's socks and underwear were not good enough to give away, nor could I throw away such personal things, nor did I want to keep them. I had an idea. I chopped them up into tiny pieces transforming them from socks and underwear into stuffing - I opened up one of the loosely stuffed jumbo cushions in the sitting room and swelled it with what had been Tim's most intimate pieces of clothing. I sowed up the cushion with manic satisfaction. I removed the remaining things from his wardrobe to mine until I could find good homes for the remaining articles of wear. Forever I will keep his misshapen slippers that long protected his poor swollen feet with the other mementos of his life. His body had gone first and now the vestments belonging to his physical life followed. Tim's wardrobe was empty.

Always having been a bit of a loner I was starting to have trouble with my own company for the first time. Without Pasha it would have been awful; I find it hard to tolerate people who don't like dogs after February when my own species of Homo sapiens combined couldn't begin to give me the comfort he produced. Still the prevailing emptiness could not be neutralised by Pasha, 'The Falcon & Firkin', 'The London Apprentice', Covent Garden or the occasional visit of a friend.

Disposing of Tim's clothes had a lot to do with 'stillness' giving way to 'loneliness'. A good friend who lost his partner too from AIDS described a feeling of abandonment. I knew Tim had loved me and had left unwittingly but the growing sense of hurt and desertion was the same as if he had intentionally packed his bags and left me.

Now I could see that my pilfering of the bottle of morphine and the letter had been my expression of being dragged to the gateway of (Tim's) death and being forced to look it squarely in the eye. I'd stood on the threshold of life and death with Tim. He had no choice; he had to cross the threshold and die. I could have chosen death but I had a choice. He didn't. I was not meant to die then. The idea of dying with him was less painful than parting and living on without him. But I didn't follow. I stayed behind. I watched him cross over into Death's Great Garden of Mystery. He turned and faced me. We didn't touch or kiss. We smiled and said Goodbye. He turned to death, I turned to life. I had been caught in between the currents of life and death and had been shipwrecked on the shore of life. I had survived Tim's death.

CHAPTER 5

March

Survivors in the lifeboats of the Titanic described the stricken vessel as still comforting - looking enormous on the calm water with all its portholes and saloons ablaze with light. Many passengers fully expected to return to the liner once the 'alarm' had passed. Yet already separated forever from the mother ship and their loved ones left on board; some of the lifeboats stayed dependently near to the dying ship. Only when the Titanic foundered and the tiny open boats faced the vastness of a freezing dark Atlantic night were the survivors truly adrift at sea four hundred miles from the nearest landfall.

Similarly with the turning of the calendar to the first day of March, St David's Day came a new season - spring. As a Welshman the Patron Saint's Day of Wales had always symbolised the end of winter. Now I was further separated from the short dark winter's day holding Tim's death; and cast into a new season alone. With this distancing between us, blending with the loneliness I already carried was a capacious sense of insecurity adding to the emotional ballast of bereavement. I now realised that my time with Tim if not the happiest and easiest the last few years had been in total the most stable and secure period of my grown years.

March 1st I poured turpentine substitute over the cardboard box which had protected the urn containing Tim's ashes. The box had a round label on it with Tim's name, date of cremation, and cremation number 280254. I felt a little self conscious in the garden as I set fire to the box in case any of my neighbours overlooking observed what must have appeared strange behaviour - yet the ancient rite of purification by fire seemed the appropriate form of disposal. Afterwards I watered the ash into the soil with the red watering can.

March 3rd: I burnt the official envelope containing Tim's certificate of cremation; and I watered that into the soil too. In the early evening once the light began to fade I burnt the actual certificate of cremation and the receipt for £9 that I had paid for the urn. The certificate took fire easily, rose gently into the air, blackened, settled and crumbled over the deep purple early flowering 'Helleborus orientalis'. Whether one files away such papers, disposes of them in the rubbish or destroys them symbolically as I did they are an aftermath responsibility to be dealt with.

You the reader might think what a drama I made of disposing mere cellulose - but to me they were not just papers and cardboard any more than a relic of the Cross is mere cellulose. Because I looked upon these 'death papers' with such awe; their disposal had to be fitting; and what method could be more appropriate than fire one of the four simple substances - earth, water, air, fire of which all material bodies were held to be compounded in ancient and medieval philosophy.

That I knew Tim was not to be scattered or interred on hallowed ground I could dispose of the certificate of cremation, otherwise needed for the church authorities. The box, envelope, certificate and receipt were trappings of death from what I saw as Tim's 'death-time' i.e. the period existing between his last breath and his ultimate return to Mother Nature - shortly his ashes would be scattered and washed by rain into the soil of Epping Forest to nourish the plants or to permeate down into the water-table below. Tim would be no more.

I didn't want to be left with these morbid papers that I did not believe belonged beyond Tim's 'death-time'. However weird my burning rituals might have appeared they allowed for Tim to be freed from the earthly shackles of funereal bureaucracy. I would only keep the death certificates out of necessity - they somehow belonged to my life perpetuating in my role of executor, and not to Tim's 'death-time'. Approximately twelve hours had passed between his death and his name being inscribed on the certificates.

Tim's life had been synonymous with exactly that - life. Even the day he died he lived for most of it and fought hard to live on. When I first came to stay with Tim for a weekend long before I ever knew we were to become boyfriends and that the house would become my home, my first impression was of a happy fun house - bright wallpapers and colours everywhere. Now the same house felt like an ante-room to a tomb chamber - the garage where Tim's ashes reposed. Once the ashes had been scattered 'death' would have been much taken out of the house; the associated papers burnt this already allowed for a little 'life' to come back into the house again. How I would ultimately get 'life' back into every room, corner and object where the shadow of death dwelt I did not know; but this was my task and I'd opened the way for it. Somehow by helping to free Tim's life from death's trappings I felt a surge in my life-force within.

March 7th was the seventh day of the third month of the year; a day that began unprepossessingly but ended eventfully - where in the course of a few hours in the evening I experienced the most significant change in the balance of relationships obtaining both a new best friend and additionally a new lover.

At 7pm I attended the first meeting of The Mildmay Mission Bereavement Support Group. Normally in life one gets to know people through either work or social métiers; this was different; that we had each lost our partner from AIDS in the latter half of 1990 proved a common denominator bonding us together and dissolving our many differences of gender, sexual orientation, race and religion; the moral being HIV can and does affect anyone and everyone. There would ultimately be nine of us - two heterosexual women Linda and Maria, and seven homosexual men Nigel, George, Vince, Keith, Nittin, Bevis and me; and two who couldn't make the first meeting. It was with Maria I had an immediate empathy that would lead to the development of a profound relationship which I had never had previously with another woman.

We had all had close links with The Mildmay which had cared for our partners within the hospice itself and at home courtesy of The Mildmay Home Care Team. Still we were not patients so we were all very impressed with the efforts laid on for us - a cold buffet spread of flans, sandwiches, salads and cakes. This initial meeting was an informal get together, the two counsellors Annie and Carol facilitating the group. The only 'work' we had to do at this first session was to introduce ourselves, our dead partners name, when our partner died, and our thoughts of the care our partner had received from The Mildmay. I was so moved by each individual story that when it was my turn, by chance the last, I was choked and just shook my head - I couldn't say a word. Later Annie returned to me and I just managed to blurt out my piece. I had in fact looked forward to the group but was completely caught off guard by the flood of rising emotion within. I didn't cry and quite resented the fervid emotional charge of riotous unconstrained clamour that seemed determined to unseat me. Afterwards I realised that such a 'safe' environment, and the understanding of the others had helped me release those weighty feelings; it felt wrong but wasn't. Such backlogged emotion has to be spent if one is to move through the process of grieving and to be ultimately absolved from bereavement.

That night at The Mildmay I found people who spoke my language of existence - (AIDS) bereavement; and therein the antidote to all the months and years of isolation that had gone before - I had found my equals and for the first time in ages I did not feel lonely - until the 9pm finish. Our first of seven sessions was over until the next month. Some drove off from the car park, a few shared a taxi. I found myself alone in Hackney Road. Nobody was there. I couldn't face going home even to a waiting dog with a wagging tail; and another lonely drink at 'The Falcon & Firkin'. As if on cue a number 6 open platform Routemaster stopped abreast of me at the bus stop outside The Mildmay as if inviting me on board. I had no prearranged plans to do anything after the group; the bus made my mind up for me so I jumped on board and rode it to Covent Garden. For a while I wandered aimlessly - around the Royal Opera House, through the market, I called in on my Godfather in Maiden Lane but he wasn't in. I crossed the road to the gay 'Attic Bar' above 'The Peacock'.

Everything Shirley had prepared me for happened. A dark Italian entered soon after me. And so I met Max. He came home with me. Any nervousness I might have had dissipated. Though my libido had been adversely affected by the demands of caring for Tim; and though my libido would see-saw with the ever changing conditions of bereavement ahead of me; that I began to function again sexually was a great confidence boost. Gil said that her role was not just to validate illness but wellness too. Though sex can be a carrier of catastrophe; and I had been through a stage of seeing sex as something equating only with disease and the deformity AIDS produces; ultimately sex has to be the greatest expression of life. My sexual renaissance was a very important step in the healing process.

Perhaps Max should have been a secret clandestine lover but I'd had quite enough of secrets. He was a reality in my life, in my bed. Just small things I had taken for granted in Tim's lifetime - someone making me a cup of tea in the morning, someone taking Pasha for a walk; brought life flooding back into those dead voids Tim had left behind. Again I understood things I hadn't before: One of Tim's colleagues had died following an accident. Within a couple of weeks the surviving boyfriend had a new woman in his life that proved a lasting union. People had thought it disrespectful; that he couldn't have loved the dead girl - only now I could sympathise and understand that these unkind views of outsiders amounted to no more than hogwash; the greatest solace is the touch and bodily warmth of another human being. Gil said that often the first relationship following a bereavement isn't the lasting one; however unsuited or suited is no less important to the needs and vagaries of the bereaved one.

And who are others to judge us? 'What we can give you is limited', Andy and Glenys truthfully said once the height of the drama - the death - had passed. Why should we suffer alone in grief for even one day? One will suffer; but one doesn't have to do so alone. The Romantic image of grief doesn't allow for the reality of grief; that new friend(s) and lover(s) are often a part of early bereavement. Some people have a friend who can step into the void such as Brahms did for Schumann's wife Clara; and did so before the death of Robert Schumann; though in no way invalidating or negating the love Clara held for Robert.

'His head was beautiful, the forehead so transparent and slightly arched. I stood by the body of my beloved husband, and I was at peace. All my feelings were taken up in thanks to God that Robert was at last free, and as I knelt by his bed I was filled with awe. It was as though his sacred spirit was hovering above me. If only he had taken me with him.

His dearest friends (Brahms and Joachim) walked in front (of the coffin), and I came unnoticed behind. It was best this way. He would have liked it so. So with his departure, my happiness is ended. A new life is beginning.

Clara Schumann'

It's no different whether a great musician such as the pianist Clara Schumann or 140 years later an anonymous gay man as myself; the sentiments one is left with for the deceased are the same - relief the suffering is over, the desire to die as well, feeling the person's spirit nearby, the ending of one life, the beginning of another.

I had not such a friend as Brahms; instead I found Max. Reactions varied. He lived up to the image I held of Italians - fiery and reactive and not by any means easy; but not without a kindness of his own. Peter Day not even meeting Max rang to say he'd heard 'the good news' and thought it wonderful that I wasn't alone; that Tim would be pleased; not to feel any guilt; not to let anyone make me feel guilty. An actor friend Frank said my friends had speculated I wouldn't be alone for very long.

Still, I was very different to how I'd ever been before when entering a new liaison; I was compromised by bereavement and discovered that whereas Tim and I had become involved very quickly with each other both domestically and emotionally; now the physical and emotional space I could make over was severely limited. Never before had I needed my own space so; when I didn't get it intolerance and irritability crept in.

When Tim died I was befriended by Patrik in Sweden who had lost his partner Göran a year before Tim. This new friendship developed through the medium of correspondence. When I later found I was having problems with my side of the new relationship I wrote to Patrik. This was his reply…

You write me that you now can't give the same attentions that you gave to Tim. No wonder - after such short time after Tim's death - but that doesn't prove that there should be something wrong with what you can give. Each relationship is different and each circumstance is different - if we always compare we will forget to live and to enjoy.

Hopefully we are able to select the person we want to be with - but we can not choose the circumstances under which we meet. They can be bad. But with patience, understanding and love we can overcome the bad timing of a meeting.

What Tim taught you - I am sure he would want you to practice - and he taught you to love, didn't he?

Love, Patrik.

I remember asking a colleague at Crusaid, 'How is X ?', a man who had been very depressed and withdrawn following the death of his boyfriend. 'He's met a policeman.' The answer had an overlay as if to say well now that he's got a new lover he must be 'over it'. If people think that because you have a new lover/companion that you are excused from bereavement; they couldn't be more wrong.

The subthemes of bereavement continued inevitably. I reawakened the balcony in front of the sitting room windows not just by stepping out there; but by clearing not only the dead plants from the previous autumn, but all the window boxes and tubs as well - they would not be planted again. It was not a large area but the one that demanded the most attention in high summer - watering twice daily without exception. Tim's last summer the balcony had looked very pretty with trailing geraniums tumbling through the railings, red pelargoniums and pink mallows creating a festivity of colour. That it had pleased Tim pleased me; but its maintenance had become just another round of my daily chores. Now that I had to look after everything I decided to streamline the running of the house - the front and back gardens were quite enough to look after. The hardest part was dismantling the wooden stands Tim had made for the window boxes against the back wall of the balcony; but the job had to be done. When I returned home from the tip and drove onto the forecourt and looked up at the balcony I was pleased I'd taken charge of even this one small area of the house but the stark change left me with the same wrenching feeling I'd had when passing through the New Year hour; that my life was increasingly separating from the life I'd had with Tim; with few comforting reference points in lieu of the many I had lost and was still losing.

It was a poignant experience returning to the venue of The Mayflower Theatre in Southampton where Tim and I had seen so many productions of The Welsh National Opera on tour (for whom he had worked when we met), now to see Verdi's 'La Traviata'. Previously we had gone by train or been driven by friends; and Tim arranging everything. The responsibility of now arranging all aspects of the outing reflected the consequence of bereavement - arrangements for Pasha to be looked after for the day, the tickets, servicing the car for the journey, checking the route, etc. - these things wouldn't even register in ordinary life. Again I felt Tim's loss; and the freed mustering and mobilizing side of my personality that Tim's dominating character had never allowed. It's like learning to walk again; what's gone before counts for nothing; that I had travelled to the other side of the world by myself; did not make a straightforward 60 mile car journey easy now. At the age of 33 basic happenings of daily existence took on the colour of virgin experiences of life.

This was the first time I'd left London since collecting Pasha from the farm. 'La Traviata' was based on the novel 'The Lady of the Camellias' by Alexandre Dumas, the true story of the novelist's love affair with The Parisian courtesan Marie Duplessis. She wore red camellias on the days of the month when she was 'not available' acknowledging a physical fact not generally referred to in polite society (menstruation). When I got up on the morning of the opera I had cold feet; once again I wanted to drop out of something arranged - but when I opened the kitchen blind I couldn't believe my eyes - the first flower of the blood red camellia in the garden had opened overnight. I would go to Southampton. Many times during bereavement one does have setbacks; but equally there are many times when little things happen that make the seemingly impossible possible.

With the heroine of the opera dying of consumption; certainly since the advent of penicillin any production of 'La Traviata' would have been Romantic i.e. remote to experience; that modern audiences would have been unaffected by tuberculosis unlike the days of 'Traviata's' première (1853) when everyone in the theatre lived under the threat of tuberculosis, the scourge of Victorian times. Göran's bold production, drawing from his own HIV experience, gave this piece back to a modern audience with contemporary relevance: suggesting a modern courtesan who acquired HIV as a result of a decadent life style, and died of tuberculosis as an AIDS related infection. I remember what Peter Day said following Tim's HIV diagnosis, 'We are living in the seventeenth century again'.

Additionally I was time warped back to the opening night of the same production in Cardiff three years before. I had gone with Hywel to escape from London for a weekend; for a rest from the tensions generated at home from Tim's refusal to discuss or acknowledge his HIV status, his refusal to be counselled; and the worries of his increasingly disturbed behaviour from such explosive emotional containment.

To then be so unexpectedly confronted by HIV in theatrical form was an allegory that helped me think about the unthinkable. When Violetta, the heroine died, I had a glimpse into the future holding Tim's death. How? When would it happen? I started to panic. Hywel and I were staying at my parents' house; on our return there all my worries and tensions boiled out of me and for the first time I broke the confidence. All my contained anxieties of one year and a half poured out. Hywel was drawn into the collusion i.e. maintaining the confidence and having to pretend he didn't know in Tim's presence. Doctors kept telling me Tim would come out of the denial phase but he never did - until just before his death; but not too late to release Hywel from the weighty burden he had long carried so magnanimously.

The combination of the unfamiliar drive to

Southampton, the grim truth of 'La Traviata', memories of the night of the première, the late drive back to London - I was tired beyond description for what was in reality just a pleasure day out. But I was glad I had made the trip; for by laying ghosts from the past, I awakened the present to free the future for new experiences.

One evening, quite spontaneously, as I walked from the kitchen into the sitting room I picked up a pile of assorted papers of mine from the worktop next to the sink. I'd given them no thought for the last three months. I carried them into the sitting room and placed them in the centre of Tim's large black and steel desk in the alcove. I didn't yet move Tim's things but in that moment and action I made the desk mine. I made a cup of coffee and began to look through my things. They told the story of my last few months of life with Tim. On top was my notebook. Underneath there was a yellow handbook for counselling training courses at The Westminster Pastoral Foundation for the autumn 1990 intake. The application date had long passed. Tim had been too ill for me to apply. After settling in London I'd wanted to train as a counsellor. I didn't have a profession. I wanted and needed one. Following some very helpful counselling in my early 20's for the coming-out difficulties I'd experienced as a young man within my family I'd wanted to work to support gay men. In the face of the AIDS Disaster a counselling career seemed meaningless. Would there be any gay men left to counsel or be counselled? I binned the handbook. I next looked at the red hessian bound diary Tim had given me for 1991. I had always kept a personal diary. He'd given me one every year since we met. But this one would remain blank. There were receipts for paint and wallpaper for the redecoration of the kitchen and invites to Christmas parties. Over the years I had

had encouraging success getting various articles and short stories published. I'd wanted to be a writer. Words whether spoken, written or read had always been very important to me; but no more. There was nothing to write about. Everything seemed futile. I'd lost and abandoned all my personal and professional plans, hopes and dreams. Without Tim all meaning and purpose to life had been extinguished. At the bottom of the pile was the final copy of the last thing I'd written and completed only shortly and by no coincidence just before Tim died.

'Fifth Night Out'
A Short Story by Rob Lewis 1990

The Arabian pool lay silent, undisturbed yet he could hear free water outside the hull. Alexandria beckoned. He saw the island of Pharos again, the tranquil Pool of Ptolemy, the turbulent waters of the Mediterranean beyond. He saw in his memories Arab boys beings ducked playfully by older men. Ahmed stood aside from his friends on the edge of the pool - but his image faded; these waters had been captured, subdued.

He retreated to the Turkish baths. He had them to himself; the mosaic floors, gilded beams, carved pillars, the dull red ceiling. The lantern lamps cast an eerie glow, his eyes roved exploring every detail to stop his mind from wandering back. Still, the room caused him distress, he yearned for Ahmed. His earlier visit had been as difficult; the steam room had suffocated him, the cold douche had stunned him. The masseur had arrested his muscles but his thoughts had found unwelcome freedom he had not been able to govern amongst the Middle Eastern surroundings. Rubbed, slapped, kneaded, the masseur impelled him back to Alexandria 1895. Alone, he thought it would have been easier at this later hour, and fortified with whisky, but it was not. He should not have come. Once more he made his escape, leaving behind his guilt, to forget amongst his own kind. He could not invoke Ahmed without memories of the ruin that love had brought him.

Before he could climb to the life he now lived five decks above he heard the sound of sobbing. A class barrier door stood ajar. He pushed it open. Bare rivets and naked lightbulbs categorised third class quarters. His surprise intrusion upon an Irish émigrée made her drop a leather pouch from which spilled seeds. While he helped her gather them up he learned she was homesick for Ireland, her mother, and all that was familiar she had left behind. The uncertainties of a new life now filled her with fear, and all she possessed was the pouch of willow seeds she would plant in the New World to remind her of home. It seemed preposterous to him that an uneducated steerage passenger could diminish him, but she had, despite his fine clothes and cultured tongue - for she had the conviction to reject a sterile existence and follow frightening adventure to chance finding happiness.

Desperately he needed reaffirmation of his being as husband, father and master. Four decks he climbed to the reassuring Edwardian foyer. The parlour suite his family occupied was quiet; his wife, her maid and the governess were asleep in their rooms, but his manservant had not returned from his usual Friday night off. He heard his son's soldier toy playing its drums. He looked in on the boy but he had fallen asleep again. He loathed the mechanical toy, its mocking gaze, and knowing eyes always ridiculing. He longed to smash it to pulp but his son couldn't sleep without it. Every beat thundered through his drunken senses threatening to demolish the fragile barrier he had raised to keep the past at bay. A shot more whisky to steady his thoughts but he had to leave; he couldn't bear to hear the automaton's drum roll.

Despite the cold of the open promenade and his wanting of a topcoat he remained on deck. He walked to the promontory overlooking the poop deck trying to drive the echoes of drumming from his mind. He breathed deeply, forgetting. Invisible against the railings he let the darkness erase the officer's condemning eyes. Light mustered momentarily in the entrance to the steerage quarters below. Something in the manner of one of two emerging men identified his manservant; no doubt with one of the other valets or one of the boys from steerage. And even if it wasn't him he knew he would be down there somewhere, flirting as he did in London with the boys of Piccadilly. The clandestine rendezvous below him was swallowed by the darkness and silenced by the steady roar of the funnels.

Even in this most isolated of places aboard he could not escape rude reminders of the past. How he envied his manservant; not only was he at peace with his sexuality, he professed it to be natural, neither learned or acquired, an inherent part of his being. But how could it be so? Everything about his society and upbringing had such inclinations to be a corruption - a malediction. Yet before Ahmed there had always been that desire. It was like belonging to a club he had never asked to join, that would not accept his resignation, a life member however much he refuted membership. As he gazed out over the wake he wished there was a levelling influence that could give him the freedoms his man enjoyed; he had been conditioned for too long that his predilections were unacceptable.

The whisky was working, he calmed. He stepped out of the bitter darkness into the Verandah Café. Only the gay set remained, a sole group drinking highballs. They were always there, always laughing, smiling and beautiful. They left, no doubt heading for the livelier Café Parisien. Drum - Drum - Drum, Drum,. Drum. His eyes followed the dapper young man wearing a striped blazer who had incited so much comment that evening refusing to dress for dinner. He pondered how such indecorous behaviour becomes acceptable hotheadedness when ones father is a magnate and one of the most illustrious passengers on board. If he had the gall of the youth and went one step further challenging the moral propriety of the time he knew he would lose more than access to the first class dining saloon.

He was glad to leave such ruinous thoughts. The revolving door that led into the smoking room maintained the solemnity of the only male preserve on board; laughter and the high pitch of women's voices being unable to ford the seals of the rotating doors. Ironically he liked this vast room least of all. Every crossing finds a huddle of bachelors around a card table, and this maiden voyage was no exception. The cloistered gathering was taking advantage of the Purser's lenience in allowing the room to remain open after eleven thirty. Just as he thought he had found some respite he noticed that one of the players who had thrown in his hand, had focused his attention onto him. He ordered a hot whisky and lemonade to silence the drummer boy, but still he pounded. With his desire grew his anxiety, his temples throbbed, his heart palpitated. Guilt annulled, he left before the steward returned with his drink.

Bewildered, he wandered directionless. He crossed a deserted foyer and entered another corridor. It led to the lounge. It too was silent and empty. Though the chandeliers were extinguished a few wall lights permitted the Louis XVI decor to be admired. Enough light shivered on Artemis, Goddess of the Hunt, with raised arrow in one hand and a stag grasped in the other. While he looked at the statuette on the mantelpiece he knew he was both the hunted and the hunter; hunted by guilt, hunting for ....., but he would not cast his memory back beyond the orchestra playing music from the new 'Der Rosenkavalier' that evening; for while he heard Strauss he was safe from the percussion of the soldier toy.

Crossing the threshold of the principal foyer he found at last an interval in his wanderings. In this loftiest of spaces the ship's architect was busy scribbling notes. Wherever seen he continually perfected his creation. He looked up from his notebook and beckoned as the foyer clock struck midnight. The twelfth chime faded away. And the clock stopped. April 13th had begun.

The architect reminisced of the night back in 1907 when his ships were born as sketches on a napkin, drawn almost indifferently after dinner with Lord Pirrie at Devonshire House. He had seen their keels laid and watched their hulls rise above Pirrie's Belfast yards. He had attended their launchings and followed their fitting out with paternal interest. Aboard during their sea trials he had sailed on

Olympic's maiden voyage and now Titanic's. There were numerous minor problems for him to correct; already he had drawn plans to convert the reading and writing room into more cabins. It was far too large and had remained virtually empty for in these modern days ladies would simply not withdraw. He motioned over the horizon - tugs were preparing to urge Olympic into the Hudson, the pier would be vacated awaiting Titanic. Olympic would make headway, the partnership would have begun. He had waited five years for this day when his two ships would be in service together, one eastbound, one westbound. He reckoned at some point in the early hours of her fifth night at sea Titanic would pass Olympic, their first Atlantic meeting. And when Gigantic joined them the threesome would be complete. Unconquerable, Olympic personified the quintessence of 20th Century Man which Titanic was confirming and Gigantic would indelibly approve.

The architect's proud thoughts contrasted harshly with his own life's echoes: Alexandria 1895 - discovered with Ahmed - that gloating accusing officer - cashiered. Only a hastily arranged marriage had saved him from social ruin. The alliance had snuffed out the rumours assuring his respectability whilst his wealth guaranteed his wife's position in the beau monde. It was ironic that they were one of the most popular couples in society and onboard; nevertheless the marriage was a sham. He cursed himself for the cross that bedevilled his career. He cursed his brother who had consummated his marriage. He cursed the codes of his class which conditioned him to live in such splendid isolation. He detested his useless hedonistic life. With no alternative he had to continue as he had gone before, easing his way through each day with whisky, his only consort, always there to keep him company, dulling the present and keeping the past at bay. Normally he liked this timeless hour of midnight when Time stood still for an hour as she did on westbound crossings; for while Time dozed there was no past to remember or future to fear. Too much had happened that day focusing on his guilt, the aimlessness of his existence, the fickleness of Society, and the emptiness of his marriage for him to share the architect's triumph. The greater his sense of desolation, the greater was his yearning to see his son, his only glory; to leave the architect, the foyer, and its clock with its wretched figures of Honour and Glory crowning Time.

In the semi-darkness of his son's room it was easier to imagine a sturdy oak beyond the curtains than the waters of the Atlantic forty feet below. The boy's eiderdown had slipped off the bed so he stooped to pick it up. Whisky-footed, he stumbled against the bedside-table. The drummer boy lurched and played its winding down tune. Throwing the eiderdown around the small form lost in the huge bed he retreated.

He poured himself another tumbler of whisky, and a second. But it was no use. He could not escape the past - that moment of disgrace had haunted him these seventeen years. He shouldn't have explored the sub decks, least of all visited Titanic's Turkish Baths; for probing her deepest secrets he had challenged his own, and revisited Alexandria. In succumbing to Titanic's temptations he had succumbed to his own. He should escape before his manservant returned to assist him with his déshabillé; now vulnerable to his passions unbridled by whisky. It was too late, he was there.

Fifth night out from Southampton, Titanic largest ship in the world stood still in the water. Ice-splinters danced in the air like a storm of fireflies amplifying the lights of the boat deck. He had never seen such coronas of sparkling light before, a phenomenon of the ice-field they were drifting in. He assisted his wife, maid, son and governess into a lifeboat assuring them it was only a precautionary measure. Many were refusing to enter the boats preferring the security of the mother vessel than a perilous drop to the sea sixty feet below. He breathed a sigh of relief when the lifeboat touched the water with a little splash.

His manservant had disappeared to shepherd a gaggle of maids to another lifeboat. They had been standing just inside the foyer entrance looking awkward and a little frightened - boundaries unclear, the written and unwritten rules of society by which everyone lived no longer applied. Maids and ladies, there seemed to be no appropriate etiquette for the events in progress. The excitement of the untoward and the icy air had sobered him up. A distress rocket exploded overhead, perhaps the situation was more serious than previously thought, she was noticeably down at the bow. He decided to take a look below to see how high the water had risen. The funnels bellowed letting off steam.

The foyer was thronged. Some were in nightclothes with just a blanket or coat thrown around their shoulders. Others were ludicrously dressed in their new motoring coats as if to go for a drive in the country which was all the rage. Only a few were impeccably dressed - it was the first time he had seen the gay set without a smile; he wondered how the young ladies in their ankle-arresting hobble skirts would ever cross the gap between the boat deck and the boats swung out on their davits should the ship need to be evacuated.

As he descended the staircase he was unprepared for the sight that met him in the foyer below. There amassed gawping steerage passengers. They huddled together like sheep in awe of magnificent and unaccustomed surroundings. Just like the peasantry who marched on Versailles 123 years before, they gazed in cowed wonderment at interiors never seen nor imagined. The herd shifted uncomfortably on the black and white chequered floor. They looked disbelievingly at the statuary, pillars and panelling. One dared to reach out to touch a pineapple carving atop a newel post. Furtive glances from smaller groups classified the bourgeoisie from second class. They tried to look at ease but were as keen to absorb the beauty around them as the proletariat. It was the downcast look of isolated couples and individuals that gave away their superior class, not giving a second glance to familiarity of environment.

Revolution: Where in Europe that night he wondered would be found such Egalité, Fraternité between the classes? The atmosphere held of a fancy dress ball but nobody was enjoying the event despite the brilliant lighting, warmth and lively beat of the ragtime band. He was now part of the crowd tableau himself. For a moment Titanic succeeded in convincing him all was well - but the stairs were a little disconcerting. The side flights to each half landing pitched him against the balustrades, the main flights facing aft seemed to be levelling out, his feet touching the treads before they ought. It was worse then being drunk. B - Deck, C - Deck, he was alone. D - Deck, down, down to the Turkish Baths. All was dry but watertight doors blocked his path to the Arabian Pool. He touched one. It was bitterly cold and covered in running condensation. He shivered thinking of the wanton icy Atlantic subjugating the warm fresh waters of the now flooded pool beyond the iron barrier.

It looked as if her bulkheads would hold. Having satisfied himself that the adjacent Turkish Baths were dry he decided to go back on deck reassured the ship would float. Then astonished he watched a steady stream of seawater run in through the door and across the floor. In moments it became a torrent, the torrent a river as it searched out the boundaries of the Cooling Room. A jet of water burst through one of the oriental screens veiling an unsecured porthole. Water trickled down the walls oozing between the exquisite tiled panels. It ran along the bottom of the gilded beams overhead, dripped onto his shoulder and dissolved the starch of his collar. The bronze table lamps burned defiantly, the lapping waters scattering pretty ripples of light over the walls. Water fanned out from the immersed porthole drowning a table - mirror obliterating his reflection. The annulling water overpowered; the mirror impotent, something gave way within; he glimpsed Ahmed, smiling, beckoning. Water now swirled around his legs, he had to leave. Titanic was sinking.

Outside, the stairs which had been so hearteningly dry were now a stepped waterfall. The pale green water laughed at Man's hubris as it sloshed over his shoes as he climbed to E - Deck. Something gave way below, perhaps a bulkhead. Water boiled up the stairs, surged, calmed. Eerily lights still glowed in the flooded stairwell. He climbed to the next deck and rested a moment; all seemed in order. Only the tilt of the deck revealed anything was amiss. The serenity of the room maddened him. It was too quiet, too warm, too still - the subtle lighting casting delicate shadows over the walls of the reception room and dining room beyond. It was too complacent. He didn't know how the ship should appropriately meet its end but it shouldn't be like this. The room should have been fighting for its life but British to the end showed no recognition of impending doom; just a flicker of fear as the first table lamp fell.

Higher, higher he climbed reaching the foyer. He hardly recognised Titanic's architect, the urgency of his step gone, a strange pallor whitening his face. The creator turned away and he watched the man he had so envied make his way towards the main lounge like the builder of the pyramids to be entombed within; a man for whom fate had singled out to counterpoise glory with damnation.

It was here only two nights previously the architect had prematurely shared with him the maturity of his dream. And not two hours ago he had been sitting quietly here waiting for the midnight hour when he first realised something was wrong - the glass dome overhead ceased to rattle and he knew the engines had stopped. And here now it dawned on him he had not the night to live. What a resplendent tomb he thought, all those left aboard unwilling sacrificial victims, necessary offerings so Man would not dare set himself above the dictums of Mother Nature again. In that moment he saw

Titanic amongst all Man's monuments to his own greatness in all their transience and vulnerability. While Man's testament to his own glory decayed around him, his loves for his son and manservant emerged as the only intransient truths. Whatever time was left, he had at last found his own time.

He grieved for one last glance of his son. He trod carefully along the stairs to B - Deck and climbed the steepening deck to his suite. The lithograph of his son had fallen onto the floor but remained intact in its frame. He sat on the edge of his son's bed; still a glimmer of warmth held under the heavy eiderdown in the hollow where the boy had so recently slept. With a thud the automaton toppled onto the floor. Its expression had changed - the mocking eyes and jeering look had given way to a fixed smile for it was a painted toy. Titanic had absolved him from his years of guilt.

The lights began to glow red, the dynamos were failing. He looked out at the desolate scene of drifting humanity amidst the ice-floes. It was hard to believe that the select party toasting Titanic's investiture with Olympic had been displaced by his solitary witnessing of her end. Momentarily the lights came on again in full brightness extinguishing the scene beyond. In the square ports he saw reflected behind him his manservant, Ahmed. They approached one another. Reconciled, they plunged into the Pool of Ptolemy. Liberté.

Most passengers will have retired, and long before the brief encounter of the leviathans would occur. The gay set might linger in the Café Parisien but he doubted they would chance their amorous pursuits for a passing ship in the night. He could not think of anything that would effect a distraction from the card table in the smoking room. And considering the punishing cold outside he doubted if any from steerage would seek their open deck spaces for an unrestricted view of Olympic's revelation. However there would be a few of us committed individuals congregated, each scanning the darkness for the first glimpse of Olympic's running lights. Our eyes track the horizon - only the absence of stars denote where the sky gives way to the sea. Spotted, she grows quickly in the night. On she comes Olympic. She is upon us, all her saloons blaze with light, the darkness abates and the night stands aside patiently. Then as swiftly as she has come, she goes, her masthead lights attendant stars guiding her through the darkness. The night rolls in and the ocean assimilates every sign of Man's passing.

It was an allegorical piece about life, death, homosexuality, victims, survivors, guilt and separation - and most of all of an indiscriminate moment of life after which nothing is ever the same again. Just a few more yards and the Titanic would have cleared the iceberg and they would have talked of a close shave. If Tim hadn't gone to San Francisco for an interview with Kurt Adler, the Intendant of The War Memorial Opera House he wouldn't have had that deadly encounter. He may have had another, he may not. I didn't think in terms of prebereavement or bereavement; I just knew I was going through a massive psychological trauma unlike anything I had experienced in my life; that I could neither avoid nor circumnavigate. There was no map or handbook. It was frightening and certainly in control of me; like being possessed by an alien entity. In a routine session with Shirley I lamented of how Tim's death had taken away all my aspirations. I asked her for a booklist of other men's stories so I could read about other men's similar experiences of loss especially around AIDS. I was looking for identification such as I'd started to find at The Partners' Group. But the meetings were a month apart. I couldn't wait. I wanted to try and get a handle on things and find some coordinates so I might be able to reorientate myself to the rest of the world and all the normal things of life which death had dispossessed me from. I was very surprised that there were no such published testimonies. Shirley suggested I write the book that I would have liked to have read. I dismissed the proposition as audacious - but the idea stuck. Just ambling home a few days later on the No. 6 bus, the three words 'The Fighting Temeraire' flashed from nowhere to the forefront of my mind. When I got home I opened my notebook. On a blank page I wrote 'The Fighting Temeraire'. I had the title. The book had begun.

The final words of my years of diary writing were not only the final words of prebereavement; but also the first words of bereavement - and the first words of this book.

I made many short visits to The Mildmay's chapel for quiet moments of thought and contemplation; to temporarily escape the daily demands of bereavement; only the sanctuary of the holy space giving me a sense of emotional security that I'd lost with Tim's death. There I felt less vulnerable than even in my own bed. I was more than comfortable with the holy space by the time I went to Covent Garden early one Saturday morning to see the rector of St. Paul's Church to discuss Tim's memorial service scheduled for May. I arrived long before the first tourists; the shops were still shut; only a few cafés open. It was reminiscent of Saturday morning dress rehearsals, arriving early on the motorbike, Tim going to the theatre, me wandering around the piazza until curtain up. Once again I bought a coffee in the café which I had always frequented; but this time I headed away from the Royal Opera House, this morning St. Paul's was my journey's end. I had walked past the imposing rear porch of the church countless times but now I went there for the first time. It was the first church to be built in England after The Reformation, known as 'The Actors Church' where people associated with the theatre are commemorated, where Bernard Shaw set the opening of 'Pygmalion' - this was where I had come to secure celebration of Tim's life. I sat in the deserted church gardens, an oasis of peacefulness in the centre of one of Europe's busiest tourist traps. Most unexpectedly in this veritable haven of solitude I felt Tim's physical presence once again. It was familiar by now. I didn't see it as a metaphysical visitation. We hold people within us when they are alive and near. When they die they remain within us and their presence 'nearby' can still be invoked. I was comforted. I knew he had spent many a moment here during rehearsal breaks. I would not look around, I would not see him. He wasn't there. He was dead. But something of him remained within me.

At 10 am I met The Very Reverend David Elliott. He took me to the vestry where we talked firstly of Tim's Christian beliefs. I was able to reiterate my conversation at The Mildmay of the previous month with The Reverend Peter Clarke; his time with Tim two nights before he died that established Tim's Christian faith. 'What did he die of?' came the next and anticipated question. 'AIDS', I replied. There would be no lies, deceits or cover-ups. AIDS had claimed his life. That was why I was there. He understood the relationship and asked a little of me. He was very happy to conduct a memorial service for Tim within a Christian context. He provided me with a framework for the service - he would welcome the congregation 'that we gathered to remember the life of Tim', followed by a Silence for our each and private thought for Tim, then a hymn 'to break the embarrassment' for everyone to join in; then a centrepiece of readings, singing, an address of my choosing; he would then end the service with prayers and a blessing for Tim. He agreed that my longing for all aspects of Tim's life had to be invoked for him to be mourned. This included Pasha; he told me of a memorial service he had conducted where the deceased's cat had been represented by a singer from the musical 'Cats'.

Successful as Tim's religious advocate my fledgling belief, though lagging far behind Tim's, had been nurtured. I sat once more in the gardens outside - my boundaries of Covent Garden had now extended to include St. Paul's. Here I would come often too - I had 'lost' the Royal Opera House but been 'granted' a church. Tim still felt close by - I sat a while longer but I had things to do. I left through the passageway connecting the gardens to Henrietta Street. I pushed into the hordes now swarming the market. I was on my own again, alone but not lonely. It was a brief moment where I actually felt ok and normal again. By the time I reached the bus stop to go home the feeling had gone but I'd had proof however transient that I could feel ok once more, however momentarily.

March 23rd, the day before we scattered Tim's ashes I

received the following letter from my mother:

My dearest Rob,

I have thought a lot about Sunday and you asking me about prayers, psalms or words for the occasion ..... I have duly looked thro' bibles and books of prayers and poetry and come to the conclusion that under the circumstances the most suitable would be The Lord's Prayer. It is used for all forms of service - we all know it from our childhoods, it is a lovely and all embracing prayer. I enclose six little cards .... as Kate will be staying that weekend she might like to have one too.

Perhaps you may have some flowers from the garden to strew about too - even if it is only one blossom ... just a suggestion. We shall be thinking about you.

Much love always, Mum xxx

To encourage me forwards so as not to come to a standstill with Tim's final departure she enclosed a card with the letter of spring flowers. On one inner face of the card was the inscription 'The Lord bless you and keep you'. On the facing blank page Mum had written the uplifting message from the bible in her own song like handwriting...

'For, lo, the Winter is past, the rain
is over and gone;
The flowers appear on the earth; the time
of the singing of birds is come,
and the voice of the turtle (dove) is
heard in our land'.

The Song of Solomon

I had almost grown used to the little shrine I had created around the urn containing Tim's ashes. It dawned on me this was 'his' last day at home; 'our' last day at home together. I needed to be alone at home. I can well understand concentration camp inmates in World War II who constantly threatened and intimidated with no chance of peace, space or privacy couldn't begin to move through the grieving process for their loved ones lost until liberated; one can only move through bereavement in gentleness, peace and space. The presence of the dearest friend or lover would have caused me the most intolerable anxiety; there are many times in the course of bereavement, and this was one of them when it is imperative to be alone.

I propped open the door connecting the hall with the garage. I played meaningful music from 'Fidelio', 'Capriccio', 'The Ring of Nibelung', and the religious music of 'Verdi's Requiem' - I was familiar with the beautiful music of the Requiem but this night I heard it for the first time in the spirit in which it was written - a mass for the dead - Tim, and the living - me. With a clear voice I read The Lord's Prayer and a poem by Christina Rossetti.

Song

When I am dead, my dearest,
Sing no sad songs for me;
Plant thou no roses at my head,
Nor shady cypress tree:
Be the green grass above me
With showers and dewdrops wet:
And if thou wilt, remember,
And if thou wilt, forget.
I shall not see the shadows,
I shall not fear the rain;
I shall not hear the nightingale
Sing on as if in pain:
And dreaming through the twilight
That doth not rise nor set,
Haply I may remember
And haply may forget.

I then felt 'he' needed quiet moments alone too. So leaving all the doors open, the heating and lighting on I slipped out to join the Saturday night crowd at 'The Falcon & Firkin'. I was taken back in time to nights I would leave Tim at home for a half hour break. One final time I returned to him. I called his name and kissed the urn. I was ready to scatter Tim's ashes and my coveted role of carer and partner. I do not believe there is any such thing as weird or strange behaviour in bereavement. However bizarre my evening's ritual might appear to the reader I can say unequivocally that it was a necessary part of my evolution through bereavement; in acknowledging and accepting Tim's death, the end of our union, and my progressive individualism.

The day of March 24th unquestionably passed as the emotional pivot of the month. Waiting for the arrival of Tim's sister and mother was a solemn and nerve wracking time. I so hoped that the ceremony would be REAL, with no artificial airs, neither hysterical nor emotionally restraining, or a cold and heartless affair; that I could create the moment to reveal the conversation Tim had had with The Reverend Peter Clarke two nights before he died; that we could then unite to read The Lords Prayer - for Tim to be fittingly mourned. I picked a purple-tinged magnolia bloom from the garden tree to place at the foot of the forest tree in Epping Forest where we were destined.

The doorbell rang. Having been told he wouldn't be coming I was surprised to see Tim's father on the doorstep when I opened the front door. I was gladdened he could forsake his own sense of funereal propriety i.e. that Tim's ashes be interred; and recognising Tim's wishes - never conformist and conventional in life, he would not be tamed in death. We set off. I was so glad for the companionship of Andy. Following the awful forlornness of Tim's funeral I had been determined I would have the support of at least one good friend or family member of my own. When Tim's mother had telephoned and said, 'You are a good navigator, we don't need anyone else,' I had been prepared and stuck to my guns. I gently reminded her of the love and support Andy and Glenys had shown Tim, and Tim's measureless affection for them. She had the rightful support of those dear to her; I needed such support too. His mother's feigned joie de vivre contrasting with Angela's icy coldness was their two very different ways of dealing with the situation. It did not encompass mine and I knew would provide no opportunity for the reading of The Lord's Prayer or one of Christina Rossetti's poems I had in my pocket. I was so glad for the private time I'd had 'with Tim' the night before; the magnolia flower would be my poem, my prayer.

We set off. I pulled into a parking area amidst the trees. We retraced the path Andy and I had followed a month earlier. In only a few weeks the grass had grown, a green haze of forming leaves covering the trees; but there was only one tree we sought - we entered the clearing. I handed the urn to Tim's mother. She plunged her hand into it as if into grief itself; circling the tree she surrendered her son to be enfolded in the embrace of Mother Nature. Then most unexpectedly she cupped the urn with her two hands as if holding the Holy Grail itself and thrust it towards me; this abstract deed more eloquent than the words she could never say, 'Now it is your rightful moment'. My first handfall blew all over Angela, I gasped; but by the time I finished scattering a few handfalls my blue blazer was whitened too. With an ethereal expression Angela completed the task; her coldness gone she now lovingly ended her brother's last moment of physical representation - his metamorphosis from live body to dead body to ash to finally integrate with mother earth; from which we all originate to which we all return. Tim's father stood aside throughout with a look of horror that at any moment one of us would hand him the urn. His mother planted aconites around the beech tree. The ceremony had been performed. This was the moment for a prayer, a poem - I laid the bloom in the fork of the beech tree.

We walked back to the car along the rising, winding, falling paths of Epping Forest. I wished his mother could let the tears roll that glistened in her eyes. Emotion welled in me that I could not repress. I was so relieved Andy was there to comfort me. But Tim's family intense dislike and disapproval and embarrassment of any emotional demonstration blunted mine. I cried but no tears fell. The ceremony had been more real than the funeral; but not real enough for Tim to be mourned. There was one final chance for this to happen - the memorial service.

I did not feel up to driving so Andy drove us home. They all came in for a coffee before Tim's family returned to the country. Kate who was staying made both the coffee and the conversation. The dialogue took a turn that kept everyone's private thoughts at bay - a no man's land conversation that not only allowed for no union of the family's grief with mine but prohibited any such development. The sense of division was exemplified by his father asking if he could light his pipe turning first to his wife, then daughter, then to Kate who said, 'It's not my house', - and looking towards me as if to say 'Why don't you ask Rob'? Her prompt was not only disregarded, I was completely ignored. It could be construed that it is *de rigueur* for a gentleman to ask the ladies present and not the men for permission to smoke; but it was the unspoken subtext, and Angela's acting out that was starting to rankle. She waltzed into the kitchen and started to noisily throw open cupboard doors looking for an ash-tray for herself. That was the issue - Tim had died and all the boundaries were awry. Since I'd first met Tim this was the very first time they had been to the house together and he wasn't there. It must have been difficult for them as it was for me. But it was clear and apparent they would not be entertained by me. Tim's parents had bought the house for him but he had bequeathed it to me to live in. Though it was my home now they were neither going to endow themselves the status of guests, least me householder because collectively they could not accord me status of partner. This was the day they had seen their son's/brothers ashes scattered, and nobody could or would deny them the grief they must have been feeling. Somehow the trivia of who smoked what or not had become a metaphor for their collective devaluation of the feelings I carried to the patronising maximum of friendship. There was a gulf between our two realities that would not be resolved this day or any other. I was starting to feel so uncomfortable that I left the room as if to do something upstairs, I found the atmosphere unbearable. Though I'd seen my partner's ashes scattered - the tangible end of my relationship with Tim; the fire of my grief had been effectively doused for the day, and I could not but feel a little angry.

Still the ceremony had taken place, not as I would have liked it, probably not to their liking either, but a respectful compromise as it often has to be when contradictory parties are brought together and neither having absolute control. Later in the day, alone again I dismantled the shrine returning photographs, music scores, books etc to their customary places. I hid the empty urn on one of the garage shelves until I knew what to do with it; I would have burnt it that night if it had been made of combustible material. The chamber containing Tim's three motorbikes was once more a garage again.

Not to read but to just have nearby I was tempted at bedtime to take to my room the bible my grandmother had given me on my 9th birthday and the little green covered book of poems by Christina Rossetti that my mother had given me for New Year 1989. I took no books to bed. Instead I walked to the clearing at the bottom of the garden. There in the darkness invisible like words in a closed book were the petals of prayers and sepals of poems I needed - the budding life of the magnolia tree.

And so another ordeal of bereavement was over.

The following Sunday, March 31st saw the collision of the third month anniversary of Tim's death with Easter Day. The stresses of bereavement were taking their toll; in a counselling session with Shirley a few days prior she said a lot of bereaved people describe a feeling as if they are going mad; and that was exactly how I felt. No wonder in retrospect. The twelve weeks since Tim's death had seen the greatest emotional, spiritual, intellectual and sexual revolution of my life. Turmoil would be a better word at this stage than change. The price and shortage of bread in Paris 1789 erupted into The March on Versailles to petition the King; similarly the tensions of bereavement culminated in my emotional overload late Sunday afternoon.

When Shirley read the following paragraph in an early proof of this book she wrote 'too many notes' in the margin against my summation of all that had taken place since Tim's death. She was right; there are too many notes for you the reader to read comfortably. But I decided to leave the list intact as I had written it because it was an even less comfortable experience for me to have 'lived' each one of those notes. You the reader have options - read it, scan it or skip it - I had no such choices; you don't in bereavement; and it was the total of each of those 'lived' experiences that brought about an emotional quarterly review that Sunday afternoon:

- I'd said my last goodbye; registered Tim's death; chosen a coffin; collected his personal belongings from The Mildmay; passed through my first New Year without him; bought a suit; fallen in love with Andy; chosen music of 'Cléopâtre' for funeral; carried Malcolm's beautiful red roses to funeral; informed people of the death; received letters of condolence; written replies; introduced myself to solicitor; searched for papers and documents in role of executor; cleared house of medicines; been upset by Tim's obituary; collected his personal effects from Royal Opera House; been comforted by his sister the night before funeral and shouted at by his father for return of car; received letters and documents from solicitor; seen Pasha lose the farm; watched Pasha grieve too; Angela had imperiously requested return of heirlooms and possessions from the house; I'd written a letter of complaint to The Royal London Hospital; a letter of thanks to The Mildmay; and many many business letters in act of taking over full responsibility of running the house; met Kenneth Richardson to discuss the mounting of a memorial service; collected Tim's ashes; created a shrine; visited Epping Forest; 'returned' to Covent Garden and Southampton; had 'experiences' in the park, at the Royal Opera House and St. Paul's; hurdled our anniversary and St. Valentine's Day alone; attended a Service of Remembrance at The Mildmay; discovered a nascent spirituality; the house had 'died'; I was slowly reawakening it; I'd met Shirley and been befriended by Patrik, Stella, Ruby and Julia; I'd 'lost' my old circle of close friends; embarked on this book; taken down utility room light and removed malfunctioning alarm system; waited, waited for confirmation date of memorial service; lost the tiny financial boundaries I had lived in; started to worry and sleep badly about my ability to keep the house going with a rising overdraft; the issue of my HIV status had surfaced to be addressed; I had emptied Tim's wardrobe; made a will; stuffed a jumbo cushion with chopped up underpants and socks; burnt letters and papers; visited the rector of St. Paul's; attended first Partners Bereavement Support Group; met Maria; met Max; rediscovered my sexual identity; scattered Tim's ashes; and now faced my first Easter Festival without Tim.

Now I did not have the emotional ingenuity to leapfrog, escape, avoid or confront the four day festival of Easter; I was too weary. I wanted the world to stop; but of course it didn't. The afternoon of Easter Sunday I invited Max to Greenwich. It seemed I carried the essence of every single thing I had lived through since the night of December 30th. My thoughts reeled - registered death - suit - roses -

medicines - solicitor - shrine - sex - St. Paul's - ashes - TIM - our last two outings had been to Greenwich; visiting the newly opened Queens House with Ken and his wife Jo only the previous October; and one month later having afternoon tea with them in their house on the hill overlooking Greenwich. I didn't lay these two ghosts; I raised them - I missed Tim, I needed him, I wanted him, I yearned for him. I had to go home. The best photograph I had of Tim was on his opera house security pass. I needed to look at it. I emptied all his small personal effects from the small box I'd put them in after he died. I rummaged through the pile of cheque books, passports, credit cards, personalised address labels and 'Timmy' shoe laces, motorbike badges etc - until I found the security pass card for The Royal Opera House. Only after I'd put everything back into the box and secured the lid did I realise the box had contained the last Easter egg I'd given Tim the year before; that I'd had to borrow the money from my father to buy I had been so broke. Just those words on the lid 'Bendicks of Mayfair, Handmade Easter Egg' were enough to fulminate the strains, stresses, changes and new responsibilities into a Niagara of tears. This was the first time I'd cried since before he died. The last time had been the day I'd been told he was never coming home again; that deluge had been for Tim and the life he was being forced to relinquish which included his farewell to me. These tears were for me and the pain of the life I was being resolutely propelled towards which would not include Tim.

But there is no going back. In the words of Claire Wheatcroft's dove of peace card she designed for The Mildmay - 'Onward, Ever Onward!

CHAPTER 6

April

April was my birthday month. A good friend Geoff (now deceased himself) faced his birthday soon after the death of his Italian lover Riccardo. He responded by organising a large party. How brave, how bizarre, how unnecessary I'd thought - now I did the same. It wasn't brave or bizarre - it was necessary.

I received many cards with kind words but most people failed to appreciate that though it was my first birthday without Tim; it wasn't the first sad one by any means. In fact Tim's full blown AIDS diagnosis had come on the afternoon of my 32nd birthday two years before with the discovery of a Kaposi sarcoma lesion on his upper palate at a routine check up. A surprise birthday card from Tim's nurse Debbie summed up the day perfectly, 'I hope you have a very happy day but I am sure it will be tinged with sadness too.' We all have the capacity to hold grief and joy in parallel; just because one is in mourning it doesn't deafen you to the song of birds; and just because one may laugh at a joke it doesn't negate the ache in the heart. I was one year older, 34; now that I had left the age of 33 that I had been when Tim had died I felt further separated from him. Tim had been part of my 33rd year of life; he would not be part of my 34th. I needed people around me to distract me from memories of happier birthdays past; this was a day Tim had always indulged me with surprise parties, excursions, meals, etc. Those very precious memories I would always revere along with the backgammon set he'd given me for my previous birthday. My day orientated around the dust covered board game - it was the only comforting reference point I could focus on. I could not yet touch it. Would I play again? With whom would I play?

April saw no major dramas or surprises. Onlookers would have seen my life outwardly less harried and settling into a familiar pattern - just a restrained continuum of gentle awakenings, unpreventable setbacks, tiresome business matters, and important aftermath obligations. Once having passed the emotional hurdle of my birthday at the end of the first week of April I wondered whether the phenomenon of bereavement was in fact assessed too highly; that although I'd had a hellish three months that in actuality bereavement is a short lived affair and that I was coming out of it. But these insolent thoughts were completely overthrown and demolished by the rude beginnings of GUILT which surfaced soon after my birthday and became the incontestable theme of April and beyond.

Annie stated at the second meeting of The Partners Group that during these early stages of grieving that the process is akin to the defrosting of a frozen bag of peas - from the outside in. Her metaphor was true. Though I had functioned intellectually and sexually from soon after Tim's death i.e. written coherent and effective business letters, replies to letters of condolence, and begun the first draft of this book; and although I'd won back a powerful sex drive; emotionally I had lagged far behind. It had taken four months for the shock and numbness to fully lift so freeing the emotion of guilt that I was now confronted with. Guilt, a key element of the over-ruling phenomenon of bereavement, would come and go, mutate and reappear in countless forms over the following two years so sculpturing the form of my life ahead. Tim had been absolutely right when he'd said of Geoff on the death of Riccardo, 'It's not now but in the months ahead it will hit him.'

Guilt arrived as it does with a released memory. In the long haul of caring for a loved one the needs and wants of the patient inevitably displace one's own; and though one rises to the demands of nearly every occasion; there will be moments and times when one doesn't get it right. I remembered the night Tim called me as he so often did to make him a cup of tea for the chronic cough he suffered in his last months; a symptom of progressive heart failure. When I put the mug of tea by his bed he looked at me, his eyes begging me to stay with him but I was just too tired. I can recall him now saying, 'Thank you very much, I am sorry to have woken you' - as always polite, yet willing me to stay. I did not. And now I reprimanded myself for my 'selfishness' quite blanking out all the nights I did sit with him until he slept; and sometimes while he slept.

And I remembered one awful day: Tim had been given some more bad news; that he'd had the maximum of chemotherapy and radiation for the Kaposi sarcoma lesions that a body can take; and was instead to have injections of the very toxic drug 'Interferon'. 'It's another step down into the grave', Tim said. He was very upset and anxious for himself though he tried not to show it. I was very upset and anxious for him too; but I could not show my feelings, he needed me to be strong. I cooked a meal, took Pasha for a walk, and did some routine household chores trying to create an atmosphere of normality. But there was no such thing as normality anymore. Did he cry? No. Did I cry? No. In fact we were both angry. Tensions started to rise. At bedtime his anxieties got the better of him. Quiet with his own thoughts all evening he suddenly delivered a torrent of hurtful and disparaging remarks against me; without even thinking I pushed him onto his bed. We were both shocked by our own and the other's actions which dispersed as quickly as had manifested. Closeness settled in again. We both regretted what we had said and done and used every opportunity to show tokens of love for the other which proved healing for both of us. We talked until the early hours until Tim finally fell asleep. We had both acted out. If words had been used instead Tim would have said, 'I'm angry, I know I'm going to die now'. I would have said, 'I'm angry that I know you are going to die now'. Of this we did not speak. I switched the light off and slipped quietly from the room for he was by now too ill for us to sleep together due to the sensitivity of his skin affected by the Kaposi sarcoma lesions. But with the hindsight of guilt all I could remember was, 'I assaulted a person with AIDS'.

Examples like this now impinged on my consciousness weighing me down with remorse; when guilt like this first strikes it renders one almost physically handicapped. Guilt for the past mutated to guilt for the present - survivor guilt. I felt guilty for being alive. Why Tim? Why not me? He had been physically bigger and stronger, more talented, multi-lingual, destined for high office - who was I in comparison? That Tim was so displaceable; then maybe I/we all prize our life and importance beyond its veritable worth. Or is it just Natural Selection? Nobody could be more worthy than Tim to be granted the stay of life; that he wasn't; I was less so surely. Glenys asked me, 'Have you gone back to the gym yet?' I could have fitted it into my weekly routine if I had wanted to do so - I did not. How could I begin to enhance my body when Tim had lost his altogether? But for walking Pasha out of sheer necessity, I nevertheless relinquished for the first time ever in my adult life my love and need of active exercise; and consequently my physical fitness faded.

I'd never had enough money to follow fashion. For the first time in my life I had financial resources (albeit on temporary loan). I could have gone out and bought myself some new clothes. Instead I gave away to The Mildmay my favourite shirts and T-shirts. I began to dress shabbily and scruffily showing little interest in my appearance; an old blue blazer became my costume of mourning. I didn't consciously say to myself, 'I must pay penance for being alive and surviving Tim' - but subliminally I did.

Nor did my budding relationship escape the ravage of guilt. I felt I had 'errored' and broken the one rule to qualify as a member of The Partners Group - I had a lover. The only way I could attend the second meeting and face my peers was to tell Max I couldn't see him for a while. It seemed only absolute space and time could appease the tonnage of guilt I carried that seemed to be getting heavier by the day.

Initially I believed that these sessions, one month apart, so widely spaced could be of little benefit. I was wrong. In retrospect and considering the potency of the emotions unleashed, examined and purged; a two hour monthly meeting was quite sufficient. I am doubtful whether any friend or friends could bring about such extraordinary group dynamics as happened at the second meeting. It needed a structural setting - a room at The Mildmay, a circle of comfortable chairs, a group of similarly bereaved, and most importantly Annie and Carol the counsellors. This allowed for the unique atmosphere of a group session where one was freed from the written and unwritten rules and constraints of society of how one should conduct oneself. This was not the work place or a social environment. Here there were no boundaries; we were shorn of the necessity to maintain emotional distance from one another; this allowed for a shared vulnerability; yet for uninhibited interaction and open exposure of our pains of grief. Here one could say things that you could not share with your best friend or partner.

The counsellors had not experienced our forms of loss; and did not need to do so to expedite our onward course through bereavement. Annie knew what she was talking about and was absolutely right when she stated that we had all been left carrying a lot of wreckage, more than any individual could be expected to bear alone; that though we all had good friends; maybe some were sagging a little from our leaning on them; maybe some had had enough of our woes; that by coming to the group we could give them some respite also; that this room and space and time was ours to use in whatever way we each wanted - to listen, to talk, to cry, to laugh, to share, to express anger; that here we could 'be' ourselves, without any of the camouflage one uses to protect oneself from the unsympathetic and non-understanding amongst whom we often live and work; that here we were safe assured of love, support and understanding.

Since the first meeting I had already met Maria socially. She knew of Max's existence. Twice I tried to confide in the group, twice I was interrupted by latecomers. I gave up. Maria shared my disappointment.

Of all the group meetings it was this second one that proved an awesome experience; for all of us - but at the same time one not to be denied. Annie simply asked us all if in turn we would each like to say a little about the dying of our partner. The initial small talk evaporated and a hushed atmosphere fell. Again I had looked forward to attending. I hadn't come expecting or prepared to cry; I didn't want to but I knew I would as I developed a band of pain above my eyes across my forehead that I get if about to. I felt foolish; but did it really matter? I could see that everyone else felt the same as well; and just hung on to get through. Yet neither I nor anyone else seemed to have the slightest desire to leave. It seemed so strange that I could sit so tightly on my feelings; yet a simple situation, sight, object, phrase as in this case from Annie, can cut through one's control to the reservoir of molten emotions one contains within; the force of which surprises the bereaved person him/herself when vented so unexpectedly; especially when one is only dealing with facts as they had happened - the memories of which are familiar and always close by. I was transported back to the night of December 30th and the stillness of Tim's room three floors above where I last saw him and bade him farewell.

I was the last to be called to speak. I was profoundly moved by the death stories recounted, that by the time it was my turn I was speechless. I shook my head, I couldn't say a word. Most of the group was quietly crying. If I tried to say anything I knew I would cry as well. I didn't want to. They waited. It felt like standing in the Roman Coliseum waiting to be slaughtered by lions. In a few breathless sentences I blurted out the circumstances of Tim's death. I cried so much relating this that George left his chair to hug and comfort me. Were these the tears I had not cried at Tim's death bed scene?

Who better to say of any of our individual death stories, those words of battle-won experience, 'I understand' than any of those present that night. Our joint understanding like an emotional safety net held by the other listeners allowed for us each in turn to tell our story knowing we would be caught should we fall. During (early) bereavement one has little if anything to give other people; yet at such a group meeting the flip side of one's own pain becomes another's palliative. On occasions like this there would be nothing comforting in being surrounded by strong emotionally invincible people; there is something very reassuring to see one's own vulnerability mirrored in others.

'This is the pits', Annie concluded, 'it will never be so painful again (it wasn't), there's only one way to go now - up.'

For a long time afterwards I tried to fathom the working dynamics of that evening. I had described Tim's death by word and letter quite a few times; and thought about it many times - all with next to no emotional response. If I had recounted word for word to one or more friends in a pub or at home what I said that night at the group I know I would not have cried. Why now four months after the event could I have such reaction; the others too? It wasn't just a coincidence the tears came at The Mildmay. Why? I can best explain as follows: In a social setting I would have just been narrating an event passed from the present standpoint. But in that controlled setting of The Mildmay where most of our partners in fact died (some at home) we brought the past to the present - I relived Tim's death without the sense of shock and numbness which had so inhibited my emotional response the night he died; hence the flood of tears. Annie had in fact led us to the beginnings of bereavement; for those days our partners died had been the true genesis of The Partners Bereavement Support Group, not in fact the first meeting the previous month. Now we could move forward together.

What I do know is that it was an especially painful experience; and especially healing. I do believe that without my attendance at the second Partners Group my bereavement would have unfolded quite differently. Bereavement is a phenomenon that can be influenced. Certain criteria such as denial, repression, lack of privacy, threat, intimidation can perpetuate it endlessly; that love, gentleness, calm, space, peace and understanding are vital elements for the healing of the pain one is left with on the death of a loved one.

A number of us were much in need of restoration by alcohol following the meeting and sought the nearest pub we could find - 'The Penny Farthing'. I was sitting in a triangle with Maria and one of the gay partners. Then came his surprise revelation that he had wanted to share with the group but not been able too - his new lover! He felt guilty because some of his old friends had found the presence of the new lover impossible to accept; I was well aware some of my friends had doubts and difficulties too about my new relationship. We empathised with one another; that our peer group then endorsed our new relationships our guilt lessened.

I remembered reading a book about the Jewish diarist Anne Frank who died in The Holocaust. There were many family photographs of Anne, her sister, mother and father from happier days before the war. At the end of the book was one photograph of the sole survivor - the father - with his new wife taken after the war. I had asked myself 'How could anyone remarry so soon after such devastating loss? Could he have truly loved his first wife and daughters?' Only now years later I had the true answer. Of course he had loved them and always would; and would hold that love for them always close to his heart; and by getting Anne's diaries published kept them all alive; and not to be forgotten. If you kill new love or the chance for new love on the outside I believe you harden the love that you hold next to the heart; so it remains a pain and can never comfort, sustain or continue to enrich one's life anew. Only now as I write this paragraph on May 10th 1993 i.e. 2 years and six months after Tim's death do I appreciate that the capacity to both love and be loved is the greatest richness in life to seek, to have and to give.

April's awakenings began with my first return to Wales to visit my parents. I had made the familiar journey by car or train a hundred times. On this occasion I drove. Similar too, but on a larger scale it took me back to the morning following Tim's death when I had driven the mile to The Mildmay - everything was recognisable, nothing was recognisable. A route I should have been able to follow blindfolded I took the wrong road at Shepherd's Bush. This wasn't because I had relied on Tim's navigational skills. It was because I had always functioned in Tim's lifetime, whether with him or not, as a moon functions to the gravity pull of its planet - Tim had been my emotional gyro-compass and I'd lost it; I functioned clumsily on my own manual control.

As I gunned the car along the open expanse of the M4 leaving London increasingly behind I was overtaken by an unexpected anxiety that some people might describe as a mild form of agoraphobia. To compensate I reached back to the image of my home in Hackney that I'd always carried with me when away from it - it no longer fitted being more of Tim's colourful personality. All I held was a monochromic image of the house with a few dabs of colour here and there that I had been able to inspirit into it of my own. Driving onto The Severn Bridge that spanned the upper reaches of The Bristol Channel I left England for the first time since Tim's death. Bridge repairs caused the traffic to slow and stop. Stuck in a line of cars and lorries hundreds of feet above the sea I was nowhere; not in London far behind me and the life I'd led with Tim; and not yet in Wales ahead where I'd led my life before meeting Tim. I'd lost all my security, hopes and dreams with Tim's death; but for the time I sat motionless on The Severn Bridge, and the car rocked by strong winds, I felt freer and more liberated than ever before in my life. I was my own free man and not without choices. As I drove off the bridge and passed the 'Croeso I Cymru' (Welcome to Wales) road sign I wondered what of my old self I would find and unite with in my hometown. I now headed for where I had lived when I first met Tim. But already Y Ddraig Goch (The Red Dragon) - the symbol of Wales dominating the road sign - reminded me one thing would never change; I was, still am and always will be first a Welshman. Some things are outside and untouched by bereavement. Neither Tim's life or death made any impression on my Nationality.

AIDS is the greatest 'outer'. I wondered how things would have been with my parents if they'd only learned the nature of Tim's illness with his death; consequently Tim's/my homosexuality; or if I'd had to hide and conceal both all along. But my coming out ten years before had given them much time to come to terms with my homosexuality; and it had been my mother who had read the signs i.e. Tim's changed behaviour and guessed the truth of his illness long before I told them; my parents were allies.

There were inevitably ghosts to lay - repeating the walk around Cosmeston Lakes that Tim had made with Pasha early one morning only two months before he died; returning with Barbara to the pizza café on the beach Tim and I had frequented during the opening days of our relationship. But surprisingly it wasn't sentimental and precious memories that caused a problem but guilt that unexpectedly raised its ugly head again.

But it was guilt from the present that resurrected guilt from the past. For the first time in years I was time warped back to my teenage years, almost half a life before; and reminded of the guilt I had battled with in trying to come to terms with my homosexuality; which then seemed a heinous crime against my bourgeois upbringing and background. I didn't want or need these sore bygone memories refreshed, but guilt is an omnipotent force. But in reviewing a late teenage crisis from the standpoint of an early 30's crisis I was able to come back to the present with a comfortable acceptance of my homosexuality. Though I was weighed down with the guilt that comes with bereavement; I no longer carried the guilt I had once felt for being gay. Though my visit to my hometown invoked it, my departure returned it to the past where it belonged; and strengthening the foundation of my new reality.

Socialising was impossible but for those friends who knew the nature of my relationship with Tim and the cause of his death. At my last visit only three weeks before Tim died, his condition, my role of carer, the very existence of the relationship with some of my parents friends, had been well secreted behind a convincing cover of falsities. Now I chose not to endure those agonizing questions, 'Got yourself a girlfriend yet?' 'What do you do in London?' I could just imagine the reaction if I'd answered truthfully those habitual questions fired at me had I put myself in the position to be asked and returned to the yacht club and rugby club - 'No I haven't got a girlfriend and I never will have. I am gay and my boyfriend of many years has just died of AIDS.' At this point I wasn't (gay) political enough or emotionally strong enough to challenge provincial middle class Wales; but nor would I endure those agonizing questions or enter into any collusion and play act a heterosexual/non-AIDS bereaved role for the sake of others. Instead I chose to socialise by myself going to an anonymous bar near the pier where I was not known and could be alone with honest thoughts. As a youth I had always tried to go with the grain, to fit in for an easy time, no longer; now at the age of 34 I felt stirrings of rebelliousness for the first time.

I felt alienated from this inward looking society by the experience of Tim's death and all aspects of life related to it; I had grown beyond their limited experience; I did not belong there socially anymore - but I did still belong to the rocks, waves and cliffs of Lavernock Beach. I will never lose my fascination for the sea; it was reassuring to watch the mighty tides (the second largest in the world after Alaska) rise and fall; taking away flotsam, depositing jetsam; that this powerful phenomenon was unchanged comforted me greatly.

Because I had met Tim while living and working in Penarth I had assumed that the most painful store of memories to face would be of my hometown. My first visit since his death proved this was not so. Penarth held memories of my childhood, boyhood and youth, troubled and happy times; the beginnings of my relationship with Tim was just another 'colour', albeit a beautiful colour, of that emotional backcloth that made up my Welsh background. While watching a rising tide surge one day my mind opened up a little; unblinkered to think of places that would be meaningful and painful to return to: Aix-en-Provence where we spent our first summer holiday; North Wales where we spent our last holiday together; now a memory indelibly scored on my mind released itself from that special week we spent in the north of the principality - I was overdue from a walk along the beach with Pasha. Unknown to Tim a debris field of jellyfish had been washed ashore slowing progress. Tim was concerned. Getting back to the house I looked up to see him standing in the window waiting in his yellow jumper. Could I ever bear to go back to Aunty Mary's and look up at that window again?

Paris will be hard to face. We had stayed with friends there many times and made countless stopovers. In fact as tourists we probably knew it better than our own capital. At the beginning of our first visit we bought a guide book for Paris and its environs and progressively ticked off museums, palaces, churches, etc. visited. We chose increasingly to tour the less well known sights, but no less interesting, such as La Chapelle Expiatoire, the site where the bodies of the guillotined Louis XVI and Marie Antoinette were discovered where the beautiful white marble chapel was built; 'Les Gobelins' where the famous French tapestries and Savonnerie carpets are still made on the same looms and in the same manner as in the time of Louis XIV.

But it is the very last place we visited, The Chateau of Vaux-Le-Vicomte I must return to one day. Built by Le Vau for Nicholas Fouquet, Lord High Treasurer of France to Louis XIV, and with its exquisite formalised water gardens by Le Nôtre, it became the model for Versailles. But one muggy overcast summer's day in 1988 it existed solely for Tim and me; we had it virtually to ourselves as if all the absent tourists we had expected to see by the coach load had known what we did not; that this was to be our last excursion from our time in Paris, and so left us alone. After touring the chateau we set off to explore the gardens but Tim tired quickly and I left him sitting on a stone balustrade quietly reading. I headed for the distant statue of Hercules on the hill, the focal point at the end of the gardens half a kilometre distant. I first walked around the vast parterres in front of the chateau marvelling at the geometric lawns, clipped box hedges, flower beds, ornamental ponds, fountains, statues and topiary. I kept turning back to wave to Tim who would look up from his book and wave to me. Though the axis of the gardens ran from the chateau to the distant statue I headed for; my avenue of procedure stemmed from Tim - he was my castle, I was his statue on the hill. I descended a course of steps to a lower terrace and walked along a broad parterre set between two large fountain ponds. Once more I turned. I wanted to go back to Tim; he knew it by my indecisive step and waved me on. A rectangular pond lay across my path but was easily skirted. I turned again and waved to Tim, distant now. I dropped down to the lowest terrace losing sight of him altogether. Now the path to my goal, Hercules, at the end of the vista was blocked by The Grand Canal, a vast and formalised stretch of water running at a right angle across the estate. The sheer dimensions of the gardens, its formal beauty, my solitariness against the stillness and quietness was overwhelming - almost frightening; I could have been a ghost. To reach the base of the hill on the other side of the water I had to circumvent the Canal, and walk its entire length along a waterside path bordered by beech trees, cross a footbridge by a shallow carriage crossing where the Anqueuil, a natural stream fed The Grand Canal, and then backtrack along the facing bank. Now I felt strangely and uncomfortably separate from Tim. I climbed steps guarded by statues of lions and squirrels to a terrace overlooking the Canal from where I looked back to Tim. He was just a speck in the distance; I waved, perhaps he waved too. I walked around the pond atop the terrace and climbed the grassy slope to the gilt leaded Farnese Hercules by Tournois terminating the vista. From there I looked back along the entire length of the gardens of Vaux - down the hill, across the obstacle of The Grand Canal, up the steps of the terraces beyond flanked by perfectly placed urns, vases and statues, along the parterres to where I had left Timmy. I could not see him anymore; he was beyond the range of my feeble vision. Still I waved. Tim who I sometimes called Hawkeyes because of his extraordinary long distant vision told me on my eventual return he saw me wave from the hill top afar and waved to me. I want to go back to that statue on the hill and look back to The Chateau of Vaux-Le-Vicomte. I will not wave. And nor will I see Tim. He will again be beyond the power of my sight; but maybe he will see me from afar; and if not I can remember when he did when once again I will be alone and separated from him.

But of all countries, provinces and cities we travelled through there is one special place I shall always remember but could never find again. We were en route by motorbike from the South of France to Paris via The French Alps. We stopped in a high alpine pasture somewhere near the border of Switzerland, spellbound.

Meadows of alpine flowers - Fritillaria, Campanula, Gentiana, Dianthus, Aquilegia stretched as far as the eye could see in palettes of colour. I stepped away to take a photograph of him standing on a rock. A huge frog appeared, we laughed. It hopped away. I was mesmerized by his ethereal expression and appreciation of the astounding beauty of the world; against its unforgiving brutality and cruelty. He is gone and I am here; but of that moment the rock remains, the headstone of his good life.

I returned to London with the gift of an old Arts and Crafts oak wash-stand cabinet from my mother. It was not just tailor made in proportion for the near furnitureless garden room; it was most importantly the first NEW addition to the house. I had completed the painting and decorating of the garden room only months before Tim had died. It was carpeted and contained only a sofa bed bought for Tim's imagined decline and confinement to ground floor that in fact never happened. Otherwise the room was barren of furniture, curtains, pictures, etc., but also virtually devoid of memories. We had spent just one evening there listening to a recording of Gluck's 'Iphigénie en Tauride' which Tim had been contracted to translate from French to English for Surtitles for The Royal Opera House. CD'S were still relatively new, he'd bought the box set for the new CD player on the bookshelf. We listened to the music but all I could hear was his cough. I started him off doing the first few lines; but he was too tired and it would never be done. Gil had visited him there for one hour one afternoon. During his last week at home he'd listened with his mother to Margaret Price singing Schumann and Schubert. Otherwise there was little to recall; the room had served principally as a thoroughfare to the garden or utility room; we had always used the larger first floor sitting room.

I built on what Julia told me following her father's death; that her mother had gained much solace from completing things planned. This spurred me on to tackle the garden room. The room had absolutely stopped, seized up in Tim's time holding me to the past. But just by placing the cabinet in one corner I moved the room on into my time - never to be again as when Tim last saw it.

I then confronted the filthy window sill that had not been cleaned since before Tim's death. I cleaned and replaced two tall Japanese vases exactly where Tim had sited them for I couldn't improve upon his choice of placement. I replaced an ornamental papier mâché duck in front of a wooden bowl of cornflower heads still tinged with blue from a bunch of flowers Andy had given to Tim the year before. I then added a marble egg from the upstairs sitting room, a Japanese figurine from the spare bedroom given to Tim by a singer from Madam Butterfly. I completed the task of bringing alive the window sill with the additions of a tailless Manx cat given to Tim by his landlady from his many visits to The Isle of Man motorbike races; and a soapstone latticed candleholder that Kate had given to us for Christmas only five days before he died - only now I took it out from its wrapping from my wardrobe where I'd put it out of sight. Two existing ornaments of my own - an ugly stone bee and a chipped terracotta owl - I smashed them to pieces. A pattern was emerging that would apply to everything from a window sill (in this first instance) to friends; from the airing cupboard to the kitchen and garden - there is no change, there is change, there is loss, there is new.

By the end of April I had bought a table lamp and shade for the cabinet where I could hide the unsightly answer phone on which I could place the book Malcolm had given me for my birthday. I bought a modern desk light for the upstairs sitting room so transforming Tim's desk to my writing desk where I have written this book. What one friend perceived as needless luxuries were in fact my successful attempts to scatter spiritual life back into the corners of spiritually dead rooms that a death leaves behind; for after Tim died every room, picture, cushion, ornament, book, saucepan, towel 'died' too. Every item has to be brought back to life by just looking, touching, stroking, holding, picking up and replacing in same or new position; and in quite a few cases can not be integrated and has to be given away, sold or destroyed altogether. Now I fully understood the preliminary task I'd undertaken at the beginning of March, like a foundation course - to burn the 'death' papers for they perpetually scattered spiritual darkness. By the end of April I had created a few isolated spiritual glows around the house.

Everyone deals with bereavement in their own way. In my case I had chosen a middle course between the extremes of Dickens' character Miss Havisham from 'Great Expectations' who froze her home on being jilted by her lover; and those people who leave, unable to remain in the house they had shared with their loved one. Like the phoenix a new house was rising within the old with renewed youth and vigour to live through another cycle - my cycle. To visitors it might have appeared at a glance to look much the same with a few changes here and there; to me there was one house before Tim died; and another since as surely as if I had moved home altogether.

There were fewer aftermath responsibilities this month; not major ones but no less important. One morning it just seemed the right time to 'deal' with Tim's razors and toothbrushes; a set of each in the shower room and bathroom. Tim had once scratched the initials of our nicknames on the handles of the razors to distinguish them. I didn't want to part with them but it seemed wrong to keep them a day longer. I put his in a plastic bag and placed in the kitchen rubbish bin. I felt so awful I retrieved them - and added mine. I went to the chemist around the corner and bought myself two new razors and two new toothbrushes - just how one aftermath task can dominate a whole morning of ones life. I regret not keeping his razors with other personal mementos of his life; but one doesn't get everything right; one does make big and little mistakes in bereavement; one does have regrets.

His shaving bowl and brush were still sitting on the shelf in the bathroom untouched since his last morning at home. I opened the lid. The shaving soap I'd given him as a present from Penhaligons in Covent Garden had dried and shrunk away from the sides of the porcelain bowl; surprisingly 'Penhaligons' was still clearly readable on the bottom of the soap. I had intended to leave it in the bathroom forever never to be used but just as an objet d'art. But a few days after disposing of the razors and toothbrushes I deposited the bowl and brush with my growing horde of keepsakes; so adding to the voids in my life that Tim's death had already left - an ominous gap on the shelf in the bathroom.

My Aunt Mary and sister Diana had both given me some money for my birthday to buy a shrub for the garden with which to commemorate Tim. While in Wales I bought two winter flowering vibernums to take home. Once planted I realised I had bridged my inability to touch the garden. Aunty Mary and Diana had given the garden back to me by the nature of their 'enabling' gifts; the garden now moved into my epoch. It's a slow step by step process. I was then able to move with pleasure some sage bushes Tim had planted in the front garden the year before to a safer site in the back garden. It slowly dawned on me that for the first time in my life I had a garden of my own; to now continue and builds upon the creative process begun by Tim and his mother who had laid it out.

It was this month the salt for the water softener and the bulk bought dog food ran out. These were fairly straightforward household responsibilities for any householder/dog owner - but new for me; this had been

Tim's domain. I had no idea where he had bought either. The nearest pet shop didn't supply the brand Pasha was used to. I tried another - he wouldn't eat it. I never in fact discovered the whereabouts of Tim's supplier; but I made arrangements with another pet shop that was prepared to give a discount for bulk order of Pasha's favourite dog biscuits. I discovered an invoice for salt that I remembered being delivered only days before Tim's final admission to hospital. Though I had written the cheque for Tim to sign he had given me instructions to give to the delivery man of where to store the salt; still totally in control of the running of the house. Now I was. These first new deliveries, mundane matters of routine for some were small victories for me. Only now four months on was I aware I was slowly growing into my new position of householder; it takes time to readjust; and I was still adjusting. I was not paralysed by decision making, nor was I absolutely used to it - I was just moving along the way.

The arrival of any long grey envelope with orange first class stamp askew postmarked Sussex presaged a matter of (Tim's) estate to be dealt with. Carrying out their duties strictly according to the directives of The Law Society, I was growing streetwise to the fact that any letter from the solicitor could well bring me further anxiety, and mind consuming if not time consuming tasks - but most of all further emotional adjustments to make. The endpoint for the solicitor is financial i.e. to pay their final fee account. What would be the endpoint for me? I still don't know two and a half years after Tim's death; but it's not financial. April's harvest was three letters...

April 5ft: Previously I'd had to contact a local estate agent to ask for the selling price of an identical freehold property a few doors away and to furnish the solicitor with this information. The solicitor now confirmed by letter the market value estimate of the property they would put in the probate papers for the government valuer to react to.

April 16th: I was advised that because Tim had just completed the purchase of the freehold a few months before he died that I was now responsible for the insurance of the property - and from the time of his death. I was now asked to fill in a building insurance proposal form based not on the market value but the rebuilding costs. For this I had to measure the dimensions of the ground floor rooms, apply a formula multiplying the number of floors and bedrooms against the insurance rating figure for the London postcode area I lived in. But before I had an opportunity to buy a lengthy tape measure a third letter arrived on the heels of the second.

April 18th: I received the long awaited Oath Will and Inland Revenue Accounts for my signature alongside that of the other deponent, Angela. I was advised that this had to be accomplished in the presence of a solicitor in front of whom I had to first swear The Oath of Executor. This I did. Holding the bible I swore the oath:

(i) We desire to obtain a grant of PROBATE OF THE WILL of the aforenamed deceased.

(ii) To the best of our knowledge and belief all the statements and particulars furnished in this account and its accompanying schedules (Inheritance Tax, Capital Taxes Office) are true and complete.

(iii) We have made the fullest enquiries that are reasonably practicable in the circumstances, etc.

A warning alongside the boxes where I tendered my signature with Angela's read: An executor or intending administrator who fails to make the fullest enquiries that are reasonable practicable in the circumstances may be liable to penalties or prosecutions.

While holding the bible and swearing the oath I felt grave about this signing formality, not because of the warning notice but for two other reasons: Angela and I were validating Tim's maximum of domestic and artistic achievement which on his death was transmuted into money i.e. the value of his home and hard-earned, hard - won savings - this took me back to the climax of his life on December 30th when his will took effect; I also desperately hoped I measured up to Tim's expectations of honouring his affairs, home, possessions and money - but most of all that I honoured his good memory.

With a new reel tape measure in hand one Saturday morning I completed the insurance proposal forms as requested by solicitor. Though the solicitor was justly administering the estate of the testator (Tim); the arrival of such letters as I received on April 16th brought changes to my life the solicitor could not have imagined; nor were responsible for, despite effecting those changes. It was a very strange experience to measure the house and discovering it was not nearer a square shape as I had always imagined, but very narrow across the front and nearly twice as deep. My perceptions of the house I lived in were changing because I was changing. It seemed I was in the process of moving into a new home I already lived in - I was.

I was spared too many downbeats this month, but not altogether; guilt seemed penance enough. How emotions restyle in only a few weeks. Only the month before without a twinge of guilt I'd needlessly worried about my ability to function sexually. Now following the first broadside of guilt I was near sexually disabled on a number of occasions. This was very demoralising as it would be for any man homo/heterosexual. My full sexual confidence would be won back, and more completely than ever before; but not easily, nor without setbacks.

I let down two friends at very short notice which just added fuel to the fire of guilt. Tim's former boss John had booked to take me to the theatre to a comedy. It was a generous hearted thought but on the day I was repelled by the thought of laughter. There were smiles in my life and the odd joke but carefree laughter for now belonged to the past; hilarity was not part of my present existence. I cancelled at very short notice.

Margot wanted to meet for a coffee at Euston before boarding her train for Scotland. A colleague and friend of Tim's her initiation substantiated she valued me as a friend too. But that Saturday morning I was still in bed at the time of our appointed rendezvous. I didn't turn up. I was exhausted.

I complained to Shirley that I was getting hitherto unexperienced bouts of exhaustion. She reassured me that many people complain of such weariness and fatigue that they believe they are physically ill; that this can come with, soon after, intermittently or long after the death. Additionally the stress of bereavement can manifest in all sorts of different ways: panic attacks, sleeplessness, sweats, palpitations, stomach upsets, rashes, etc. In some cases symptoms can be severe and debilitating; the bereaved person needing added specialist help; but no less abnormal than mild physical and nervous symptoms.

The biggest disappointment of the month was that it became quite clear in the closing days of April that the confirmation date for Tim's memorial would not be established in time for the service to take place in May. There just wasn't enough time for invitations to be printed and distributed, for The Order of Service to be designed by Francis, for friends from abroad to book flights and make travel/work arrangements. Wasn't Tim worth it? Weren't people aware just how important it was for me and for him that he be collectively mourned? Letters and phone calls had brought no response. I didn't want to be actively involved, I had stresses enough to carry; I wanted someone else to rescue the lost memorial service; I didn't have the energy to make another phone call or write another letter; so I did nothing.

April

By now I had survived four months. Survival was the word. At the second meeting of The Partners Group Annie had said that one day we would feel we were living again and not just surviving. It's like that and in retrospect I don't see how else it could have been then. I had lived on Red Alert for four years prior to Tim's death. It would take more than four months to switch to Amber. Green would be better still; but better Red Alert than the lights go out altogether.

CHAPTER 7

May

I picked up a heavy jug full of kitchen utensils and hurled it across the room smashing to smithereens against the wall of the dining room, implements flying in all directions. A large storage jar followed shattering against the kitchen door, basmati rice exploding everywhere. Bedlam. With this destructive outburst I dramatically entered a new phase of bereavement - ANGER; to be the core experience of May and other months ahead.

Stressful circumstances had proved the release catch for the reservoir of anger that had built up in me over the past four and a half years since the beginning of the story with Tim's HIV diagnosis. Whereas in January and February a neutron bomb wouldn't have produced a blink of anger, now Friday lunchtime May 3rd I had lost my emotional balance and knew it. Vulnerable to my own thoughts I was frightened of what I might do next.

The week before Pasha had fallen ill with a severe ear infection. The steroids prescribed by the vet made him lose control of his bladder so I'd had to sleep downstairs with the backdoor open for him to have free access to the garden; still there were many puddles to clear up both day and night when he couldn't get out in time. By the morning of May 3rd I was really tired having had little sleep the previous week. I was still upset about the memorial service; the day before I had a string of phone calls from people anxious to know if a final all-out effort had been made by 'the powers that be' to establish a date. Kate had cancelled a holiday in Paris to be available for the service - now I had to tell her there was no memorial service. My parents and Kirsten urged me to contact The Royal Opera House. Still I did nothing. The morning of May 3rd I had an appointment with Shirley. I was so exhausted I could have slept on the floor. Afterwards I had tasks to do: I was supposed to go to the electricity showroom and arrange for the supply to be transferred from Tim's name and billed in mine; then to try and find a shop that would rewire the worn cable of the Hoover. Instead I went home - I was just too tired. I arrived to find the inevitable puddles to clear up - and another message on the answer phone concerning the memorial service. I made a cup of coffee and sat down to write to The Royal Opera House; but that was as far as I got. This was one letter, one stress too many. I'd had enough. I'd really had enough. I erupted with rage.

I was fatigued from disturbed nights with Pasha and concern for the dog, I was aggrieved that Tim would not be mourned in May - but these were mere scratches on the surface. As a scratch on a champagne bottle allows for the great pressure within to rupture along the line of the score mark; so the anxieties surrounding Pasha and Tim's remembrance allowed for the expression of a much deeper seated and explosive anger within.

I was angry there was a virus called HIV. I was angry it had claimed Tim and taken him from me. I was angry with Tim for dying. I was angry with Tim for leaving me. I was angry he'd left me with so many problems and all responsibilities. I was angry with myself for being angry. I was angry. ANGRY, I was tired of coping and having to cope and be controlled. I wanted, I needed to be destructive. But once I'd vented the anger I bitterly regretted breaking the jug and storage jar Tim had bought in a local pottery, and denting the kitchen door. Though the wave of anger had passed, I didn't feel myself at all. I was not in control and found myself in an extremely vulnerable position. I was vulnerable to myself and my unfettered emotions. I needed help.

I wasn't surprised Shirley corroborated my anger as a normal part of bereavement; I was surprised when she said she had been expecting me to 'break'. 'Had Tim been very angry during his illness?', she asked. 'Yes', I replied. 'Have you been angry before?', she continued. 'Not like this', I answered. 'Were you the pacifier, the placater?' 'Yes'. 'So you had been repeatedly left upset and hurt having mopped up his anger like a sponge over a long period?' 'Yes.' Then you shouldn't be surprised should you that your store of anger has started to come out now, should you?' What could I say when she provided such a logical explanation for such uncharacteristic behaviour. She concluded that I shouldn't be surprised if I was angry, very angry again. I left wondering how, when, where an 'anger attack' would strike again - I just knew it would.

I do believe that an HIV diagnosis exacerbates any weakness/flaw in somebody's pre-existent personality. Before Tim's diagnosis his mother had once asked me if I had ever experienced the 'big bang' as if warning me Tim had a quick temper. 'No', I answered truthfully. Tim was highly strung, would not bear fools gladly and could be embarrassingly outspoken - but had always been very polite and respectful towards me. We had always avoided any major rows or arguments by both being always desirous to 'talk it out'; that is until a few days following his HIV diagnosis. The weekend after his diagnosis Tim succumbed to a bout of flu. Was it just flu? He was extremely anxious for himself. I was worried for him. Still he was determined we would go to the country for the weekend for him to discuss the forthcoming new

production of 'Norma' at Covent Garden with his boss John. I
told Tim to stay in bed until it was time for us to go. I took
him a cup of tea at the appropriate hour saying it was time to
get up wondering if he might not feel well enough to go. He
did - a dogged determination not to give in to illness or to be
compromised by HIV was one of Tim's hallmarks of living
with HIV; anger was the other. I was wearing a green
lumberjack shirt and a pair of blue braces he had given me in
Canada that he liked me to wear. 'Take those stupid f.....g
braces off', he yelled at me. I was stupefied - he'd never
spoken to me like that before. I was so shocked I said nothing.
I did nothing - I would not take off my braces. I understood
even then where his anger had come from but I was very hurt
by his unkind words that in my concern, love and hurting for
him he could hurt me so. Unknown to me I had taken on
board his first bout of anger and not without some sense of
resentment. The emotional landscape of our relationship had
changed irrevocably.

Now I began to remember examples, and some appalling
examples, of Tim's stress related anger. From December 1986
to December 1990 there were dozens and dozens of minor
and major squalls of anger from Tim. However upsetting to
experience if I was the focus or just the witness they bore
measure of the great anxiety and pain he carried; and because
he could never escape that pain his outbursts could happen
anywhere, anytime and for no apparent reason...

'We came home late from The National Film Theatre
where we'd passed a gentle evening watching 'A Room With
a View'; that I'd put a bowl of oranges on his desk instead of
the usual place on the dining table was enough to provoke a
monstrous expurgation of anger from him completely ruining
the evening. Again I understood the source of his anger; that
he needed to be angry; but I did not need it. So I left the
house and caught the bus to 'The London Apprentice' to give
him time to cool off. Sure enough on my return he was the
definition of tranquility itself; I was not.'

'Following a performance of 'Don Carlos' at Covent Garden he had another tempestuous reaction. We had been chatting amicably with friends in The Crush Bar and made to leave continuing our conversation as we descended the long flight of stairs to the foyer. In the seconds it took to cross the vestibule to the street he had a complete Jekyll and Hyde change of personality; he became extremely angry and ran off. I followed in hot pursuit and caught up with him in the alleyway alongside Bow Street Police Station. He calmed as quickly as he had angered dismissing the episode as if it never happened; and I never understood and never will what provoked this sudden and disturbing mood change.'

'The worst ever which almost ended with violence and police involvement took place outside The Royal London Hospital. Tim had always said that as long as he avoided admission to hospital he would be OK and would remain well. Following his first major illness and consequent admission he had to make major readjustments to find a new standard to live by to accommodate a new set of circumstances - the transition from HIV asymptomatic to HIV symptomatic. Because the hospital food was very poor in quantity and quality I was allowed to take him out for a meal one night. We went to a favourite Indian restaurant of ours in Brick Lane. I wasn't surprised when he insisted on walking so sapping his limited energy resources. The food was wonderful and comforting - a reminder of the good times we had shared and hoped to share. I saw no trouble ahead. I wanted to order a taxi to take him back to the hospital. Again he insisted on walking but just did not have the energy, so we waited by a bus stop in Whitechapel Road. Then I started to get worried, not because he showed signs of anger, but of extreme childishness. He had always been a prankster but now seemed to have actually regressed to childhood. He hid in shop doorways and danced around me like a child's game. But this was a deadly game. My response was parental. 'Now Tim come here', I said. 'No', he danced defiantly; but it was a tragic dance for he was like a rag doll, I could have cried. 'I've got to get him back to the hospital, I need Gil's help', I said to myself. I was out of my depth, but there was no-one else there, I had to take responsibility and deal with the situation. Mercifully a bus drew alongside - but he threw a complete tantrum about the price of the ticket; the innocent child becoming a very angry man again. 'Hooligan', shouted a woman passenger. I bustled him up the stairs to the top deck. 'Only two stops to go', I said to myself willing a set of red lights to change to green wondering what would happen next. Tim vibrating with rage pushed me out of the way and ran down the stairs with renewed vigour. Once more I followed him. He leant around the glass door separating the driver from the lower deck and grabbed the unsuspecting driver by the lapel. The man swore at Tim, braked and stopped the bus dead in the centre of the road switching on a loud panic alarm. This was a bad dream; but I had to keep my head. Passengers were alarmed. The driver opened the partition door and made a movement as if to strike Tim. A blow could be fatal; Tim was recovering from blood clots on the lungs. This time I pushed Tim out of the way and stood between them. I said in a very loud and commanding voice telling not just the driver but all the passengers as well so the situation wouldn't escalate, 'He's not well and I'm taking him back to hospital.' Immediately Tim came off his anger and the driver cooled who said, 'You should take him to the nearest f.....g loony bin.' I looked the driver dead in the eyes and said, 'Open the doors.' He did exactly as I asked - he got back in his cab, shut the partition door, turned off the alarm, pulled the bus over to the pavement and opened the centre doors. I pushed Tim off the bus. Immediately he regressed to childhood and danced off again, skipping and laughing. I grabbed him and led him childlike back to the ward and put him to bed. He pulled the sheets over his head and refused to come out. I was totally unsympathetic by now and feeling really pissed off and stressed out. I went home. I rang the night staff and told them what happened; that he wasn't well enough to be let out again by himself or with a companion. She promised to advise his doctor in the morning. Quarter of a bottle of vodka was left in the kitchen. I poured it into a very large glass and drank myself into a stupor.'

'On his 39th birthday, only six months before he died, he overcame months of exhaustion and asked me to drive him to the John Lewis department store in Oxford Street. He bought a set of blue enamelled cast iron saucepans he'd long wanted. He then asked me to drive him to Tottenham Court Road where he bought a sofa bed for the garden room. We had a bacon sandwich in a café - it was just like old times when we went shopping together after I first came to London. He started to tire so I suggested I drove him home for a rest before we went out with Andy for a meal that evening. He refused to heed my advice and insisted on driving to another department store miles away. I knew trouble lay ahead. Sure enough he caused an awful scene discharging his monumental anger onto an inattentive shop assistant. He stormed out of the shop quite mad. I pretended I didn't feel well and said I wanted to go home - a ruse to get him safely home. It half worked and would have if my nerves had been able to cope with his dangerous and reckless driving narrowly avoiding a number of collisions. I wasn't sure he wouldn't even crash the car on purpose. He had become quite unbalanced. At a set of traffic lights he began to yell abuse at a driver alongside. He was very distressed knowing this was his last birthday; but last birthday or not, AIDS or not, I could not cope with this situation. I demanded to drive. He refused to swap places. I got out of the car. If he was going to kill himself he wasn't going to take me with him. He truly frightened me to the point I wondered whether the virus was affecting his brain. But once I'd escaped the situation I began to worry what he might do and walked home the way he would have gone fully expecting to come upon the scene of an accident. When I eventually got home he was in bed, the curtains drawn, having ripped up all his birthday cards and cancelled the reservation at the restaurant. He gave back to me my birthday present of The Symphony Fantastique by Berlioz, his favourite composer. It was very hurtful. It took the whole afternoon and Andy's persuasiveness for Tim to be enticed back to normality. A happy morning had given way to a hideous afternoon but ended happily at a pizza restaurant in Bloomsbury. Ironically a former colleague of Tim's entered the restaurant and sat at a table nearby clearly suffering from advanced AIDS; and died in fact three weeks later. This unfortunate man's dilemma didn't provoke anger or denial from Tim but extreme compassion; and he seemed to get in touch with something in himself that he could accept; that he had not been able to accept earlier that day - his own impending death.'

Tim never made reference to any of his outbursts - if he even remembered them; but I will never forget them. I wonder how Tim would have coped with such gargantuan outpourings of wrath on my part if the positions had been reversed. Similarly to mine I could only hazard a guess.

A few days before he died Anne his nurse said, 'If there's anything you want to say to Tim say it in the next day or so.' I knew 'the time' was close at hand. I remember looking at him sleeping peacefully and said to myself, 'This is the end of your anger Tim' - he didn't have the strength or energy to be angry anymore. All that I could say to him was all that I could ever say, 'I love you Tim.' And unrecognised by me the anger passed into my possession.

And now five months later May time saw the harrowing early days of my emergent anger. Yet reflecting the ambivalent nature of bereavement came the most pleasing of reawakenings. Max asked, 'Why do you keep dead twigs?' pointing at the leafless branches of my one and only houseplant - a poinsettia. 'Why don't you have some flowers in the house?' I flamed red. Of course to him it looked like a leafless almost dead plant because it was. But to me it was the beautiful Christmas plant holding the moment when the staff of The Ambrose King Centre (STD) Clinic presented it to Tim only weeks before he died - his emotion, my heartbreak. 'Take it home and look after it for me until I come home', he said cradling it like a doll in his wheelchair. Though I have always been successful with plants; whatever I tried to do with the poinsettia it dropped its leaves one by one from the moment I brought it through the door. It seemed determined to die with Tim. I'd already decided that when it was completely dead I would bury it in the garden. When I shared this private story with Max he seemed very moved; and with great respect asked if he could prune it. I made no objection. From that moment it came back to life sporting an abundance of new little green leaves within days. It was saved. I understood why my mother's azaleas were so important to her, a gift from my father following a heart attack; that as long as she kept them going he would be well - and twenty three years on successive generations of cuttings taken from the original thrive, and my father is well. Though Tim had died I saw the sporting shoots as a balm and antidote to the memory of the unbearable pain of the day Tim had been given the poinsettia.

Max gave me two Busy Lizzie plants for the garden room; but they upset me profoundly and I didn't know why. The beautiful flowers seemed to scatter 'darkness' about them; I found their presence almost impossible to bear. I wanted to throw them out but I didn't want to hurt his feelings; and I felt very mean to nurture such ungenerous feelings for such warm hearted gifts. I took Pasha for a walk to think about it. 'Throw out' was the key word. Again I remembered - in my numbness after Tim's death I had thrown out all the house plants save the huge weeping-fig tree in the sitting room. Flowers had become symbols of death for me : vases of daffodils from my mother and me surrounded Tim at his death, and a basket of hyacinths from Gil; the bouquet of roses from Julia for Tim that arrived too late, the morning after his death; the freesias in the coffin from his mother, narcissi and mimosa atop from me; my sixty red roses for the funeral; a gesture of white chrysanthemums, carnations and tulips for me from an opera singer; pots of red cyclamen and red azaleas, simple bunches of flowers and ornate arrangements flooded the house in the days following the death. When the last cut flowers died towards the end of January I threw them all out as one does with dead flowers - all the potted plants too including ones of old. I put the vases away on the top shelf of one of the kitchen cupboards and closed the door on flowers. All I could see in flowers was death and grief. But walking past the budding red roses of The Rose Garden in Victoria Park I realised that these red roses belonged to my time now; and I was not dead - flowers could also be symbols of aliveness. I returned home with thoughts overhauled, to discover the apricot and pink flowered plants were true sources of growth and life ongoing. Max had given me back flowers.

I bought some of my favourite flowers - anemones at Liverpool Street Station and arranged them in the square glass vase I had given Tim as one of his 37th birthday presents - and placed it on my desk in the sitting room. I had vowed I would never use the vase ever ever again; yet now whenever I am especially sad or especially happy I buy myself anemones for the square glass vase.

There was a furtherance of awakenings. I bought a carpet for my bedroom. I completed the decoration of the room with the hanging of three opera programmes I had framed - 'Fidelio', 'Capriccio', and 'Götterdammerung'. They represented the operas in rehearsal and production spanning the transition period of Tim's last valiant attempts to work, his final illness, and his death. The spout of the watering can split. Just a piece of garden apparatus it was something Tim had been holding early on in our relationship when I first realised I had fallen in love with him. I searched garden shops and ironmongers until I found the right one - only a plastic red replacement was acceptable.

I bought some new bedding. Something as basically essential as sheets provoked me to look at the tumult of towels, duvet covers, flannels and pillowcases in the airing cupboard. I was getting used to the pattern of change that touches everything in bereavement. I wasn't ready but in due course I knew I would clear out the airing cupboard - favourite bed-linens would remain; there would be losses of worn and brash covers I had never liked, black flannels and red towels; already there were new sheets, there would be additional gains many more.

Only when Maria told me of her difficulty in changing brand of soap, paralleling mine did I realise that small indulgences are a real part of bereavement and should thus be included - hence this paragraph. Maria had always used 'Pears' soap because that was what Roger liked. One day she was in a supermarket and reached for the usual brand. She hesitated. Instead she wanted to buy 'Simple', but still Roger's influence swayed powerfully over her; but eventually her will ruled. I had an identical experience. Habitually reaching for a block of four 'Imperial Leather' soaps I chose instead a block of four 'Lifebuoy' soaps. The sensation of guilt was real - Tim did not like white. There was a noticeable absence of white in the house. I do like white and wanted to introduce it to the house, but felt extremely guilty for modifying Tim's projected plans of colour schemes for the house - and introducing mine; even something as insignificant as white soap - for he would not have approved. It wasn't just soap that Maria and I were obtaining but the expansions of our own fledgling solo identities. Unless one can make seemingly minor changes to one's life; one will never successfully make the major changes that need to follow to complete the transformation of a 'successful grief'. Queen Victoria is an outstanding example of 'unsuccessful grief'. She would not have exchanged soap of Albert's choice for her own. And far from dealing with Albert's clothes, long after he died she was still having them laid out for him to wear in the evening. Many years on she remained locked, frozen in grief in the time of Albert's death.

Eighteen months after Tim died major plumbing repairs and alterations necessitated the redecoration of the shower room resulting in a much admired white and chrome design of my conception; so losing the grey, red and black design of Tim's that began with my purchase of four white bars of soap.

In May there were the habitual losses too. The pattern was becoming so predictable that before I even entered the garage one Monday night to put out an old box of wine bottles for the rubbish men I thought of the two other storage areas - the loft and utility room and wondered what else I could jettison. Whereas a normal week of life had produced one or a maximum of two sacks of household rubbish; now five months into bereavement successive weeks saw the rubbish men take away six, fifteen and one time twenty four black sacks of rubbish. One neighbour asked me if I was moving! Boxes of beer bottles and wine bottles followed the first box, wood Tim had collected by the ton from skips, old rolls of wallpaper, an old bucket and mop, more magazines I discovered in loft, one of the benches I dismantled in the garage, oil cans, dirty rags and brushes, dustbins, boxes of miscellaneous electrical fittings, two broken stereo systems, bricks, a rusted barbecue, a rotten garden tub, broken cameras etc. 'Let time pass' seems to be a patronising cliché when people say it following a death - yet they are some of the wisest words. After Tim died I vowed I would keep forever the kennel he made for Pasha; yet when it eventually fell apart with rot I had no difficulty in getting rid of it. The one difficulty I had in May was getting rid of the soda fountain. It had been given to Tim as a present. I didn't like the drinks it made, they always went flat quickly. Tim liked it. We agreed to differ - it was his house, his soda fountain. Now it was my house and my soda fountain. I did not like it. I knew I would never use it. Not without some guilt it followed all other things that Tim's death had devalued to being redundant and unwanted. But overall it was becoming easier to get rid of things; progressively less guilt accompanying my decisions.

May the 3rd was the meeting of The Partners Support Group at The Mildmay. I didn't want to talk about my anger outbreak; but as the months went by and I learned of similar expressions of strong charges of emotion from others - even from Gil following the death of her husband - I slowly accepted anger as an essential part of bereavement; and that ultimate acceptance helped me through this recurrent phase.

George spoke for those of us who had been left with financial security - 'I've always been broke, in debt, borrowing and in love (he'd been with his partner for 17 years); now I've got more money than I know what to do with thanks to an insurance policy - it's nauseating.' I too had money to come from Tim's estate and had already borrowed against my legacy to maintain the house and myself, to begin improvements and additions. I was more than grateful to Tim for looking after me but financial and material gain could in no way compensate for lost love - it was nothing to celebrate. Like most people I'd always found it hard to make ends meet. All things were now possible but I wanted none. Tim's death had already radically altered my views on the want of material possessions. I could no longer see things as status symbols, luxuries and comforts. I saw Tim's family's heirlooms as sources of anxiety; the house, its upkeep and maintenance a responsibility; the motorbikes and car as problems. Not a hoarder by nature, nor a monk who had taken the vow of no worldly goods I steered a new found course of minimalism ultimately working towards an attractive and functional house - with no excesses. The house was undergoing an irreversible process of change; from reflecting predominantly Tim's personality to now mine; the evolvement beginning with Tim's death and will end with my own.

I began to read the one and only book I would read in the

two years following Tim's death - 'The Long Road Home' by Wendy Green; a story of heterosexual widowhood. It was the comparisons and contrasts between her experience and mine that allayed my doubts of there being enough material for a book giving me a single-minded determination to complete this book. Her honesty about a widow's sexual resurgence gave me the fortitude to be frank about mine. I was very moved by her account of a period during her husband's illness when he was 'beyond reach' that correlated to my experience with Tim. I felt quite elated to read of her outpouring of anger too - towards the DHSS: an official in a busy office behind a screen couldn't hear her and she had to raise her voice repeating ever loudly, 'My husband has just died.' The official responded with the sympathy of a stone oblivious and unconcerned of the pain it caused her to vocalise the grief in her heart. She stormed out seething with anger. We all have our own way of exorcising a death. Wendy Green wrote 'The Long Road Home'. A mother and daughter who had lost their mountaineer son/brother had to climb to the summit of the mountain he had died on. If I was a gay fisherman and had lost my partner I might need to hunt the biggest shark or marlin in the seas. Wendy Green's book helped me; and convinced me of the purpose to write this book. I hope it may be useful. For the last seven years I have talked to my diaries, to Gil and Shirley, to Pasha and the animals I feed in the park. My hope is that when this book is published and taken from me I won't need to talk to the squirrels anymore.

The proverbial letters from the solicitor countered the sentimental face of bereavement reminding one again of the business side of death - and the business side of life - listening to an inane conversation between two City gents on the No. 6 bus as it went down Threadneedle Street towards The Bank of England I realised that though the mantle of grief had banished all pettiness from my life; I had forgotten that this was not so for everyone - that trivial matters do occupy the minds of the non-bereaving who live in the 'real' world; and though only one seat behind I was still very much in the underworld; and anger loomed near.

I was notified by the solicitor that the papers in connection with Tim's estate had been submitted to The Probate Registry and that hopefully Grant would be issued shortly; that then the solicitor would be in a position to gather in the assets of Tim's estate. I would have been extremely perturbed if I'd know another two years would pass before matters would be agreed with the Inland Revenue and the final estate account papers be signed by Angela and myself; and the final discharge of Tim's wishes be exercised. The legal processing of a will in the United Kingdom can be a long drawn out and very costly affair - the total legal fees amounting to more than nine thousand pounds!

But one letter, as happened sometimes, prompted me back to the heartbreak side of bereavement. Apparently one of Tim's premium bonds had posthumously won a prize. Angela and I had to endorse an application for payment to Tim's estate. Tim had been lucky on a number of occasions and had won five prizes, once twice in a week, each time the house resounding to the sound of his jubilation - but now as I signed my signature of executor; without the echo of his laughter the house stilled.

But the most important letter of May written or received was the one I wrote to The Royal Opera House. I'd said to Kate I couldn't write the letter, she said I could; now I was able too - my disappointment, depression, and determination not to be actively involved in Tim's memorial service had transformed to a creative determination to be actively involved; to win back and secure the memorial service; and to have the biggest degree of control possible. The stress of losing it altogether or a further waiting game was just too much to bear with so much anger running close to the surface. It was a great tribute that prominent opera companies and artists had offered to combine forces, and in such a notable venue as St. Paul's Covent Garden; but it was evident that in five months the two companies had not been able to establish a date with the church. It didn't matter where or how but that it took place. This could happen in Westminster Abbey or an open air mass in Victoria Park. That The Royal Opera House and St. Paul's were only a few hundred yards apart it seemed I should ask those two establishments to find a convenient date; and if the Welsh National Opera en bloc or individually could then collaborate all the better - if not there would be assembly enough. Writing the letter I was inebriated with zeal as if asking a King for a Pardon for a loved one. Could The Royal Opera House possibly have understood my demanding, arrogant, emotional letter? I attempted to explain the need for Tim to be mourned, so he could rest in peace - and only I could effect this. On completion and posting I realised that in addition to having taken on board Tim's anger I had acquired his forthrightness that would remain after the anger eventually dissipated.

Within days September 12th was named as the date of Tim's memorial service.

Yet before Tim could be mourned by his own company another member of the staff of The Royal Opera House would die similarly. In his last days at work Tim had optimistically bought a street map of Madrid. I found it reminding me of the working holiday we had planned in Spain that never took place. Tim had been scheduled to have talks there with a Spanish director about her new production of 'Carmen' at The Royal Opera House; and I would have accompanied him on this particular trip. But he died. I could not go to Madrid - but I could go to see 'Carmen' now in performance. But while the audience, I included, saw Carmen killed by her soldier lover a real life tragedy was taking place in the wings only yards from where Maria Ewing lay feigning death. The stage manager of this particular performance - his last - would die alone at home a few days later. I'd known many people prior to Tim's death that had died of AIDS, but this was the first case since. Peter's death acted as a flashback to the friends and acquaintances I'd known and lost. I had not known him well at all but held no less sympathy for him, his friends and family than if we had been close. I wondered how he would have felt on Tim's death; his own only five months distant? Our modern salutation 'How are you?' is derived from the old days when those words had grave import and significance. Prior to HIV death was common in opera houses - but only on stage. But at The Royal Italian Opera as Tim's workplace was called last century any season would begin with the certainty that by the end of it many members of the company and regular audience would have died - as in all sectors of Victorian society; when the beginnings of a cough or fever could portend a fatal and incurable illness - as today for those with HIV. Now the Arts are feeling a revival of the sombre mood that pervaded the whole of nineteenth century society; that will ultimately touch everyone directly or indirectly unless a control or cure for AIDS is found.

The month drew to a close as it began with a fearful anger response from me, roused by a four day visit from a German couple - Claus and his beautiful wife Jutta. They were old friends of Tim's from Munich. He had stayed with them often while working in Germany, and they had made a number of visits to London; but by chance I had never met them. We knew of one another. They asked if they could come and stay for a few days en route to The Isle of Man motorcycle races. They wanted to meet me and to ask questions of Tim's life and death. Of course I agreed; I wanted to meet them too. I knew Tim would want and expect me to extend the arm of hospitality that he would have. However a few hours before their arrival I realised I wasn't ready to entertain anybody.

I remember entering Tim's bedroom to make up the bed. The room was so quiet it was motionless; retaining a stillness I had not yet been able, nor wanted, to displace. Out-of-bounds almost to myself I could hardly bear to intrude at all and I felt extremely resentful I was being forced to bring premature life back to the room. I thought of sleeping there myself and giving them my bedroom but that was out of the question - I couldn't imagine ever sleeping in that room again. (Vince told us at The Partners Group that following the death of his partner he vacated the bedroom they had shared to sleep on the sofa - never to return). Additionally I had to bring life to the kitchen and adjacent dining area; and returned to the large Tesco's supermarket at Bow - I wasn't ready for any of these things.

I had to leave the underworld for the real world. The resultant experience was the light hurt my eyes for I had grown accustomed to the twilight.

I really tried to fulfil the role Tim would have expected of me; externally I succeeded. I was welcoming, happy, and as generous as possible. I took them down the Thames on an open riverboat; a beautiful blue sky above but my spirit was in the depths below. I made valiant attempts to 'make conversation' at breakfast and to entertain them in restaurants. Internally it was just too painful to bear and I knew I wouldn't survive these four days without a response to the stress their visit had engendered. I wanted to cry but there were no tears to fall.

One morning I took them to the local Post Office to buy them travel cards for a day's sightseeing. I didn't understand the different prices for the different zones; nor did they. Instead of explaining the shopkeeper banged the counter with her fist saying, 'You are wasting my time.' I smarted with rage and told her she should be more helpful and less rude considering the money I'd spent in her shop over the years. 'Why should I', she said arrogantly? We left.

I took Claus and Jutta to the bus stop and waved them off. I started for home but an awful anger welled in me of monstrous proportion. The insufferable rudeness of the shopkeeper had ignited the fuse of my anger barrel. I started to shake, my heart pounded, my mouth went dry. I went back to the post Possessed and out-of-control I marched back to the Post Office and vented a tempest of rage on the woman until I was spent. I had become Tim. I was Tim on his last birthday berating the shop assistant he assailed. I was Tim on the bus outside The Royal London Hospital. I was banned after swearing at the woman and have never been back. Now I really was frightened of myself. I really was going mad if I wasn't mad already.

'No you're not', asserted Shirley, 'though we may have to talk of 'transference'.' She showed me that additionally feeling pressurized to do things that I wasn't ready to do I had been forced to take on Tim's role exchanging the post of follower for leader. Though I had always helped in many different ways when people came to stay, Tim had always been the overseer. 'Did you feel you were Tim?', she asked. 'Yes', I answered incredulously - how could she have known? I told her these onslaughts of anger were unlike anything I had ever experienced. I didn't feel they were of my persona; but of Tim's. She explained the phenomenon of transference. When one is in an angry situation as I had been so many times with Tim during the course of his condition and illness there are two faces to that anger situation - Tim's and mine. In recall I had often returned to the experience and relived it from my side - the hurt, anxiety and fright; but I also returned to the experience from Tim's side so reliving his anger; hence the feeling of being possessed. 'It's really taking it out of me', I complained. 'Good', she said, 'did you hear what you just said?, that's exactly what it is during - it's taking it (the anger) out of you.'

The relief was enormous when Claus and Jutta left. Again I was bowed with guilt - for they were such lovely people. I quickly stripped Tim's bed, retied the curtain ties, shut and locked the windows and closed the door. I washed 'our' white and blue teapot and put it away to gather dust. It would be a long time before people came to stay again.

May

Despite the rise of my anger this month, May ended on a gentle creative note. Where some might plant a rose or tree of remembrance, the fifth month anniversary of Tim's death saw me raise my own permanent garden memorial to him, a five-piece volcanic-stone temple-lantern. A neighbour commented on the beautiful 'Japanese Temple' - it was in fact Javanese from The Merapi Volcano, carved in Muntilan near The Borobodor Temple. The garden with its twisting gravel path leading through flanking herbaceous borders to the secluded clearing by the magnolia had always been wanting of a focal point. Now one friend described my garden as looking like a children's story. Providing the natural focus for the garden the stone temple - lantern allowed for me to light a candle on special days of observance such as Tim's approaching birthday, and the not-even-thought-about-yet first anniversary of his death. On the night of May 30th I lit a scented candle aptly called 'Woodland glade' (where Tim's ashes had been scattered), the scent mingling with the heavy sweet perfume of the Mock Orange Blossom overhanging. My spiritual awakening began at The Mildmay, expanded to include St. Paul's, Covent Garden, and now included my garden sanctuary.

CHAPTER 8

June and July

Six months distant from Tim's death, I was approaching the halfway mark of my first year of life without him. Comparable to crossing a rope bridge strung across a yawning void I was centre span and at my most unsteady.

If I didn't have emotional hurdles and aftermath clear up issues enough to deal with; additionally June and July saw a succession of difficulties occur that I had to battle through and survive. These were hard testing months: just because a loved one has died, it doesn't mean one is assured amnesty from life's unsympathetic sway. As I would discover grief multiplies problems to almost unmanageable proportion.

The very first day of June an old friend Jill invited me to supper. It was the first time we had met since Tim died and was a happy reunion - until I talked of the temporary shrine I had made of Tim's urn in the garage. She laughed and completely belittled its significance and importance. She told me her 'crem story'; that a friend had once worked at a crematorium and told her that all the ashes were mixed up; and that the ashes in Tim's urn probably hadn't been his anyway - and so what if they were. In her opinion once a person was dead they were dead and that was it. She gave me her advice, 'Put it behind you and move on'. I smarted with indignation. Though Shirley had taken me through the grizzly details of Tim's after-death from body bags to bone grinding cremulators; though I knew the ashes were his, I was still profoundly upset by her mocking insensitivity. She thought me far too serious and pinched my cheek and tried to make me see the 'funny side of it'. It was all I could do not to storm out. She thought me touchy, indulgent and oversensitive. She was right. I was.

By sheer coincidence a few nights later, while leafing through the stack of 'Sea Breezes' magazines on my bedside cabinet I came across the following passage relating to the loss of H.M.S. Hermes sunk by the Japanese in World War II.

'By 10.50 the Hermes was dead in the water and heeling badly and then suddenly 20 minutes after the attack began and with some of her guns still firing, she plunged beneath the calm blue sea. With the Hermes gone the aircraft turned their attention to the Vampire which they clinically finished off in ten minutes.

There were no burial parties to recover the dead after the battle and no makeshift wooden crosses mark the spot where they died. There was no funeral for them, no kind brave words above a battlefield grave, or proud salutes, and no tunes of glory. For the crew of the hospital ship Vita, which rescued 600 survivors, there was no time to think of the dead.

In later years, while the dead of the battlefields were honoured with individual headstones in impressive regimented graveyards, those who died at sea were given the single impersonal proxy headstone of the memorial at Plymouth. Even the terminology is different for the victims of war at sea. For those who die in a land war there is the reassuringly final 'Killed in Action'. The men of the Hermes and hundreds of ships like her, were simply 'lost at sea' or 'missing in action', almost as if there was some doubt, and that they might yet be found.

Sociologists and psychologists now realise how important and reassuring a coffin and a funeral are to the bereaved. They provide a consoling dignified parting, an opportunity to say 'Goodbye', and a *finality which allows the future to begin. For the families of those lost at sea there are no graves to visit, nowhere to lay a wreath and say loving words above a father, a son or brother. There is no comforting headstone, with a name, a number and a regiment. For them there are only the lonely years ahead; forever wondering what had happened to the young man who sailed away and never returned.*

Sea Breezes

By this account I was 'lucky' - I'd 'had' the body, the coffin, the funeral, the urn and the ashes to qualify my grief. One of the members of The Partners Support Group told us how comforting it was to visit the grave of his policeman lover. Similarly, though temporary, my shrine in the garage had been a focus for me to pit my grief against; and since the scattering of the ashes, for those of us without a grave to visit, the names in The Book of Remembrance in The Mildmay Chapel are not just the beautiful words of the calligrapher - they are the words of the headstone, the epitaph, where I can take flowers for Tim. And for one friend, Tom, the name of his Maltese friend in The Book of Remembrance is very special - the only evidence and testimony remaining of the man's many years in London.

Jill's enduring friendship was very important to me; I had not forgotten her many acts of kindness, love and generosity to me over the years; yet I couldn't pretend I hadn't been wounded by her remarks. I wanted her to understand how important Tim's ashes had been to me; and had helped in the very slow process of coming to terms with his death; so I wrote her a letter gently explaining - and the sense of hurt dissolved away. We can become very righteous and propriety about our grief.

How a few wrong words from a relative, friend or colleague can compromise a long standing relationship? June 5th was the date of the fourth Partners Group at Mildmay. Everyone had their own 'Jill story'. Intentionally or not words can fall upon the ears of the bereaved like salt in a wound. Even at this stage six months on when our emotions were thawing out, our sensibilities remained raw and susceptible, and the impact of words can be quite different to that of their intent.

- Better to have loved and lost than not to have loved at all -
- Now you are free to do anything you want -
- What you need now is lots of hard work -

Ultimately whether there is absolutely any right or wrong words I do not know. But the three examples above though harmless a few years on impinged like thorns in the flesh for me, Malcolm and Maria, following our individual losses.

It's not just untoward words but incidents too that amplified how compromised we were by grief. You would think that for bereaved people there would be some respite from further life-stress and traumas. But it's not so at all. And I wasn't the only one learning this. A member of The Partners Group was diagnosed HIV and had to take this on board with his already heavy load of grief. Another member was burgled and lost some precious sentimental belongings and mementos. I know of other bereaved gay men who have been made redundant, and one man who was knocked down and badly injured soon after the death of his partner. Ones threshold to cope with stress is lowered by the increased sensitisation that comes with grief and can remain for many months, and in some cases years, following the death. At the June meeting of the Bereavement Support Group we acknowledged that the problems we encountered individually would have been less so in the lifetime of our partners.

My tally of bad luck was less dramatic and far reaching than for those illustrated above, but no less erosive in aggregate. Unwell again with another bout of fevers, chills and sweats; Pasha needed an operation on his ear and required close attendance. Finding noise burdensome I hardly ever switched on the radio or T.V., only listening to particular pieces of music. A long standing noise problem with an obdurate neighbour and her two daughters with protracted sequences of car hooting at all times of day and night I now found intolerable - an intrusion to the peace and quiet I needed to work things through. All the lights fused. I was unfooted on the stairs by one of Pasha's toys, fell and hurt my back. The gas boiler broke down. It didn't seem possible that anything else could happen. I was wrong - while giving Ralph a lift to The Mildmay a car pulled out of a side street without looking and smashed into the back of the car. Aware of my anger blasts Ralph told me to keep calm. In fact I felt quite numb and switched off both the engine and my emotions and let Ralph and Max accompanying sort things out with the other driver.

Though I had no control over the antagonistic forces of life; I could and had to activate a positive and creative countermeasure to growing despair or I was going to go down. It was at this point I turned to my much neglected and overgrown garden for succour where I found safe haven. Weeding between every shrub, pruning and removing some oversized bushes altogether; in this routine maintenance I slowly brought life back to every leaf, flower, pot and clod of earth; so bringing refreshment and revitalization to me.

With so many concurrent problems I now had to face the fast-approach of June 9th and what would have been Tim's 40th birthday. I anticipated the day with dread - a tiger-trap of depression into which I would have plummeted. How could I side-step the day? I couldn't. I had to confront the day head-on, and from talks with Gil I devised a stratagem.

Tim was dead but it was still the 40th anniversary of his birth. I decided to mark the passing of June 9th as a commemoration day; to hold a remembrance celebration; a just opportunity to say thank you to family, friends, colleagues and counsellors for the help, love and support they had shown both Tim and myself. Including the convalescing Pasha I compiled a list of thirty to honour.

Strangely though both Maria and Max hadn't known Tim, without their individual practical and emotional help I couldn't have carried it through. Succumbing to another bout of 'flu', I gave up the idea; but at 'The Conqueror' following the June meeting of The Partners Group Maria helped me rekindle the plan for the celebration; so earning her place at the occasion. Similarly Max accompanied me to Oxford Street where I wanted to buy copies of Berlioz's 'La Mort de Cléopâtre' that I wanted to give each guest; not because it had been Tim's funeral music but that it was one of his favourite pieces of music by which he could be remembered. Unfortunately it had been discontinued. I was so overly disappointed again I gave up. Life seemed to thwart me at every step. 'Does it have to be that particular piece?', Max asked me. I'd had a fixation it could only be 'Cléopâtre' - but of course it could be any music Tim loved. So I chose an assortment of requiems, operas, oratorios and songs by Strauss, Wagner, Berlioz and Beethoven. And still fighting off the 'flu' as the day neared, without Max's practical support in preparing for the day it would have been gruelling if not impossible to achieve; so he too won his place at this unique event for which there seemed to be neither rules nor guidelines.

For each guest there was a collection of gifts representing Tim's life and loves. With everyone gathered in the sitting room I went up to my bedroom to get the surprise bags of presents. Tim's boss Jeremy had procured a bundle of carrier bags from The Royal Opera House Shop. With a red tag I had labelled each one into which I put a chocolate motorbike, a scented candle, a Mildmay mug sporting a motif of red and green balloons, a C.D or tape, four photographs of Tim, and a few balloons. In every bag I put a postcard from the large collection Tim had amassed over the years from his visits and travels to museums and art galleries. And I had chosen a card that seemed pertinent to the friend e.g. for Maria for whom Egyptology was an enduring fascination I chose one featuring an Egyptian artefact. On each card I wrote 'In Remembrance of Tim's 40th birthday', and a personal message of my own. Though I'd allotted myself a bag of gifts too I didn't give myself a card; sensitively Max bought one and placed it in my bag on which he wrote, '9 GIUGNO 1991. In Ricorrenza Del 40 Compleanno Di Timmy' - featuring two dolphins. Thereafter dolphins became my logo of life-after-

Tim.

Whereas my birthday party two months earlier had had a forced sterile quality; Tim's Remembrance Day did not. The atmosphere was extraordinary. There were more good tears shed than at Tim's funeral; and more laughter in the house than at any time since Tim's death. And at some point in the evening everyone present, and at a later date those who could not attend, composed their own personal message for Tim on a large white card I had placed on my desk with a pot of colourful crayons...

Dear Tim,

If spirits carry memory and thoughts take wing. Remember us. As you tease the Angels and we remember you.

With love, Mary (my mother)

Thanks for your friendship Tim. You are still very present to us all here tonight. I'm thinking of you often. It was an honour to know you. I love you Tim. You're still my great friend.

Always, Francis

For Tim,

Rest in Peace. And Rise in Glory.

Ralph

Dear Tim,

To see all the different people this evening, who were all affected by you is brilliant and just shows how open and welcoming you were to people. I wish I could have had more time to get to know you better.

Alles lieber, Kerstin

Dear Tim,

I get the impression you were as influential in the world of opera as you were on me with motorcycling. I shall carry on riding and enjoying it through all weathers as no doubt people you introduced into the world of opera will keep on enjoying all it has to offer. I can assure you that whether people are listening to what you were very good at or listening to me racing around on my GSX-R we will all be thinking of you as we do so. Thank you for being a major driving force in my life - you still are.

Lots of love, T.C 9.6.91

Although I wrote on the card too there was something I wanted to communicate for which no words exist. So I went into the garden to the temple-lantern. While the flame wavered I reflected upon our eternal separation. And when I went back into the house, the sitting room knee deep in balloons and brightly coloured wrapping paper did I realise that this was the 40th birthday celebration he merited; we had invoked Tim - he was there amongst us all. For the first time since he died I felt the closest thing I could describe as contentment.

In bereavement one is often at odds with both the past and the future as two happenings illustrated. After a brief visit to my parents I returned to London. It was the first return train journey I had made to Wales since Tim's death. As the 125 train neared Paddington I was overcome by tremendous anxiety. I thought I was going to have a panic attack. Why? I was looking forward to going home and Max was meeting me. As the train pulled into the station I was time warped back to my last such arrival - six months before. Only three weeks before Tim died and full of anxieties for him I had gone directly from Paddington Station to The Mildmay. This warm summer's evening under the roof of Isambard Kingdom Brunel's magnificent edifice of glass and iron I felt an echo of the chill of that lonely cold winter's night. Yet oppositely I had a very strange experience in just booking for 'Attila' at The Royal Opera House. Committing to one evening one month hence seemed to tempt hubris. Having lived on a knife edge with Tim for so long, after six months I still couldn't trust the future, not even on the reduced scale of four weeks. I only had confidence for the immediate present in which I lived - the now.

Death highlights the inequalities of gay relationships. Since Shirley's intervention following Angela's demands for heirlooms and possessions to be returned on Tim's death, the surviving family versus surviving boyfriend relationship had been nullified; now the game-pieces were being put back on the board - June 17th was to be my first visit to Tim's sister since the death, and the very first ever in my own right. The legion of problems encountered already in the first two weeks of June proved precursory to one of the bitterest phases of bereavement I was to experience. Had Tim lived, had I been a conventional partner I imagine the outcome of my visit to Angela would have been very different.

The visit. My reservations that all would not be well were justifiably founded. No sooner than I arrived and Angela had made a cup of coffee and the pleasantries were over she said, 'the car, you must do something about the car, we have no peace from him (her father), it's become an obsession, he doesn't talk about anything else. You must return it or make him an offer for it. If you decide to return it use the journey to return the things we want back. You must say something to him before he drives us all mad. You can get through it if you pretend.' By that she meant in my supposed follow-on visit to see Tim's parents that I downgrade my standing in Tim's life to that of chum or pal; and that I give up any expectancy of being openly recognised as Tim's partner. This I would not be party to. I had never intended going to the farm wearing a 'glad to be gay' badge; but I would not allow anybody, Tim's family least of all to demote and diminish the most important relationship of my adult years. 'I hope I haven't frightened you off (going to the farm)', she concluded. She had.

One didn't have to be a psychologist to recognise the phenomenon of displaced grief that Tim's father was expressing - laterally focusing the pain of Tim's death, in this case onto an inanimate object, the car, thereby avoiding the issues surrounding Tim's death. Not surprisingly Angela had declared her surviving family's stance of loyalty was cardinally in favour of the father than to the surviving boyfriend - me. The mother and daughter were clearly not going to do anything to help him come to terms with the facts; and had entered into his collusion. I would not be drawn into this game and abandoned the planned visit to see Tim's parents on leaving Angela. On the outside I was a well built strong man. On the inside I felt like a ragdoll. I loathe conflict on a good day. But this degree of stress left me raw, vulnerable and paranoid. Fledgling feelings of being ok or content for a moment hadn't matured into something solid to give me a strong inner base to fight my quarter. There was no safety or security in the world. I felt worse than at any point since Tim had died and lost all my gains of recovery. And I was angry he hadn't protected me from his family.

I tried to rationalize the issue which went far far deeper than who legally owned the car. Tim's will stated clearly he'd left all his personal chattels and possessions to me. By that account the car was mine. The previous summer I'd asked Tim, 'When is the car going back to the farm?' It seemed to be in our almost permanent keep having borrowed it countless times. 'It's not', he said, 'it's ours, my mother has bought a new car and given us the Sierra. Tim didn't like the car and wanted to change it - he didn't really like any cars being a blood-biker. I did like the car and dragged my feet; we went to a number of garages to look at cars but his final illness put any further plans to exchange it to a stop. I could find no papers of ownership, only the current MOT certificate and a cheque stub attestation that Tim had paid the insurance until the autumn. That the document of ownership was still in Tim's father's possession the car legally belonged to him.

I was upset and angry. I would be increasingly housebound with Pasha without the car having already lost the facility of him going to the farm; he was too large and boisterous to take on London Transport. Not having received my legacy yet from the solicitors I couldn't afford to buy it anyway; and even when

182

I did I had been advised by the solicitor who drew up Tim's will I might yet be liable for substantial tax payments. But these were not the issues that upset me. For Tim's father to have felt any moral obligation to me; as he would for a conventional partner he would have had to have recognised the gay relationship. This he could/would not do. Maria's support inflamed me further, 'I couldn't have coped if Roger's family had demanded or asked for anything back.' But it was her words, 'they have been so loving, generous and supportive', that riled me to almost war-footing - I couldn't say the same of Tim's family. All I had done was love and look after their son/brother. One doesn't want thanks but nor censure of any kind just acceptance and understanding; and I wasn't getting it. That the father could voice such material concern for the car - a lump of metal worth approximately £2,000, and voice no concern for me hurt bitterly. Didn't they realise I might be facing the same fate as Tim? This was a clear example of how an issue of estate mobilizes proprietary rights and hence personal worth.

Now I had little doubt that if this was how Tim's father felt about the car, had Tim not left a will I would have received little munificent consideration and would most likely have been displaced from my home; gay men having little legal standing in the United Kingdom. The moral here being that gay men must make detailed wills; and that just because cordiality and tolerance exists in the lifetime of ones partner it is not necessarily the case following death, however long one has been together, however affable had been friendships with individual members of the deceased's family. It is difficult not to become cynical.

Steering clear of any further possible confrontation with the father I volunteered to return the car without contest, discussion or negotiation writing briefly to Tim's mother and at greater length to Angela. She had declared her family's position to me, now I declared mine; not angrily or personally just truthfully as I saw it. I thanked Tim's mother for her offer of plants for the garden but said I wouldn't be returning to collect them - it would be impossible without seeing the father, and as things stood any convivialities between myself now and Tim's father could only be fickle. I wrote that it wasn't for me to challenge Tim's father's way of grieving but I could and would keep out of the way; that I was sorry I couldn't be accorded my due standing by Tim's father. I told Angela additionally if I had gone to the farm to collect the plants and been treated condescendingly by the father I would have been hideously angry so it was better I kept my distance. I told them both I would shortly return the car to Angela. I thanked them for the use of the car and how indispensable it had been ferrying Tim from one appointment to another reminding them of a distressing segment of Tim's life they had had no part of - if they were having the car back they could have some truth to go with it. Whether I was reacting only as one could to the friction and opposition I experienced visiting Angela, or over-reacted a little or a lot I can not judge of myself, not even now two years on as I write this. But what I do know, unequivocally, is that visit left me feeling discriminated against simply because I was gay - the surviving bereaved gay partner. And with this prejudice, gay rights became an issue for me.

In readiness to return the car I moved the heirlooms Angela had nominated to be returned from the house to the garage. When Tim had died a 'spell' lay over everything in the house; and nothing could be touched or moved until the 'spell' had been allayed. Time had done this. Though Tim had legally left me the contents of the house; morally some things did not belong to me i.e. the brass milk churn on the top landing with the name of the farm engraved on it was uniquely theirs. Now that time had gone by I didn't see the issue of heirlooms as a problem; but again there was an emotional spin off. The marquetry card table on the top landing and the antique dining table in hall alcove were not so easily relinquished - it wasn't the items but the ornaments Tim had placed upon them that made the task difficult. I tried to say to myself, 'they are just pieces of wood, if they mean that much to Angela then let her have them, less to clean.' But the card table was Tim's last reference to the house. I didn't want to move the dried flowers I'd given to Tim which he had arranged and placed on the dining table in the hall. Only as I moved them did I realise they were all part of Tim's home, my home, our home. With the pieces of furniture in the garage I felt our home had been irreparably violated - by Tim's own family; and considerations and sympathies for them dwindled.

In a home occupied for a long time one can walk around in the dark locating door knobs and light switches without any problem. As of habit I made a cup of tea to take to bed. Without switching the top landing light on I decided to go to the bathroom so left the mug on the card table - of course it wasn't there and I spilled tea all over the carpet. Down on my hands and knees mopping up tea at 12.30am the void of the table left me with a sickening feeling in my stomach summoning up the void of Tim's bedroom and wardrobe adjacent - and the biggest void of all - Tim. Slowly, slowly one gets accustomed to the absence and then quite out-of-the-blue when one is least expecting it something like a spilled cup of tea can take one back to the earliest and rawest stages of grief - and I was incensed that it should be Tim's own family to bring this on.

The next day I cleaned and hoovered the car for the last time. Along with the card table and milk churn I placed other things I was certain they would like to have, things not belonging to my time with Tim - silverware I would neither polish nor use, glassware that they had given to Tim for his 21st birthday, farming books, certificates of education, postcards from his mother and sister that he had kept - it wasn't for me to throw them out, it was for them to keep or dispose of, photographs from his schooling years, etc. Only with the car packed did I remember Angela had gone away on holiday, I couldn't leave the car with her. My resolution it was going this very day would not be thwarted by such a detail - so I could then settle to this major mid year readjustment. I would abandon the car on the farm and depart unnoticed. Subjectively I resented them all.

Objectively I was trying to be honourable. Yet the ensuing conflict saw me major in neither camp; I failed to resent them totally, and I failed to be irreproachably correct. Schizophrenically like a swinging pendulum my thoughts for them oscillated between sincere consideration and an almost want of revenge for their loathsome middle class materialist and prejudicial standpoint. Though I understand the use of inanimate objects - the car and furniture, to be an emotional ploy, especially for the father, to avoid facing the pain of their feelings; they certainly weren't going to show much regard for my grief if they couldn't tap into their own. This was a typical example of how an issue of will/estate can slight the grieving feelings of one of the bereaved parties; and that matters of will/estate can not be separated from the emotional, there is an inter-relationship between the two.

I asked Max to accompany me on this unrewarding furtive mission; I didn't want to go alone. How different this final trip was to all the ones I'd made before - to Oxfordshire to collect Pasha as a puppy, trips to Wales, trips to the farm - three successive weekends I had driven Tim to the farm only the summer before, countless runs to The Royal London Hospital and Mildmay shuttling Tim from one outpatient appointment to another, my solo drive to The Mildmay the night he died, registering the death the next day with his parents, collecting his things from The Mildmay, scattering his ashes with his parents and sister. I parked the car within the gates of the farm and locked it. I put the spare set of keys with a brief note in an envelope to be dropped through the letter box; and this was effected without encountering anybody. Not mentioning the recent damage to the rear light which I'd had repaired I informed them of work I'd had done on the car engine - and 'how difficult I found the whole thing'; by this I meant the gift of the car being reversed with Tim's death, and being relegated from partner to pal. What had they been doing at half past midnight the night before? I bet they hadn't been down on their hands and knees in tea and tears. What I felt might have been irrelevant to them but I wanted them to take responsibility for the disquiet they had caused me and to be aware my feelings were not just those of a 'pal'. We walked to the station and caught the train back to London. I wondered what Tim's father would do with his grief now he had the car back.

My grief seemed renewed as well - the quality of the house seemed so different - no car on the forecourt, empty spaces in hall and on top landing. Suddenly it seemed I was back to square one; whatever steps I had taken to recover had been for nothing. It wasn't just material things that were missing. I doubted I would ever go to the farm again. Slowly I realised other voids existed too. This was the time of the year we had usually been taken to Glyndebourne - it would not happen this year or ever again - dressing up again in our DJ's, the picnic, the operas - The Magic Flute, Arabella, Katya Kabanova, etc - just memories. There was no countdown to the end of The Royal Opera House season in mid July, the celebratory meal, the summer recess, the planning of our summer holiday, the holiday itself - motorbike tours of Europe. The marker buoys of summer had sunk - it seemed endless.

I felt so down I rang one of my old friends. She was too busy to see me. I felt so humiliated having reached out and been rejected I vowed I would never turn to friends ever again for moral support; I could now value more the support of Gil and Shirley where one knows that the time you have with them is absolutely yours, is inviolate and that they can give you their full focus. Shirley told me that in former rural society family formed the main natural support system of the bereaved; yet for bereaved gay men like myself whose parents and siblings live outside London, and when not just partners' but friends have died too; that the Mildmay became a haven and place of safety and security like an extended proxy family for men like me.

It was with Shirley that I tended to talk about the more immediate here-and-now issues relating to Tim's death. But it was with Gil that I talked about deeper and more far distant times of my life which bereavement released and touched upon.

She helped me see that in my resentment about the car that I too was behaving like Tim's father; that the force of my feelings were also quite out-of-proportion to the car. Even if it had been an Aston Martin, at the end of the day it didn't matter who owned it; whether it was gifted, given, bought or returned. This was about grief and Tim; and the real ownership at stake was who had the rightful ownership of Tim's life and memory. 'But something else is going on here too', she said. I looked at her quizzically. I often had the strange feeling with Gil that she knew things about me before I became aware of them. She did. On delving deeper it wasn't long before I started to make connections.

When I'd 'come-out' to my parents in my early twenties I'd been rejected and been on the receiving end of dislike and open hatred from family members and others. I had no confidence in myself as a man in any way - neither sexually nor professionally. This precipitated me into a dysfunctional self-loathing state. In retrospect I can see that it was a very negative and self-destructive time of my life. It was only when I met Tim that I began to stabilise and sort myself out and start to catch up. I flourished with him. He gave me love, security, encouragement and a sense of being in a safe place. Most of all he'd accepted me for exactly who I was. I was now revisiting and being reminded of that earlier time of my life before Tim as well as having to deal with the present. Gil helped me pinpoint and locate the common element that had so strongly reactivated the past that melded with the present. It wasn't dislike, hatred or hostility. It was 'lack of acknowledgement'. I hadn't been accepted for being gay. I wasn't being accepted as Tim's partner. Gil and Shirley's acceptance of me at this point was critical to my psychological survival. I knew my psychic health and survival depended on my ability to use therapy; the gravity pull of the past seemed stronger than a present I did not wish to occupy. And this had come about from how all the players' grieving sensibilities had been placed in relation to a crappy old Ford Sierra.

My first attempt to rally myself was a material one to replace the lost furniture. I bought a reproduction Art Deco occasional table I had long coveted. Having almost reached the limit of my overdraft facility I couldn't justifiably afford it. But made of hammerite steel, its armour-plating finish to this day I see as my battle-flag of this gruelling period.

My emotional response was escapist. When there is so little comfort in the present and the future looms frighteningly one returns to the past to seek happier times. Long before HIV clouded our lives Tim and I crossed The Rocky Mountains on The Trans Canadian Express. Not only had it been a wonderful experience, it had been a special time of closeness for us both that we had often reflected upon. One of our ultimate shared experiences, I now started to re-read the travel journal I had kept of the journey...

'Tim woke me at 3am! He had not been able to sleep and had watched the scenery go by. He got up and went to the observation deck. I went down to lie on his bunk and marvelled at the snowscape outside. We stopped awhile - I later learned a massive snowfall had blocked the track. The first pre-dawn view I saw was the train negotiating a right hand bend so that the forward carriages were visible from our bedroom, the headlamps of the train casting a golden glow through the falling snow. I dressed to leave the bedroom in our carriage called 'Château Papineau' and joined Tim to watch the dawn rise over the snow covered landscape shrouded in mists and clouds hanging over and among the mountains.'

Vague and day dreaming I lost myself in the past willingly. I 'walked' the corridors, dining room, bars, observation decks of the train trying to resurrect that sense of comfort and security now absent from my life. I was searching for him but never found him. But there was something about the warmth and cosiness of that train in a very hostile winter environment that I was compelled to return to again and again. Strangely in my introspections I never saw Tim - I could still only see him ill and dying. Annie told us in the July meeting of The Partners Group it is common to remember ones partner as a very ill person; it can take a long time to remember them as the fit and healthy people they were before AIDS struck, but eventually one will. Gil said of my reveries, 'Returning to the past is part of the process of grieving.'

And so in this period of abstraction for the first time since Tim's death the 30th of the month had passed by unnoticed; so June had given way to July; I had marked every successive month anniversary of his death until now. Probably inspired by the re-reading of my old journals I picked up the red diary Tim had given me for this year in his last weeks of life. I wrote the one world 'DOLDRUMS' across one of the early July entry dates; but it wasn't enough to spark me to restart keeping a day-to-day account of my life again. I was reassured to learn from Patrik that he too had given up many years of chronicling life on Göran's death. Contrastingly in as much as the 'last' had begun long before Tim died, e.g. he last wore a short sleeved polo shirt two years before his death due to K.S on his upper arm; seven months into life without Tim wasn't long enough to bring about all reawakenings, and some things are destined to end with the life of ones partner.

In the first week of July a letter postmarked Sussex fell on the door mat in Tim's mother's handwriting. I read the first line only. I could not read on. I asked Shirley to read them. I could detect nothing from her expression as to the contents as she read them. She finished, folded them up and put them back in the envelope. 'These are very angry letters from a very very unhappy lady', she said. 'Should I read them?', I asked. 'You won't get anything from them', came her reply. I knew I had to find the courage to read them.

Without making reference to the contents, nor taking sides, judging neither me nor Tim's mother she listened to my side of the story and attempted to put the case of Tim's mother. She accepted my reasons for not wanting any possible confrontation with the father hence my determination to avoid any possible encounter with him. She validated the car and items asked for and those I included of my own volition had been thoughtfully returned. She said it had been wrong of Angela to ask me to compromise myself and that it was not my place to challenge the father's coping mechanism. She believed deep down he was probably aware of the facts but had no facility to deal with them. She illustrated this as not uncommon with the case of a milkman father whose gay son had died at Mildmay, the father saying, 'he must have caught it from a girl while on holiday in the South of France'. Shirley believed the discovery of the car would have thrown up the death again especially for the father who would have been left holding the grief and nowhere to focus it. In as much as the voids in the house had taken me back to Tim's death so would the discovery of the car for Tim's parents. She also believed the letters (there were two) had been written one before finding the car on receipt of my letter and the other after finding the car; and before unpacking anything. She felt I had hurt Tim's mother's feelings in not collecting the plants which had been a symbol of goodwill; that she might genuinely have wanted to see me and been disappointed and hurt by my rejection.

She believed a lot of the anger in the letters was not directed at me - but at Tim; for not including her in his illness and dying. 'I am a mother too', Shirley said, 'and I would be very angry if a son of mine had AIDS and excluded me. She told me I should be aware of just how painful this must have been for Tim's family, especially the mother and unfortunately Tim's chosen way of dealing with his illness at the exclusion of the family was again not uncommon. And nor was it uncommon for (a) family member(s) to unload their sense of injustice onto the surviving gay partner - me in this case. By leaving the car as I did I had unmindfully left myself wide open to receive the full force of Tim's mother's grief that she had little opportunity of expressing elsewhere.

'Tim could have made things a lot easier', Shirley said, 'and has to take some of the responsibility for these letters.' Tim had not resolved the issue of his homosexuality and our relationship with himself or his parents. I remember visiting

Tim at The Mildmay not long before he died. He was angry. 'It was her last chance', he said unkindly of his mother who had visited him earlier. He had wanted to talk of his being gay and our relationship. She wouldn't - couldn't. Tim had left it too late. AIDS is a cruel and more effective OUTER than the action any gay activist group can muster. Shirley said they may have internalized Tim's homosexuality, they certainly hadn't accepted it amongst themselves - and they certainly weren't going to begin by acknowledging the issue of mine which my letter to his mother had reintroduced - hence the backlash.

She hoped Tim's family would overcome their prejudices about counselling to explore other areas of prejudice and bereavement. Though any or all of Tim's family were welcome to visit The Mildmay it was standard practice for family's living outside the local area of The Mildmay to be referred to bereavement counselling organisations such as CRUSE, Compassionate Friends, and The National Association of Bereavement Services. Tim's family was no exception and would be offered such services available in their locale; whether they actually took up the help available had to be their responsibility ultimately.

I took Shirley's advice to do nothing, to respond to the letters in no way, to let time pass, that no doors should be shut, that all possibilities be left open for ultimate reunion work - but to realise that a distancing of relations might be the only realistic option ahead. 'There has been right and wrong on both sides', she concluded, 'there usually is, I've often asked myself if it can be otherwise, death is such a messy and untidy affair.'

On leaving The Mildmay I boarded a No. 6 bus to go to Covent Garden to meet Tim's boss Jeremy for an informal chat about Tim's memorial service. I read the letters as the bus winded its way through the City.

Letter one:

Dear Rob

I'm sorry that you didn't feel able to call and collect the plants last week. I really don't see why you cannot accept that my husband has lost his only much loved and admired son, he wants to remember him in his own way. He is a very gentle man, a man of the country, not very 'au fait' with the big world outside; to him Timothy's happiness was all that mattered. He bought his house for him - with very hard -earned money, making certain sacrifices to do this, only anxious that he should have a house of his own. We all loved Timothy very much and prefer to remember him as we each have always known him. His private life was his own, and we respected his privacy.

He brought many of his friends home to the farm, they came from all walks of life, nine bikers once, singers, friends who were working here and wanted a bed for a night or two. They were all made welcome, as were you yourself. You created your own barrier here, by complaining to Timothy every time that you were teased or imagined some slight. Perhaps you were unaware that I was usually briefed before a visit about what not to do or say whilst you were with us. (I must say that I rather resented having to mind my p's and q's in my own house).

I really do feel that it's time that you stopped thinking as much about yourself, your feelings, your emotions, do you realise that you have never shown any sympathy towards us, Timothy's family (not even the night that he died)! After all you can hardly compare a few years friendship, with 39 years of having a son and a brother. Not once during those sad days at the Mildmay did I see you attempt to comfort any of Timothy's friends who called, you just lapped up all the sympathy that they and the nurses gave you.

I can't help feeling that Timothy would be very disappointed in the way that you are handling things and trying to rush everything, these things take time, sometimes years. Everybody's emotions are strained, and it is better to take things quietly.

There is no point in going on, you so obviously feel harassed and 'hard done-by', such a pity!

Yours sincerely, Marjorie

Letter two:

Dear Rob,

What an immature gesture! To return the Sierra and pieces of furniture and leave it at the top of the road!! (What if we had been away?) Surely it would have been more civilized to call at the house.

Nobody has harassed you into returning anything, and it could all have waited until you were ready. Unfortunately you create your own stresses and I don't know what the 'changes' are to which you refer. This continuous harping about not being able to 'afford' things is ridiculous £35,000 in a few weeks time, a rent free house equipped and furnished (can't be bad Rob)!!

Thank you for the things returned, Timothy always agreed that when he had no further use for them, that he would return them as they were articles that had in the past been left to me.

Pity rather, I was going to suggest that perhaps you might like to bring Vicky or somebody down to lunch when you returned them.

Take a bit of advice from me Rob, go and get a job or something to do, and don't keep imagining things, and getting things out of perspective.

Sincerely, Marjorie

P.S. I hadn't posted the previous letter, so this has been enclosed.

The letters were beyond anything I could have conceived: *'imagined some slight'* - overall she had been welcoming, kind and generous but I certainly hadn't imagined her salvos of abruptness and downright rudeness over the years which I'd grown to understand as her difficulties in accepting the gay relationship, and only how was I aware how angry Tim had been with his mother every time she had been rude to me; *'a few years friendship'*, - I was sickened to have the feelings of our relationship devalued and diminished; *'lapped up'* - I was in no position to offer sympathy to anyone the night he died anymore than she was; *'Nobody has harassed you'* - Angela had put the pressure on from the beginning of bereavement, now I realised the want had been Angela's own independent voice, and not as family spokeswoman as I had thought all along; *'I can't help feeling that Timothy would be very disappointed in the way you are handling things'* - she didn't actually know how I was handling things generally for there was virtually no contact or discussion between us. When I read that, my sense of integrity crumbled. In untroubled times it would have been hard to brave such a vote of no confidence, but seven months into bereavement to be the focus of such criticism and resentment proved a setback that for the first time since Tim's death brought me to a standstill. This was a typical example how affairs of estate in the settling between the surviving homosexual partner and the family of the deceased bring differing and incompatible value systems together. Given the situation of their family grief on one side of the equation, mine on the other; their family unit, my solo status; their singularly unique personalities, and mine - it couldn't have been otherwise, the outcome was predictable, it nearly always is. If one changed the names, locations, personalities to embrace every situation that has existed between every bereaved gay man and family of the deceased, the outcome is nearly always the same - embittered parties, hurtful words and deeds, sometimes even violence. The ruling dynamics transcend individualism. Thankfully there are exceptions to this rule, but overridingly problems with the family of the deceased remain a fundamental issue for bereaved gay men. Still, I wouldn't be parted from 'the letters' I carried them in my back pocket as if they had been laudatory!

Numbed I found myself back in the very earliest stage of grieving that immediately followed Tim's death. I could not muster myself for anything. It was some words in a letter from Julia appreciating the bag of gifts I had given her on the occasion of Tim's 40th birthday remembrance party that finally activated me, 'You are doing it all so right.' Slowly, slowly I began to repair my sense of self-esteem elementary to healing.

There was now the quandary of ensuring the attendance of Tim's family at the memorial service. Things could hardly have been worse between Tim's blood family and 'little' family. If his mother knew it was I who had won back the service, was organising the order of service and had commissioned invitations to be designed by Francis, I was certain she would not attend; and that would be wrong for Tim. A ruse was needed. I asked Kenneth the representative of The Royal Opera House who was marshalling forces for the service if he would 'front' proceedings; and print notifications on Royal Opera House headed notepaper in his name to be the official invitations; Francis' design to be now used as cover for the order of service sheet. He agreed. I sent a postcard to Angela saying the memorial was the Royal Opera House world's response to Tim's death. This I knew they would accept, neither challenge nor interfere in. It was an exercise in diplomacy itself that with Gil and Kenneth's help worked. I was now free to plan the order of service.

Unable to look ahead comfortably to September 12th for me, I found I could for Tim. It was not out of spite I was so determined to have as much 'family' control over the service as possible. I did not see it as a competition between Tim's family and myself as to whom loved Tim the most or vice versa. We were all important. Though I wouldn't and couldn't attempt to diminish their individual status at the service; I couldn't be so sure they wouldn't have mine had they had organisational control. I was also concerned that if I shared any of my feelings about the order of service they would be overruled and it could become another meaningless featureless ceremony. I remembered the day at The Mildmay when his mother received two of his biker friends. Rather than seeing them as ambassadors for all of Tim's motorbike friends and representatives of an important part of Tim's life she treated them as if they had blundered into a cocktail party - I wasn't yet sure how motorbikes would be represented, I just determined they would be. And far from planning it at his family's expense or embarrassment if they could co-lead the mourning with me, that the supporting love and dynamics could see Tim truthfully invoked; this could tempt them on whatever conscious or unconscious level to acknowledge why he had been taken from us; and in death they might see Tim as they had never seen him in life. Remembering the healing power of The

Mildmay Mission Memorial Service, they could have this too if they could sanction themselves. This was the task ahead.

Yet before I'd even finished addressing and posting dozens and dozens of notifications for Tim's service it was time to attend Peter's service at St. Paul's, Covent Garden. I'd never been to a memorial service before and it was a very strange experience like déjà vu back to front - experiencing the event before it happened; for in two months time in the same church with much of the same congregation from The Royal Opera House we would be gathering to honour Tim. I sat in the side-aisle back row pew. Going on behalf of Tim who would have attended had he lived, I was able to share in the combined well of emotion for another brave and talented man snuffed out in his prime by AIDS; and in fact felt far more moved than at Tim's funeral there being no emotional constraints upon me by Tim's family. As The Royal Opera Chorus thundered out Mascagni's 'Easter Hymn' I wondered how I would ever cope in the front pew leading the mourning with Tim's family if this was how I felt for Peter, a man I had not known well. After the service I wandered around Covent Garden Market anticipating panic for a ceremony that now had more than a touch of tangibility about it. I was terrified.

As executor I was informed that bequests Tim had made to a number of friends had been paid; and an interim payment of my legacy so absolving my huge overdraft. The solicitors also asked me whether or not I retained bank statements, invoices, personal accounts, etc., to help settle matters with the Inland Revenue regarding outstanding tax returns; and that The Capital Taxes Office wanted a valuation of the property for The Inland Revenue. The relief of settling my overdraft was enormous so ending letters from my bank manager as to when it would be settled, even though I had shown him a copy of the will. The largest amount of money I had ever possessed was nothing to celebrate; but that it was a measure of Tim's enduring concern and love for me was extremely comforting and reassuring. With so much running against me these two months, it was my least creative period and saw few reawakenings; but I did manage to complete the furnishing of the garden room with the addition of a wicker chair and round wicker table. With the purchase of a modern standard reading lamp I realised I had created a new sitting room!

July, I was able to strike 'urn' off the aftermath list. Following discussions with Gil as to different options of use or disposal I decided to return it to Golders Green Crematorium whence it came. To put mementos in it and bury it in the garden didn't seem right for me - I hated the thought of somebody possibly unearthing it one day. I wished it had been wooden so that I could burn it but being made of pressed metal this was impossible. To use it as a vase as some people do seemed morbidly grotesque; and I knew Tim would hate me to memorialise it. To put it in the rubbish seemed profane; nor could I just leave it indefinitely on the garage shelf. Returning it to Golders Green seemed the most respectful form of disposal. I rang the receptionist at the crematorium to make the arrangements. She advised me to remove the label on the lid with Tim's name, date of cremation and cremation number. I had to soak it off. I dried it and burnt it in the garden. I washed the empty plastic bag that still held a whitening dust of Tim's earthly remains and poured the water over the garden. To my discomfort I found a quantity of remnant granules of Tim at the bottom of the urn. I carefully placed these in the soil around his poinsettia now resplendent in summer foliage in the sitting room. Then I symbolically washed out the urn pouring the water from it over the Javanese lantern. As Max had kindly offered to return the urn to the crematorium not wanting to go there myself, it seemed right he should participate in this ritual as well; and he too poured water from it over the garden. I could begin to see how many ancient rites of purification by fire and water originated - it seemed so natural to cleanse it before returning it. The urn had fulfilled it's duty to Tim - and to me. By letting go of it, I accepted Tim's death a little bit more. I was gladdened not saddened when I put a red line through 'urn' in my notebook under 'aftermath list.'

Gil had previously asked me if I had dreams or nightmares; that for many people they are an important phase of the grieving process. Though I had occasional dreams throughout the year, July my dream phase properly began.

A recurring nightmare of my youth returned of shark attack. Latent for eighteen years it gave a measure of the stress of life seven months on from Tim's death. I interpreted it at it's face value of anxiety, threat, fear, isolation and vulnerability.

One dream upset me profoundly. I woke from it as clear and lucid in my mind as a film on T.V. I dreamt I woke up in the morning and opened the curtains to see flowers poking through the soil spelling, 'I love you', and Tim reminding me he was still with me and had not stopped loving me. I had to get out of bed and look through the window to make sure it had not happened. There were two possible origins to the dream, my recent inheritance or more likely the other - the previous day I had been rummaging through boxes in the garage and found a brightly coloured carrier bag that seemed familiar. There was nothing in it. In one of our last days at home together Tim forbid me to look in what I was certain was the same carrier bag, then on his desk. It contained a gift he had bought for our approaching anniversary which he died eleven days before. Had Tim disposed of it so as not to hurt my feelings or hidden it somewhere for me to find? In sorting out Tim's affairs I always half expected to find it - I never did. Whether the dead reach out from their spirit world to the sleeping mind of the one they've left behind; by the sheer lucidity of this dream I felt as if I had experienced a visitation from Tim himself.

The most graphic and lifelike dream I have ever had was less easy to fathom, containing both beauty and fear. I was following a stream that flowed down a barren rocky ravine. The air was warm and the sun was shining. I was absolutely alone. The course of the rivulet was interrupted by a series of interconnecting rooms through which the water flowed. The floors and steps between each room were paved with exquisite mosaics; each room was columned, supporting ornamental stone beams, and open to the sky. Though the sun streamed in through the open ceilings and between the columns, the air was frigid within. Despite the beauty of each room there was a terrible fear in each room. The very shallow water held strong currents that pulled me helplessly and remorselessly from room to room propelling me down the waterfall steps that linked each room before finally relinquishing me to the safety of the gentle stream that issued into the ravine from the last flight of steps. Perhaps it was a metaphorical dream of ones journey through bereavement, I couldn't be sure; but the crystal clear imagery of these dreams verified my slumbering subconscious was still going through further innovations.

July 22nd. I'd escaped London, home and all the problems therein for a few days restorative by the sea in Wales. I went for a walk along Lavernock Beach with Max and Pasha. The sun blazed down. The tide was high, the sea as calm as glass. I sat down on a rock to rest a while, the water lapping gently in front of my feet. Pasha walked into the sea and stood stock still examining a floating seagull just offshore. Max stooped to examine a fossil he found. Half way along the beach, mid year, the tide reached the top of the turn and stopped too, for a few moments neither coming in nor going out. Momentarily nothing moved. All was still. I was neither happy nor sad. For the very first time since Tim died I was perfectly at peace with myself and the world.

CHAPTER 9

August

Eight months into life without Tim day to day existence proceeded much as the previous months with the usual reawakenings, downfalls, business matters, and shifting balances of friendships making up the pattern of August - but it was all now in the shadow of Tim's memorial service on September 12th. As a lookout spies landfall, August was the month my rudderless mind found its compass. I sighted what would be the major reference point of my first year of bereavement. A diminishing number of weeks away it was no longer remote, below the horizon as it had been all year; it pre-empted the most acute stage of mourning this month; the process having been time delayed by the memorial having been twice postponed.

Time had separated Tim and me increasingly as the year progressed; every day passing another day between us, his day of death another day distant. From the moment his memorial service became tangible the tide turned. With the countdown started, every day passing seemed to take me closer to him. Logically I knew he was dead but on a deeper level it felt as if I was going to be with him again for one last time; to feel his presence, and be near him before he left me forever. It was a psychological mirage; but as real as our reflection in a mirror - a perfect representation of real life but nothing is there. This was necessary so I could help him go to death and he could help me go to life. I retreated deeper and deeper into the underworld of grief. On entering this mourning stage of self-absorption I felt quite remote to the non-bereaving world.

For the first couple of weeks of August the boundaries of Victoria Park well accommodated my needs for solitariness; the twice daily hourly walks around its perimeter with Pasha provided the space for me to address the voluminous issues and challenges Tim's life and death had left me with.

August 7th was the penultimate meeting of The Partners Group. Maria was the longest bereaved at fourteen months, I the shortest at eight months. From listening to the others and the counsellors I learned that one year is still 'early days'; the second year a continuum. (A friend of mine who lost his boyfriend from AIDS said after five years, 'His death was the worst thing imaginable that could ever have happened to me. It still is, it will never be OK without him, but it's absolutely fine now for it not to be OK.'). At every meeting including this one there were tears, silences and laughter. We acknowledged bereavement is like a merry-go-round on a roller coaster.

We didn't talk just about ourselves; but also of our dead partners; Tim, Davey, Henry, Dominic, Melvin, Terry, Patrick and Clinton. To not talk about the partner you love who is deceased is as unhealthy and unnatural as it would be trying not to speak the name of ones partner when alive. The group helped and encouraged us to find the right attitude towards our absent partners trying to strike the balance between extremes such as Queen Victoria's delusionary denial of Albert's death; and the absurdity of being told 'to forget the person, put the bad experience behind and move on'; both equally and oppositely unrealistic options, neither of which permit necessary and painful honest thinking and reflection.

Through her own grief experience Maria helped an aunt who had lost her husband many years before. Maria encouraged her to talk about him. The aunt contacted Maria to say how wonderful it had been to speak his name again; for fearing Polish superstition she had not uttered it since his death. Looking at all the couples in 'The Falcon & Firkin', on the No. 6 bus, in the park, the gay and straight couples listed in my address book, its very easy to feel one has been singled out, 'chosen' to suffer bereavement. One knows the statistics of HIV infection and deaths; but figures are remote to the home and environment one lives in. To sit in a room where all those present are AIDS bereaved it becomes instead a harsh shared fact of life; to know retrospectively that during those years of isolation before Tim's death feeling so alone, that in fact I was not for Maria, Linda, Bevis, Nigel, Vince, George and Keith had had similar experiences. This knowledge stayed with me long after the group finished and stopped bitterness creeping in.

Without the group I would not have known anyone who had lost their partner from AIDS in the same time period as Tim died. The greatest value of the group was being able to measure myself against how well, how badly - how normally I was progressing through my first year of bereavement; without it I would have been exceptionally isolated. We had all reached halfway house; life was OK, life was not OK - that's normal.

I was growing accustomed to the fact that bereavement in any one month, week or day called on me to function on many different levels. I didn't expect to ever have that feeling of secure happiness again that I'd once had with Tim; I knew I could never be trusting of life to say 'my life will not be foreshortened' as one friend said; but I did dream that one day I might feel I was alive again and not perpetually caught between life and death which was how it felt in August. Eight months after Tim's death it was all so different to eight months before his death - then we had been 'living' in the face of death albeit on a progressively diminishing scale; now I was 'surviving' in the face of life and only comfortable on the diminished time scale of what existed between dawn and dusk.

August 5th I wrote in my notebook, 'I have taken a shaky

control of my life again. There's no point in being passive and waiting for problems to go away. I have to be active and strong and make good things happen for me again.' - I had discovered the theory; the daunting task of applying it began.

The reawakenings continued though not without some pain. Now that I was in funds I pressed on with improvements to the house. I bought a new T.V, CD player, mirror, a chest of drawers, carpets, bedding, lamps and shades. For the first time three rooms were completed - my bedroom, the spare bedroom and the sitting room. Through material acquisitions I was completing what Tim had begun; finishing projects we had started and had in mind; and beginning to discover and follow my own lines of creative thought. The vulnerability of my grief certainly put me into the realm of low/medium paranoia. I made the house my protector.

During our last weeks together at home I had been ready to drive Tim to Tottenham Court Road. Tim wanted to buy a larger television for the sitting room where he envisaged spending his days resting in the months ahead. But his flurry of stamina was short lived; we didn't go. A month later at The Mildmay he told one of the nurses that when he went home the first thing he would do was go shopping with Rob to buy a television and wallpaper for the kitchen - he didn't come home. There was no long period of decline. He died. I didn't go to Tottenham Court Road but I did buy a new television and wallpaper.

The existing portable colour television was displaced from the sitting room so I repositioned it in Tim's room above, so displacing Tim's black and white portable - I tried to use it in the kitchen, it was useful and had an excellent picture. It belonged to me but it held Tim's identity so strongly I could never 'make it mine'. I placed it in the garage and eventually gave it to Francis. How indulgent people might think. Nevertheless memories slash raw through ones emotions many months after the death; it wasn't just an old electronic gadget; I could never look at it without remembering Tim in bed, so very ill.

I was spending quite a lot of time in the garden looking, planning and weeding. I needed to be in the garden. To be creative in just planning a hedge or a pond was a positive expression of Tim's love of gardening he'd left with my own. Now that I had won back the garden ironically the atmosphere of the garden seemed more alive in August as I cut down the dead delphiniums and poppies than when they had beckoned, grown and blossomed months earlier when I hadn't been able to plan or touch anything.

In the first wave of sorting through the contents of the house at the beginning of the year I had thrown away dozens and dozens of old magazines but had kept all Tim's motorbike and German text magazines. (Tim was a fluent German speaker); by August in a second wave of sorting through those remaining I had no difficulty in getting rid of magazines I had not and could not read when he was alive; and would not and still could not read now that he was dead - but I did keep one of each with my treasury of mementos in my wardrobe.

I read no books that year after Wendy Green's 'The Long Road Home'; but I did read every copy of the monthly delivered 'Sea Breezes' magazine that arrived on the second or third day of every month. Since a child I had always had one or more books on the go; now there were none on my bedside cabinets; only a growing pile of 'Sea Breezes' - with so many threads of continuity lost those that remain, 'Sea Breezes' in this case, take on a quality of importance quite beyond their intrinsic value.

As every month had passed the excesses of sentimentality had gradually diminished somewhat (until this month). With every successive wave of 'bringing alive' an ornament that maybe he had last touched, a corner of the garden he may have last looked upon; in this continuous re-evaluation of the property slowly Tim's dead house reawakened as mine. Watching the refuse collectors taking away redundant bags of magazines was as important as waiting for a costly delivery.

August 10th saw the most important reawakening of the year for the house. It was a hot summer's day. I went into Tim's bedroom. I hadn't been in there for weeks and the stuffiness was unbearable; but more noticeably - the room's 'stillness' had gone. This was the moment to bring Tim's room back into the being of the house. I propped open the door, opened the windows; with the suction of draught that swept through the room it became a living part of the house again. It would always be the room which had been Tim's room. But it was now a second spare bedroom.

Despite the successful transition I achieved with Tim's bedroom I had no such luck with the kitchen and garage; Tim's personality dominated both to my exclusion. How would I ever bring them back to life in my own right? This quite defeated me. I still shunned the kitchen: Tim's spice draw; mug; egg cup; The pasta machine I'd given him as a birthday present six years before; the fondue set I'd bought with love and joy, and given to him a few weeks later with love and despair that fateful Christmas of '86 following his diagnosis; the milk jug and pasta spoon I'd put in his first Christmas stocking; stories behind every piece of crockery and cutlery; bags of Pudding Rice his favourite pudding; chocolate moulds and cake tins; chutneys he had made; his fridge magnet in shape of a cream cake; tins of lentils and peppers from our last trip to France; bottles of his homemade Elderflower champagne; the Cappuccino coffee maker he had given me one Christmas; the lasagne dish I'd bought just before he died but never used; his named place mat; the teapot he had given me when he'd asked me to live with him; the cups and saucers I'd given him on our reconciliation; tins of evaporated milk he loved with Pudding Rice that I loathed - eight months after his death it was still overwhelming.

I didn't want to memorialise it all, or to 'freeze' it all as it had been in Tim's time which I had effectively done; nor to get rid of any of it. I wanted to face it all but didn't know how because there was so much to face. As people always seem to gather in kitchens at parties so did the concentrate of memories and sentiments.

I had only won back the fridge for convenience food, the

dog's cupboard, day to day cutlery, crockery and mugs. The many cupboards, shelves and drawers I just couldn't bear to face yet. An outsider would have seen a tidy undecorated kitchen. Through the visor of bereavement the new kettle I had bought shone like a candle in a dark tomb. It was new and 'alive', quite separate to the kitchen and its 'dead' contents which I could not yet reclaim.

The garage was the second largest room in the house and dominated by Tim's three huge motorbikes and piles of spares, tools and maintenance equipment. Precluding any other use of the garage yet; they represented Tim's dynamism, sexuality, manhood and life-force. Though the motorbikes were under dust covers Tim still retained this space eight months after his death. Unlike Tim's bedroom which I had treated as a private out-of-bounds mausoleum; oppositely the garage was like a 'working tomb.' Having only seldom entered Tim's bedroom until liberating it; I had used the garage on a daily basis - the water softener was there to be regularly filled with salt, I dried the laundry on drying lines strung across the garage, tools for the house and garden were kept there, after wet walks with Pasha I returned by way of the garage door to clean his dirty paws there. Though I had by now progressed through the stages of keeping the three motorbikes, to two, to one to deciding to ultimately sell all three; I realised that the final transition from Tim's house to Rob's house would only take place when the three motorbikes had gone. Tim arrived at the house physically for the first time on a motorbike; he would leave symbolically and spiritually with the last to go.

August 15th I attended a dinner party. Though the food was wonderful, the company of friends kind and convivial, overall it was meaningless. The animating force one needs for lightheartedness had gone; I felt unbearably isolated by the sparking spirits of lifefullness around me. I couldn't be myself. Nor could I pretend. I made a conscious decision to withdraw further; I could not bridge the social barrier yet.

One member of The Partners Group organised an outing to a

nightclub; I quite recoiled and declined. Though I had already formed a good one-to-one friendship with Maria outside the group; the possibility of meeting up similarly with larger numbers of friends became increasingly difficult to contemplate. However the structure and dynamics of the group within the boundaries of Mildmay; the familiar venue, the counsellors Annie and Carol - the lead horses of a disorientated team, the predictable 7 o'clock start and 9 o'clock finish; allowed for me to fraternise with numbers of people I would not otherwise have mixed with that year. It's only in retrospect I realise that in addition to providing emotional support the meetings provided in disguise a chance to meet on a social basis in our post-group overflow to 'The Conqueror' pub after the 9pm finish. At the time it seemed to be like Part II of the evening - a less serious version of what happened within the hospice - but was in fact a group of new found friends having a drink in a pub.

I began to cry this month as I had cried during Tim's final weeks of life; then in anticipation of his death, now in anticipation of his memorial service. I had seen Tim's motorbikes, teddy bear 'Edward', toy labrador 'Pudge' throughout the year and reacted heartlessly; now they brought tears to my eyes; as did a rogue nasturtium I found in the garden from a plant Tim had sown the summer before. I believe the cold rituals attended earlier in the year combined with the delays in setting a date for Tim's memorial service had equivalently left Tim on a shelf in the mortuary at The Mildmay; and my mourning similarly in suspended animation.

One day I was re-reading an old diary. I concentrated on a section when Tim had been HIV with no symptoms and I had been very anxious for him. My diary evoking life in Tim's time beckoned me back. I said to myself 'I will ring Tim at work to make sure he is OK.' I started to dial the Royal Opera House number but then I remembered. I could still get confused between fact and fantasy.

Irrespective of the uptrends and downtrends of August the month had its business matters as always to be dealt with.

Twice daily the postman delivered letters often demanding immediate attention; and at this a sacred time and it didn't seem right in this acute stage of mourning that I should have to renew a home contents insurance policy or write to the dog insurance company trying to resolve a minor but maddening six month problem of re-establishing Pasha's cover in my name.

Tragic love stories such as La Traviata, La Bohème are beautiful and moving yet quite misleading. Such romantic portrayals of death show well the emotional face of grief but none of its unappealing aspects and consequences - business - the nitty gritty of life a partner is left behind to deal with.

I did honour all my responsibilities and cleared all outstanding matters of correspondence, still I needed what I saw as my rightful phase of Romantic mourning. I went to Wales for a few days retreat where I could just 'be' with my thoughts for Tim remote from the letterbox and telephone. Business, reawakenings, downfalls, friendships, they all have their place in bereavement; yet this was the month where for the days of my retreat and contemplations by the sea, the aspect of mourning had to be inviolate from the other aspects of bereavement.

It was the first month without a letter from the solicitor. As if in its place I received a seven month awaited reply from The Royal London Hospital regarding the letter of complaint I had written following Tim's death. Though a formal letter inviting me to discuss HIV care with the Deputy Director of Inpatient Services it recalled me across the solstices and equinox to Tim's last days of treatment at The Royal London Hospital prior to transfer to The Mildmay for terminal care. Memories freshened around me; the biting cold of an empty courtyard, looking up at the room housing Tim, my loneliness, his loneliness; the sorrow of that December day returned with such clarity it was almost tangible - and all my related thoughts to that period fell off the shelf where I had left them; I had to carry them now in tandem with my mourning thoughts, I couldn't separate them for they were on the emotional side of the business letter which had prompted them.

Mourning led to its product morbidity. It was a phase I needed to experience. I see morbidity as the scab on bereavement. Scab is an ugly word and an unsightly quantity but vital to healing - similarly morbidity. I became quite fascinated and preoccupied with death and suffering. In book shops I abandoned sections devoted to art, film, opera, gardening, literature that I had formerly frequented. Images of war, The Holocaust couldn't satisfy my appetite for images of suffering and death - Japanese beheading POW, Germans herding naked Jews into gas chambers - but it was always with horror, revulsion, sadness and grief I looked at these photographs. I was relieved Shirley validated this phase as normal. I had once been told of a father who having lost his daughter scanned obituaries for notices of the deaths of other young girls; I had then thought how weird, creepy and unnatural. I was now all those things. I understood - how natural.

A film on TV coinciding with the August 14th outbreak of World War I left me so overwhelmed with grief I never thought I would recover. I thought of the good and young lives lost, those thousands lying in the vast military cemeteries that Tim and I had sped past many times on the road to Paris as we crossed the Somme. The 1918 end of hostilities did not alleviate the national grief that swept the land held by parents, brothers, sisters, uncles, aunts and lovers; and I thought for the first time of my great-grand mother who died in grief at the loss of two sons, my great-uncles; and I imagined the thousands of bereft gay lovers of the time, Germans, British, French alike trapped with their clandestine grief.

Retreats were not possible after my return from Wales but quiet moments in the chapel at The Mildmay and St Paul's, Covent Garden were possible. I had frequented both but only in August did I 'see' with my eyes, heart and head, the image of Christ on the Cross. We are told he suffered to save us all - this I couldn't understand at all; he hadn't saved Tim, his family and me from any of our respective sufferings. Yet I do believe Jesus did live and suffer horribly before dying on the Cross; that image became a symbol for my grief. I started to wear the gold crucifix my mother had given me years before which I had stopped wearing soon after Tim's HIV diagnosis. An absolute non-believer in my head for so long it was difficult to accept this degree of religious movement in my heart. Eight months into bereavement I was questioning my atheism; not quite a non-believer, not quite a believer; but already this stirring of religious and spiritual thought had a healing and comforting effect and allowed me to move through the morbid phase faster than I believe I would otherwise have done. This released me from morbidity for a more constant sadness. Gil said it could stay with me for a long time. It did.

It was this month I agreed to Angela's demands that there would be no mention of AIDS or collection for AIDS charities at Tim's memorial service. Begrudgingly I entered into their collusion perpetuating their illusions and prejudices; so that their friends and relatives would be spared the very reason we would be congregating next month. They who were determined to be spared the truth of Tim's life; I who had been spared no facts of his life, I deeply resented 'doctoring' the proceedings. But they needed to be there for Tim; otherwise it would become another incomplete and wanting ritual. He didn't just belong to me. So begrudgingly I agreed to a public perjury of the truth. So there had to be a compromise between an openly living gay man like myself and a country farming family such as Tim's family. But I was determined that through the components I had chosen for the memorial service they would be subliminally acquainted with my 'Tim' as well as their 'Timothy.'

For my sake and Tim's mother's peace of mind an olive branch had to be proffered so we could each attend the service without fear of one another following the insensitive way I had returned the car precipitating 'the letters' she had written. I bought a small scented book of verse and wrote a card apologising for the way I had returned the car (although I didn't mean it for that had been the only option open to me) and saying I had never wanted to hurt her feelings purposely (true). As I wrapped the gift I felt quite fickle but as I dropped it into the posting box it disappeared as a heartfelt gift; how emotions buck and yaw in bereavement. She responded with the following card...

24.8.91

Dear Rob,

It was very strange that you should write, (I was just about to write to you) apologising for not having thanked you for sending the mag: Opera, way back in March! I was reusing the envelope and feeling inside I found your note sort of fixed in the fold. You must have thought me very rude for not acknowledging it, I thought that it came from the Royal Opera House H! Thank you for your card letter and delightful book. (I am taking it to Austria, we leave at crack of dawn, and so somebody else will have to post this I hope!) It was a very nice thought. It has been a very difficult time for us all. I hope that Pasha is better and that you are well, and your Mother better? We will be back on the 12 Sept.

Sincerely, Marjorie

Shirley was very pleased to hear of the improvement in relations in only a month from when they could hardly have been worse. 'There has been good and bad, right and wrong on both sides, there usually is', she said.

I carried 'the letters' with me through until the New Year. One might think I should have destroyed them. Why keep them? Why on earth carry them on ones person? The answer : In a world where Tim's family were in a Bermuda Triangle of emotions; giving scrambled messages to everyone regarding the nature of Tim's demise; I was ironically one of the few sure bearings any of them had regarding the honest truth of Tim's life and last years. Is it any surprise therefore that the stimulus of the way I returned the car provoked her to unload the massive anger she was carrying - onto me. The letters did hurt badly; that had been her intention; they were my war wounds of bereavement; as validating as any letter of condolence; a severe backhanded compliment; letters that would not have been written had I not been Tim's gay partner.

Over the months I showed the letters to different friends because I wanted them 'unwritten' - taken from me. Reactions varied: sympathy for her, for me; reprimands for her, for me; Jeremy wouldn't read them; Julia was furious that I should have received such diminishing words - it was she who finally allowed for me to be purged of them, 'Put them in the book verbatim.' Maria responded emotionally and shaking her head as if in disbelief pulled out of her handbag a letter she had long carried; every word of that letter responsible for the pain she was left to carry from the man who had infected her partner so bringing about the loss of their baby, his death and maybe her sufferings to come.

Tim's family could play around with his truth but not mine. They could airbrush me from his obituary in an attempt to conceal his homosexuality and our relationship. In a letter his mother could attempt to degrade our relationship to 'a friendship of a few years'. Because The Mildmay was an AIDS hospice; before visiting Tim for the first time his father had to be told the true nature of his illness. A nurse told me afterwards that his father had convinced himself that Tim had caught HIV from a woman when he had worked in Iran. The nurse could neither challenge nor collude; only listen. But I could not play around with Tim's truth. I was the custodian of all he had been to me and left me with in its entirety. There was no part of his life I wanted to edit or that was at odds with my world view. Our relationship was founded on our common homosexuality and his death and my grief was the result of HIV and AIDS which had shadowed the greater part of our life together; and now the time I lived in. These were siege times. The rest of my life would be informed by my homosexuality. Their lives would probably not be touched again by HIV/AIDS. Mine most certainly would be.

While sorting through some cardboard boxes under the workbench in the garage full of oily rags, I chanced upon an old wooden box. I opened it to find some German gay porn magazines, phials of amyl nitrate, a cock ring, sex toys, a heavily studded denim waistcoat, an old gas mask and a torn leather jacket covered in metal motorbike badges. This unexpected discovery was a stark reality check; a further buttressing of the brutal truth - his sex life which had killed him. This was why he was dead. But still I was lucky; this gave more tangibility to why we had unwillingly been forced apart, forever. This was the reason I was in the garage on a sultry Saturday afternoon in late August. I broke up the grubby age old battered cardboard boxes and disposed of them in black plastic refuse sacks along with the oily rags and the contents of the wooden box. His death was starting to make sense to me. And my life without him was just beginning to make some sense to me too.

Eight months after Tim's death I was managing the juggling act of bereavement - the house, garden, dog, business matters. I was bringing things slowly alive again and I was bouncing back from the downbeats. I was writing the first draft of this book. The few remaining and evolving new friendships and a potential new relationship were valid and real. I was a survivor; this allowed for the concept of a life being possible without Tim. What and where that life would be I didn't know; but in the transcendence to that new life I knew instinctively that I would make the transition from surviving to living. I was cloaked in my mourning robes - but a budding feeling was forming that I would come to know as Hope.

CHAPTER 10

September

The first eleven days of autumn were my last days of mourning. Yet in the closing days of this foundation zone of bereavement the usual themes pertained.

On the upside I completed clearing the site around the temple-lantern transplanting lilies and shrubs ready for the pond I envisaged. New irises 'Cider Haze' and 'Perry Hill' were delivered from Kelways Nurseries. I continued to work on this book not losing the momentum I had established. I was reading old diaries charting our life together, contemplating on the ordinary things that make up a relationship and the profundity of events and emotions that mapped the course of Tim's illness.

The first draft of this book began with his diagnosis in 1986 and ended with his death in 1990. I would eventually rewrite the book beginning with his death because it was to date the most singularly pivotal experience of my life. And where would it end? Books have a final page; people have their last day of life, and there I guess it will end with me. Gil and Shirley far from voicing those meaningless epithets 'forget Tim', 'put it behind you', 'move on', 'get over it'; they reassured me that my relationship with Tim would find its rightful place in my panoply of lived experience; neither arresting potential life nor becoming prohibited territory; that the intense pain would pass and eventually memories would come to mind in the act of remembering which is different to grieving. So I had the theory; now the mighty task underway of putting it into practice. I no longer wished to join Tim in death. I very much wanted to live, but I didn't know how. The beckoning currents of life were not enough to free my anchors which were still dragging and entangling in the still unfathomable depths of bereavement. This intense revisiting and rethinking of past times and things is correctly described by some professionals as 'grief work'. It was hard to see I was making progress.

On the downside my grandmother lost her sight suddenly on September 2nd. I travelled to Penarth a few days later to visit her in the nursing home where she had been moved. It was a solemn time yet my reservoir of hallowed thoughts for Tim was readily available for my old Granny as well.

Business wise I received two letters from the solicitor. The first one contained Tim's outstanding tax returns to be co-signed alongside Angela's signature. The second letter notified me that a district valuer would be visiting on September 12th to value the property for the Inland Revenue. Being the day of the memorial this was not possible so I rearranged his visit for two days prior to the service. His visit was polite and courteous. Though he was just doing his job nevertheless I found an alien's presence in every room and cupboard, an intrusion at a time I wanted absolute 'stillness' everywhere again.

Bereavement produces both emotive and business consequences. Though they are immiscible they are 'mates' and often have to be managed together.

While cleaning a pair of shoes I spontaneously decided to sort out the shoe cleaning basket. A nominal domestic job still it was part of the encompassing aftermath responsibility. I disposed of tins of polish and tangles of motorbike boot laces that would never be used again. I didn't want anyone else to use them and it seemed wrong to keep them. I knew Tim wouldn't want me to memorialise them. Sentiment can exist in the most unlikely places; however trivial or momentous is all part of the same phenomenon to be faced in ones' own time if left with a houseful of possessions as I was, there being a story behind every object.

Much of my time was taken up with prememorial preparations. It was a great honour that the service was being mounted by members of The Royal Opera House, the Flagship of the Arts and The Welsh National Opera. Still it wasn't without considerable stress, essential elements for the order of service, and the post memorial gathering had to be not only finalised, but fought for. I had to write a number of letters and make phone calls that things previously discussed would actually happen. I could never have been so outspoken, demanding and forthright for myself. For Tim I would risk any repudiation. My determination that Tim would be given a chance to be mourned released a latent entrepreneurial strength in me forever displacing the 'mail boy' image I'd had of myself at Crusaid.

As Tim's lover, partner, best friend, chief carer, executor and trustee, it wasn't wrong for me to be the continuity person between his family, friends, colleagues and workmates, the motorbike fraternity, the doctors, nurses and counsellors who had looked after him. Only I could be the lynchpin. It was a rightful privileged duty.

Preparations included a need to make contact with all important friends and people who had helped colour Tim's experience. Vicky had agreed to be my companion for the service. Glen and Andy had been the only couple Tim had 'allowed' into the reality of his last year. Francis and Kirsten had been the ambassadors for all Tim's friends breaking down his emotional barricade at The Mildmay thereby letting other friends follow in those desperate last days. I gave Angela details of the order of service for her to disseminate amongst

Tim's family as she saw fit so they could come prepared. 'The trouble is we don't know who people are,' she said. While visiting my ailing grandmother my family demonstrated their continued support which was reassuring. Two days before the service I met Jeremy, Tim's boss and colleague at 'The Globe' in Covent Garden. He had been the bridge between Tim's professional and private métiers. Later that afternoon I went to St. Paul's, my time for me. An oasis of peacefulness within the bustle of Covent Garden I had it to myself. I sat in the front row where I would be sitting two days hence and contemplated. An emotional rehearsal it excited a mixture of hope and fear, excitement and dread fuelling me with adrenaline to cope. I was prepared.

Max both helped and stepped aside. This was not his time, nor my time. It was Tim's time. A few days before the service a maintenance man charged me £40 just to tell me the washing machine was defunct. Just to have broken down was inconvenient with a backlog of laundry and people coming to stay. These were the first welcome visitors since Claus and Jutta came to stay earlier in the year. But in these last few days before the memorial service when every morning, afternoon and evening was allocated, to have to arrange for the disposal, replacement and plumbing in of a new machine stressed me to the limit. I was learning that the mundane problems of life do not stop or stand aside at reverent times; and in fact seem to almost purposely orchestrate to coincide. Max responded by drawing a calming picture of a peaceful pond with water lilies and frogs as a forethought of the pond. It made me smile.

This demonstrated his unique position in my life as 'witness'. Especially at this time some might have seen him as an outsider; in fact he was on the inside observing better than anyone else how I was affected by the minutiae of life, ordinary and daily things, the stressful, unexpected and momentous.

One friend asked me if Max was going to the service. An inflection in the voice spoke the real question, 'Please reassure us that he won't be sitting with you or better still won't be there at all.' I didn't need to be told what was de rigueur. However in my opinion he had well earned his place in the congregation; that he had shared, helped, suffered within my bereavement more than anyone else. In whatever way our relationship would evolve I believed the service would prove cathartic for him, and validate the problems he had encountered entering a relationship with an AIDS bereaved partner. It would be misleading to pretend there were not moments when Max couldn't hide his feelings of exclusion during this countdown period; that my focus had returned to Tim. There are times during bereavement, and this was one of them, when one doesn't want to be loved or cared for by anyone else.

And so the day approached. It was not just coincidence but fitting that the final partners group fell the evening prior to the memorial. I was glad to be out-of-reach and safe within the group while people travelled and readied for the service the next day. It was a retreat but nevertheless a working session. We had gone to the first group very much as survivors who had been touched by death; we left the last session as survivors who were testing the water of life again. It is important to be understood; without such a peer group I would not have been. The meetings spanning seven months equated to seven safe houses, stepping stones through a journey of vulnerability and threat. Without The Mildmay Missions Partner Support Group I would have been less confident, less secure, less sure of myself.

Customarily a number of us went on to 'The Conqueror' nearby. So I could attend this last meeting Max had volunteered to meet a friend Sylvie arriving at Victoria from Paris. Unexpectedly about half an hour before the pub closed Max arrived with Sylvie and another friend staying for the memorial.

Within the boundaries of The Mildmay our meetings had been unquestionably inviolate. In the public space of a pub I wasn't sure of the 'rules', as to whether or not the arrival of my new lover and two friends was an intrusion. Because Tim had died Shirley had invited me to the support group. Because Tim had died I had met Max. Because Tim had died Sylvie had flown to London to attend Tim's memorial service the next day. It didn't seem wrong that consequences of Tim's death should overlap. Everything is connected.

Tim first introduced me to Sylvie six years before in Paris on our way to Aix-en-Provence on the motorbike. If I had been told then that six years later Tim would be dead, I would have a new lover, that I would meet Sylvie in an East End pub after the concluding session of an AIDS bereavement group I would have found it unthinkable - there was something unreal about it all.

This was the most exclusive club I would ever belong to. The criterion for membership was that one's partner had to have died in the last six months of 1990. We all had life membership. This was a club no-one wanted to join and could never resign from. His words of wit now more candid and telling than he could have possibly imagined Oscar Wilde summed up how I, we felt about belonging to our elite select group, 'I would not want to belong to any club which would have me as a member'. Out of 9 couples comprising 16 men and 2 women, 9 men had died already. I wondered how many of us would survive ultimately.

On returning home I lit the thirty six hour candle in the temple lantern in the clearing at the bottom of the garden. It would burn through the twenty four hours of September 12th. I had initiated the beginning of Tim's memorial service in the garden he had created and loved of which I was now custodian to maintain and develop.

September 12th was the emotional axis of 1991. People talked of 'a celebration for the life of Tim' but I couldn't share their view of what I saw as a tragedy. Yes we would gather to remember his achievements and qualities but only because he had died. Cut off on his ascent to his full promise; how could I forget the tears, the anxieties, his earth shattering anger at being cheated of a life he cherished. A memorial service outweighed anything that could be deemed celebratory. I would not be celebrating his death. For me celebrations were for birthdays, parties, Christmas and successes. I would be honouring and remembering him because he had died and suffered terribly. Bereavement is an indeterminate invisible quantity and quality but September 12th gave tangibility to Tim's death and the lives of all those ensuing who had known him in whatever capacity.

The day began like any other, letting Pasha out into the garden, making a cup of tea, retrieving the post from Pasha who had collected it from the doormat and deposited it gently in his 'lair' under my desk in the sitting room. There I found the following message from Peter Day.

Wednesday 11 September 1991
My dear Rob,

I know it is Tim's memorial tomorrow, I know that you will think I should be there but I will not be. Not out of lack of feeling for Timus but because he is so firmly rooted in my mind as he was that I cannot conceive of him in any other way. A memorial will somehow seem to bring that to an end, I would have to see him differently in the future. I know this is irrational, that one needs rituals to allow one to allow one's feelings to have an expression that funerals and memorials are seen as a thanksgiving rather than anything more negative, but that is not how I feel. I shall always remember him as he was: when he first climbed those stairs with you about the book as you were wary of me; when he came to tell me about the test; even when he was angry with me. Why should I give thanks for something that hasn't finished and will only finish with me? He is as present now as he was when I didn't see him, we even have our conversations when I ponder on aspects of the relationship. It maybe that I should come as support for you, but I know you do not need that. Maybe to show his parents how loved Tim was: I'd rather face them and tell them what I think.

*So, please dear Rob, don't be too upset: we must all face experiences
in our own way. This is mine. Lots of love and maybe we shall see
each other when I am back from Seville.*
   Peter

Peter was the editor of the first book I wrote and had
become a close friend of ours. The day after Tim was
diagnosed HIV he had gone to Peter to confide in him - before
even telling me. Out of all our friends and family members he
was the only person Tim entrusted in apart from me and the
medical profession. Peter carried the situation - us, our joint
anxieties and fears for almost two years until Tim's anger
phase brought about our separation. Peter felt he had to
intervene to arrest Tim's willful spiral into self destruction. He
consulted with a friend who was a psychiatrist for advice as to
what course of action he should follow. He wanted to visit
Tim's parents and tell them that Tim had become quite
unbalanced and irrational and was verging on a total
breakdown. Instead he opted to confront Tim by letter; that he
had to come to terms with being HIV. The psychiatrist advised
that the letter might cost the friendship and sadly this proved
the case. Nevertheless the letter achieved its desired effect, and
Tim began the slow process of facing up to the source of his
anxiety and anger - his HIV status. This allowed for our
reconciliation and for Tim's acceptance of therapy from Gil
Parker, something his denial state made impossible prior to
Peter's intervention. With Tim's first hospitalization it was only
Peter who visited apart from myself and unfairly received the
full force of Tim's anger. Though Tim lived another two years,
only on his deathbed did he reconcile their relationship but
died before Peter could visit. So singularly involved for the
first two years of Tim's condition, and left carrying so much I
thought he needed the service to be 'debriefed'; not so after
reading his card. I was glad and comforted that Peter should
so rightly have his great influence at the beginning of Tim's

Memorial Day.

Max walked Pasha and would shepherd Sylvie to Covent Garden so I would be free to get ready. I wanted and needed to be alone. Dressing in the suit I had last worn at Tim's funeral I discovered how much weight I had put on as a consequence of too many late night takeaways, too many pints of lager, and no exercise. No sooner than I boarded the familiar No. 6 bus I was surprised and quite unprepared to be overtaken by the feeling 'I was off to meet Tim'. In my pocket I carried the tiny Swissair aeroplane he had given me exactly one year before. Dismounting at The Aldwych I was reassured to glimpse Fiona on the lower deck, one of Tim's nurses from The Mildmay on her way to the service too.

By circuitous route I met Vicky at Covent Garden tube station; I thought it superstitious to meet anyone until the service was over. But there are no hard and fast rules so after wandering around aimlessly for a while we changed plan and rendezvoused with my parents whom I knew to be at 'The Globe'. I needed a quiet anonymous moment with Vicky to ready myself so we disappeared to a backstreet sandwich shop.

The time had arrived for us to make our way to the church. It was a lovely day just like the first time I had travelled to Covent Garden to meet Tim for a coffee after his initial production meeting at the Royal Opera House five years before. From that day until his death Covent Garden had been our domain. Vicky and I picked our way through the milling crowds. Then ahead I saw the porch of St Paul's where Bernard Shaw had set the opening of 'Pygmalion'. The Royal Opera House with its lofty fly tower dominated the market, and there we would gather after the service. Covent Garden belonged to Tim and me again, one last time. Since I had last seen him in the early hours of New Year's Eve, I had waited patiently and less patiently for this time when echoes from his life would abound forth, as if coming from him; but in fact as we tripped across the cobbles were being summoned from their long hibernation within me. Tim might almost be waiting for me in the church.

Vicky held my hand. I tightened my grip as we entered the church gardens. Already I was feeling as the night Tim had died, numbed by some powerful natural anaesthetic, far more potent than the pint of lager I had just drunk with my parents. People thronged the steps, I shook hands and said hullo to people but I was blind. Without Vicky I would have been terrified. Kenneth, the General Manager of The Royal Opera House had arranged to meet me outside. Only he seemed familiar and approachable. We greeted one another, I introduced Vicky, he handed me a telegram.

Dear Mr. Richardson,

Would you kindly pass on the following message to Rob Lewis.

As you know, Tim was very fondly regarded by so many of us here in Vancouver. We were enlightened by his buoyant approach to the work, his lovely wit and his enjoyment of life. We were all so happy for him when he met you and of course during your visit here in 1985, we thought him very lucky.

We remember him with great affection and send our deepest expressions of compassion to you.

Sincerely,

Kathleen Speakman	*Bruce Johnson*
Joan Voisine	*Peggy Jameson*
Debra Harrison	*Joan Dreidger*
Margaret Ryan	*Staff and Company of*
	the Vancouver Opera

I read kind words that honoured Tim and recognised both our relationship and my position that day as the bereaved partner. Yet it seemed ironic and sad that I could only read such a telegram on the steps of a church in the circumstances of death - though gay men can have traditional baptisms, confirmations, funerals and memorials, there is no provision for a valuable and loving relationship to be formally acknowledged on consecrated ground in life.

Tim's family was ahead in the good hands of their escort Jeremy who had volunteered to chaperone them. While they made their entrance I was glad to have the telegram to read, to distract me from them and everyone. I didn't want to talk or be spoken to other than by Vicky or Kenneth so defined was the aura of anticipation enveloping me; the completely irrational feeling that as I stepped through the door into the church Tim would be there waiting for me.

A polite distance between me and his family seemed correct. Tim's very absence for which we congregated uncovered our vulnerability to one another. Once Tim's family was seated, Vicky and I crossed the threshold of St Paul's. Ruth, who had worked in the Producers Office, performed her last courtesy for Tim as she handed us copies of the order of service. We walked down the aisle and took our places with Julia, Kate, and Kenneth. The quiet companionship already distanced the unrewarding memories of Tim's funeral and ash scattering.

The cover drawing for the order of service that I had commissioned from Francis O'Connor had well captured all aspects of Tim's life. He had created a composite drawing of a motorbike, music bars, Pasha's head, and of his own volition added a large line drawing portrait of Tim. When I had seen the preliminary sketch I had been shocked, not that Francis had taken his rightful liberty as artist to express what he felt appropriate, but because all I could 'see' in the lines that made up Tim's face were the ravages of AIDS. I asked Francis to redraw it more lightly thinking Tim would look less ill - he didn't. When I looked at the same drawing many months later I didn't 'see' AIDS, just Tim! AIDS had impressed itself into the constitution of my mind; and for a long time distorted all my sensibilities.

On the back were the final four lines of verse from Mozart's opera 'Die Entfuhrung aus dem Serail', representing our dog's place at the service who Tim had named after one of the characters in this opera.

'Long life to Pasha Selim
honour to his domains
and let his brow be resplendent
with rejoicing and glory'

In that simple line drawing Francis had caught the essence of our exuberant dog. I was very proud of Pasha and the defining role he had played in our life and Tim's illness. Oblivious to the service now underway I was comforted by the thought of him snoozing at home and probably on my bed but as intrinsically important this day as everyone present. I wondered what Tim's family thought of the design I had commissioned of 'Tim' who was so different to their 'Timothy'.

The situation was comparable to The Temple of Abu Simbel in Egypt as day breaks on February 23rd and October 23rd. On only those two days of the year the axis of the sun aligns with the axis of the light shafts that had been cut one hundred and eighty feet through the rock; the morning sun streams through the doorway of the antechamber lighting the interior, shedding its sacred beams on the four Gods in the inner sanctuary, Ptah, Amen-Re, Rameses the Great and Re-Harakhty.

And now at 2.30pm on September 12th 1991 all the people in Tim's life were gathered within the sanctuary of St Paul's Church, Covent Garden. The altar, the natural focal point for the eye to rest on, here all the coordinates of Tim's battle were focused, the very reason for our assembly: Tim's fateful flight to San Francisco in January 1980 where he contracted HIV; the discarded newspaper on a bus in Cardiff where I first read of AIDS; the death of Edward in New York, the first person I knew to die; my HIV test in May 1986; my negative result giving Tim false confidence to be tested; his HIV diagnosis December 20th 1986; his AIDS diagnosis on my birthday April

6th 1989; Tim's death December 30th 1990; his funeral January 4th 1991; the scattering of his ashes, March 24th 1991; and now his memorial. The organist stopped the preludes he had been playing, the rector stepped forward. If I had ever been a Calvinist predestined to be at St Paul's this day and time it was the night I had met Tim. In the brief few seconds before he spoke all the coordinates of the past and present lined up. Something had stopped within me the night Tim had died. Emotional hawsers snapped and now catapulted me across time. I had a strange sense of having being propelled from my last moment with him to this moment without him.

The Very Reverend David Elliott welcomed us all to his church to remember the life of Tim.

A moments silence followed for us each to have our own thought for Tim. I couldn't think to order but in the silence I could hear the bustle of Covent Garden Market beyond the altar wall where buskers performed on the rear porch to a happier throng of people than within the church. This time the juxtaposition of life and death seemed so right; they do exist side by side, unlike the night of his death when it seemed so wrong.

Then followed the hymn 'The Lord's my Shepherd', something the whole congregation could participate in. Falteringly we all began to sing. Then a few strong voices led before a great wall of sound washed over us from The Royal Opera House Chorus seated in the choir stalls above us at the back of the church.

My voice gave out all together, not because of the amplitude of the chorus, but because of Kenneth's intuitive choice of hymn. I made the connection that the words were the same as the psalm that Peter Clarke the chaplain of The Mildmay had recited with Tim two nights before he died. The Royal Opera Chorus sang with a might for Tim, words he had barely been able to muster to croak.

'The lord's my shepherd, I'll not want;

September

He make me down to lie
In pastures green; he leadeth me
The quiet waters by.
My soul he doth restore again,
And me to walk doth make
Within the paths of righteousness,
E'en for his own name's sake.
Yea, though I walk in death's dark vale,
Yet will I fear no ill:
For thou art with me, and thy rod
And staff me comfort still.
My table thou hast furnished
In presence of my foes;
My head thou dost with oil anoint
And my cup overflows.
Goodness and mercy all my life
Shall surely follow me;
And in God's house for evermore
My dwelling-place shall be'

I had asked Julia Carson Sims to choose the first reading. The extract she read from 'The Mint' by T.E Lawrence was inspired.

'I walked over to my bike, which lived in the garage hut opposite. Its tyres never needed air, its engine had a habit of starting at the second kick. My Brough is a top gear machine, as sweet in that as most single cylinders in middle. I chug lordily past the guard room and through the speed limit at no more than sixteen. Round the bend, past the farm, and the way straightens. Now for it. The engines final development is fifty-two horse power. A miracle that all this docile strength waits behind one tiny lever for the pleasure of my hand.

Another bend: and I have the honour of one of England's straightest and fastest roads. The burble of my exhaust unwound like a long cord behind me. Soon my speed snapped it, and I heard only the cry of the wind which my battering head split and fended aside.

The cry rose with my speed to a shriek: while the airs coldness screamed like two jets of iced water into my dissolving eyes.

Once we so fled across the evening light, with the yellow sun on my left, when a huge shadow roared just overhead. A Bristol fighter, from our neighbouring aerodrome, was banking sharply round. I checked speed an instant to wave: and the slip stream of my impetus snapped my arm and elbow astern, like a raised flail. The pilot pointed down the road towards Lincoln. I sat hard in the saddle, folded back my ears and went away after him, like a dog after a hare. Quickly we drew abreast, as the impulse of his dive to my level exhausted itself.

The next mile of the road was rough. Over the first pothole the Brough screamed in surprise, its mudguards bottoming with a yawp upon the tyre. Through the plunges of the next ten seconds I clung on, wedging my gloved hand in the throttle lever so that no bump should close it and spoil our speed. Then the bike wrenched sideways into three long ruts: it swayed dizzily for thirty awful yards. Out came the clutch, the engine raced freely: the bike checked and straightened, as a Brough should.

The bad ground was passed and on the new road our flight became birdlike. I dared, on a rise, to slow imperceptibly and glance sideways into the sky. There the plane was, two hundred yards and more back. Play with the fellow? Why not? I slowed to ninety: signalled for him to overtake. Slowed ten more: sat up. Over he rattled, hoping I was a flash in the pan.

Open went my throttle again. I crept level, fifty feet below: held it: sailed ahead into the clean and lonely country. An approaching car pulled nearly into the ditch at the sight of the race. The Bristol was zooming among the trees and telegraph poles, with my scurrying spot only eighty yards ahead. I gained though, gained steadily: was perhaps five miles an hour the faster. Down went my left hand to give the engine two extra dollops of oil, for fear that something was running hot: but an overhead Jap twin, super-tuned like this one would carry on to the moon and back, unfaltering.

We drew near the settlement. A long mile before the first houses I closed down and coasted to the crossroads. The plane caught up, banked, climbed and turned for home waving to me as long as he was in sight.

I let in the clutch again and eased my bike uphill to the aloof cathedral. I stabled the steel magnificence of strength and speed at the west door and went in: to find the organist practicing something slow and rhythmical. Like a multiplication table in notes, on the organ. The fretted lacework of choir stall and spandrels drank in the main sound. Its surplus spilled thoughtfully into my ears.'

Lawrence (of Arabia) himself being gay and a motor biker, Julia could have found no better reading to represent the important place and part motorbikes had played in his life; the sense of freedom they gave him, his unaffectedness despite the grandiosity often associated with his profession, his solo individualism and freedom which his bikes always gave him and at times when he struggled with our relationship, rebelliousness to middle-class convention, and their symbolism of his male sexual potency. 'I hope there are motorbikes on the other side,' he had said not long before he died. Moments before my great-great-aunt died she said to my mother, 'And now the greatest adventure of all'. As an experienced stage-manager Julia perfectly concluded her reading with Lawrence's arrival at a church - the perfect continuum between a lesson and the reality of her audience; as if he had parked his Brough outside and come in to join us.

Kenneth took up the baton and stepped forward to deliver a tribute for Tim. I had not expected any humour in the service but Kenneth so rightly surprised me and made us laugh. I realised we would have failed Tim had we allowed tragedy and grief to override and displace memories of his laughter, horseplay, and practical jokes:

'Tim had an immense capacity for work and leg-pulling sometimes to the point of distraction. Once, prior to the Welsh National Opera's visit to East Germany, he managed to convince the scheduling department that nothing containing dots would be allowed past the Berlin Wall in case secrets were being smuggled in micro dots resulting in emergency action to remove all punctuation. Unbridled fury followed when the hoax was discovered!'

I believe I knew better than any of the congregation the full diversity of Tim's humour: the beguiling hoodwinker; the bewitching storyteller who could bring life to stuffed toys; a hilarious impersonator of unpopular singers; and his childish hiding games in cupboards, behind curtains and under tables. Sometimes he would get so carried away with a particular prank that it would go beyond the point of being funny. Once I returned home late, it was dark; I believed he had not yet come home. As I walked up the stairs to put the light on he reached through the balustrade and grabbed my ankle! I nearly died of fright.

Poignantly I saw first hand how, with his AIDS diagnosis his practical jokes and playfulness were transformed into a darker morbid mould. Gone was the clowning and tomfoolery - instead he began to play dead. His acting was so dreadful, so bad in fact it was funny; and though I might laugh I never lost sight of his masked message. Once when he was ill with blood clots in the lungs, I took him a cup of tea in bed. I thought he was dead. He suddenly sat up in bed laughing. It was too telling, too realistic and wasn't funny that time - he scared me. When I later told Ruth Richmond one of his doctors at The Mildmay she was aghast. But I understood, it had all been a rehearsal. Part of Tim's work had been to prepare singers to die realistically which is how so many opera's end. It is quite difficult to die realistically on stage without over-acting. It's even more difficult in real life because it can only ever be unrehearsed. Death had been destined inescapably to be Tim's final scene and we had both known it. He had been preparing me and himself. The autumn before Tim died he stopped playing dead; he must have known there was little time to live. His carefree laughter ceased as well. Only now during Kenneth's tribute did the spirit of Tim's untroubled humour reach through the years from before Tim's AIDS experience to arouse amusement once more.

Kenneth's masterstroke was a brief eulogy for the international Swedish director Göran Jarafelt. He had created many important and successful productions for the Welsh National Opera where he had met and worked with Tim. His death a year before Tim had been marked by minimal solemnities. Tim had been very upset by this considering Göran's enormous contribution to the company. I had wondered at the time whether Tim's pique was just his own fear of being superseded and then relegated to memory as well. Kenneth, as if knowing of Tim's aggravation paid homage to Göran. I knew Tim would have been very happy that his memorial was being used as a vehicle to honour Göran in the presence of members of both the Welsh National Opera and the Royal Opera House. I wondered how many of the audience had known they had been lovers too.

I had my own recollections of Tim and Göran - the night I met Tim at a dinner party I met Goran first, half an hour before Tim's arrival. Their lives, illnesses and deaths became inextricably linked through Strauss' opera 'Ariadne auf Naxos'. Our first trip abroad had been a working holiday for Tim assisting Göran on his new production of 'Ariadne' for the 1985 music festival at Aix-en-Provence.

We were happy. There were no dark clouds on the horizon. We returned the following summer, Tim assisting Göran on the first revival of 'Ariadne'. We canoed through the Ardèche Gorges, basked by fields of sunflowers, picnicked amongst the surreal purple-blue lavender hills of the impressionist painters; but things had changed irrevocably since our visit the previous summer. AIDS was no longer remote happening somewhere else to other people. It had a name - John David's lover Edward had died in New York, Colin in London only the week before we returned to Aix, and John in San Francisco. I had been through the trauma of 'the test' planting the seed for Tim to be tested. The net was closing fast, we were oblivious. Three summers later Tim already ill returned to France to assist

Göran on a second revival of 'Ariadne' in Lyons. Bizarrely both were unsuspecting of each others condition, both doomed they gave convincing performances of their own, living each day as if it was an unlimited future. Five months later November '89 Tim disobeyed his doctor's advice. With extensive skin cancer, a developing leg infection and blood clots in the lungs he travelled to Antwerp by motorbike to assist Göran revive 'Ariadne' yet again. But it wasn't to be. Tim rang in tears to say Göran had died. I travelled to Antwerp with Glen and Andy to support Tim. I saw the dress rehearsal and could hardly hold back my tears of pride that out of such sadness and grief there could be such creation. Tim said it was the best work he had ever done putting Göran's spirit into the production. The silver stars on the ceiling of the pretty opera house emulated the stars of the sky above the open air theatre in Aix where it had all begun four years before. Who ever would have thought that idyllic summer of 1985 that six years later Kenneth would lead Tim's colleagues, friends, family and partner in remembering two vibrant talents lost?

I chose the following item to represent my position in Tim's life. This was for Tim. This was for me. The Irish soprano Suzanne Murphy had generously agreed to my request to sing one of opera's most challenging and beautiful arias 'Casta Diva' from Bellini's 'Norma'. I chose it for three reasons. Tim had been working on this opera with Suzanne singing the title role for Andrei Serban's production for The Welsh National Opera when we had met. Our relationship was made during 'Norma'. I'd spent my second weekend with Tim in London. We were due to return to South Wales for Tim to attend the dress rehearsal, and for me to go back to the job I had. He said, 'Why don't you stay here, I'll come back after the dress rehearsal'. In the words of that sentence he was asking me to live with him. I said, 'OK'. And in saying that one word I left Wales, my job, my new flat, family and friends. This was the biggest decision I'd made in my life.

Just before his HIV diagnosis Tim had been looking

forward to working on a new production of 'Norma' at The Royal Opera House with Margaret Price. He thought he would die before the first rehearsal. The fact he didn't and did good work, 'Norma' became a symbol of renewed hope for him, and me; that one can achieve things previously planned; AIDS didn't destroy everything. And being the pagan prayer of a druid priestess who cuts the sacred mistletoe at night under a full moon; it well symbolised for me the romantic druidic heritage of Wales:

'Chaste goddess, who dost bathe in silver light
These ancient, hallowed trees,
Turn thy fair face upon us,
Unveiled and unclouded...
Temper though the burning hearts,
The excessive zeal of thy people. Enfold the earth in that sweet peace
Which, through thee, reigns in heaven...'

Fearful of breaking down if facing the congregation she chose to sing from the choir stalls above. Invisible to us her glorious disembodied voice floated over our heads, the perfect delivery for the most ethereal of arias. Just like any great performance in the Royal Opera House creating make-believe, the chemistry of Suzanne's memorial performance began to work. I knew Vicky was on my left, Julia on my right, but the sense of reality was of being alive again in Tim's time. Her singing released me plausibly counterfeiting the present for the past. I was sitting next to Tim at the opening night of 'Norma' in The New Theatre in Cardiff.

Norma, the Druid High Priestess has an illicit love affair with Pollione the Proconsul of the occupying Roman forces in Gaul. She confesses her secret publically to her people and is sentenced to death. And now Suzannne sang Norma's song for Tim; that we his public bears witness to his long held secret now in all our knowledge; and we gather with love to say farewell to Tim whose life force was taken from him by AIDS.

In this public deconsecration of our relationship, I felt absolved from all the lies, deceits and collusions of which I will have no part again. And with Norma mounting the pyre I let him go into the flames, into the care of death. And so we parted.

I had delegated the responsibility of the second lesson to Tim's former colleague, friend and landlady, Kate. Her capital choice of quotes from 'The Prophet' by Kahlil Gibran philosophically defined the sense of separation that death yields.

'(i) *The Prophet Leaving - The gates of his heart were flung open, and his joy flew far over the sea - how shall I go in peace and without sorrow - too many fragments of the spirit have I scattered in these streets - I can not withdraw from them without a burden and an ache - it is not a garment I cast off this day, but a skin that I tear with my own hands - yet I can not tarry longer - alone must it seek the ether - Ready am I to go, and my eagerness with sails full set awaits the wind - Only another breath will I breathe in this still air, only another loving look cast backward - Shall the day of the parting be the day of gathering? - And shall it be said that my eve was in truth my dawn? - And what shall I give unto him who has left his plough in mid furrow - If this is my day of harvest, in what fields have I sowed the seed, and in what unremembered seasons? - If this indeed be the hour in which I lift up my lantern, it is not my flame that shall burn therein. Empty and dark shall I raise my lantern, and the guardian of the night shall fill it with oil and he shall light it also. - Go not yet away from us. - A noontide have you been in our twilight, - Suffer not yet our eyes to hunger for your face. - Much have we loved you. - And ever has it been that love knows not its own depth until the hour of separation. -*

(ii) Friendship. And a youth said, Speak to us of friendship. And he answered, saying:

Your friend is your needs answered. He is your field which you sow with love and reap with thanksgiving. And he is your board and your fireside. For you come to him with your hunger, and you seek him for peace. When your friend speaks his mind you fear not the 'nay' in your own mind, nor do you withhold the 'ay'. And when he is silent your heart ceases not to listen to his heart;

For without words, in friendship, all thoughts, all desires, all expectations are born and shared, with joy that is unacclaimed. When you part from your friend, you grieve not;

For that which you love most in him may be clearer in his absence, as the mountain to the climber is clearer from the plain. And let there be no purpose in friendship save the deepening of the spirit. For love that seeks aught but the disclosure of its own mystery is not love but a net cast forth: and only the unprofitable is caught. And let your best be for your friend. If he must know the ebb of your tide, let him know its flood also. For what is your friend that you should seek him with hours to kill?

Seek him always with hours to live. For it is his to fill your need, but not your emptiness. And in the sweetness of friendship let there be laughter, and sharing of pleasures. For in the dew of little things the heart finds its morning and is refreshed.'

The dean of St Paul's returned to lead us in prayers.

18 August 1991
Dear Rob,

I got the invite to the service for Tim. I'm so sorry I can't be there, but I'm now in Los Angeles and am designing a TV series which starts shooting on September 16th. Hope to get thru London this winter - tho God knows when. I wish so much I could be there on the 12th. Hope the summer has been good to you, and that this card finds you well. Say goodbye to Tim for me, my thoughts will be there.

Love, John David

In my thoughts I fulfilled John David's request and said goodbye for him. He was the first AIDS bereaved gay partner I'd known. When he first visited us following Edward's death I had been baffled that he could still smile, laugh, travel, work, go to gay bars, etc. Now I followed in his path discovering for myself the nebulous phenomenon of gay bereavement.

Tim's favourite composer was Berlioz. His 'Grande Messe

Des Morts' would have been fitting; but even with the resources of The Royal Opera House would have been impossible to stage with the vast requirement of timpani. And so in remembrance of a performance of Berlioz's 'Grande Messe des Morts' at which Tim had cried copiously for his own death I chose the final piece 'Sanctus' from another French mass - Charles Gounod's 'Messe Solenelle de St. Cecilia'. As one would find in the sanctum of Abu Simbel just before the sun moved over and darkness engulfed, the sun would momentarily find its maximum force producing euphoria of light. Similarly with the swelling force of voices this was the end to all the 'beginnings', all the 'befores' that had collectively taken life from Tim's body on December 30th 1990 at 10.50pm. At the precise moment the chorus and singers produced their supreme sound all the ties binding Tim to life unknotted; his fight for life, his reluctance to die, his anger at being cheated of the life he cherished, his downheartedness for his promise unfulfilled - all gave way to an acceptance on my part for the death he had so bitterly and begrudgingly fought against until the day of the card of The Fighting Temeraire. Now he was at peace. With our joint acceptance he floated free and took wing.

In the silence and during The Blessing for Tim that followed my guy ropes of December 1986 'it can not be that he will die' gave way to 'it must be that he must die'.

I wanted to disappear to be alone in Victoria Park. Instead I was expected to join Tim's family and lead the congregation from the church. When I turned to leave I was so bewildered by the numbers of people filling the church I was overcome by nerves; I just could not walk out facing the seated congregation. After composing myself I tacked onto the end of the crowd swarming the aisle, happy to be an anonymous member of the congregation that spilled onto the steps outside. As we shuffled to the door by chance I found myself with Gil. Never demonstrative with me before she held my hand quelling the nervousness I had expected before or during, but not after the service. We reached the door. She let go of my hand and I stepped over the threshold, alone.

The sun of the approaching autumnal Equinox struck me, blinding me at the same time as a valedictory clap fell on my shoulder from the dean. I thanked him for conducting the beautiful service of remembrance for Tim. Nine months had passed for me during the forty minute service. Less than an hour before my mind played games with me that Tim could almost be waiting for me in the church. Of course as a piece of fact I knew he was dead, but the knowing hadn't really registered or meant anything. Now I felt it. As a flower seed needs time to germinate, grow and the right conditions to bloom so does the knowledge of a death; and for the mind to gradually accept the information, absorb it and for it to become a legitimate accepted part of ones life. Hence the phrase 'mad with grief' for the person receiving unexpected news of a loved ones death; the consequence of the minds refusal and repudiation to consider the facts. We all need a sound reality base to cope with life and its vicissitudes. We all need a rich imagination so as to be spontaneous and creative. But bereavement is an altered state of mind and takes us into a dimension where the fine balance of its constitution no longer obeys the call of logic, the persuasion of the rational, nor responds to the sound of life's birdsong, where sorrow corrupts all joy, hope and optimism. I'd never experienced such a strong sense of being in the now, in the moment. I honestly think that for the first time since the night of his death my body clock synchronised with the calendar clock. I'd won back some reality and had my rightful place in the world again. Tim was dead. I was alive.

I was not prepared for the multitude of familiar faces which met my gaze outside. I felt I should talk to everyone; I wanted to talk to no-one. If only my mind had rehearsed this moment. My eyes darted around trying to find anonymous faces to rest on. There seemed to be none. Max and Sylvie materialised to offer their formal salutations. He shook my hand and discreetly disappeared into the mingling crowd. Sylvie stepped forward to give me a kiss, but lingered a moment too long. She was brimming with tears and looked lost and confused and in desperate need of some comfort. I guessed she was missing her husband Didier who she represented. Again it was my duty to offer comfort and this gave me a fillip of renewed strength. I was startled to see my beautiful Welsh friend Menna. She had said she couldn't come but had flow in from Australia at short notice for the service. 'I needed to see how you are with my own eyes.' Now I left overwhelmed. I hugged her and momentarily hid a determined runaway tear in her long hair. Like Laurence Brough hitting the rut, my mind lurched and swaged, but held steady too. There was Big Harry The Biker with his moll, a gaggle of famous sopranos, Mum & Maria and the reassuring sight of Shirley, Annie and the nurses from Mildmay. I desperately needed a moments respite. With Hywel and Menna I disappeared into the anonymity of the market place. The short walk across the cobbles amidst the shops and stalls proved the emboldening interlude I needed.

One final time I entered Tim's work place as his rightful partner. Conveniently close to St Paul's I had boldly requested the use of The Royal Opera House for the post-memorial gathering. The vast hushed interiors contrasted harshly with the daily carnival of Covent Garden Market adjacent. Although a little punch-drunk from an overcharge of potent memories nevertheless by the time we reached The Crush Bar I was composed and ready to meet all those waiting and those following. Especially for the friends and colleagues who had been excluded from Tim's dying, death and funeral I felt it very important people were given an informal opportunity to talk afterwards; to be debriefed of thoughts backlogged these last nine months. Death brings about unthinkable changes and partitions. In saying hellos I said as many goodbyes not just to members of Tim's extended family, his motorbike chums and work colleagues most of whom I didn't expect to see again, but also to many of my friends who I haven't seen since. Whether in the backroom of a pub, amidst the gilt and velvet of an opera house, in a community hall, etc., it's important to have a chance to say goodbyes for without endings there can be no beginnings. One loses the world of ones partner when he or she dies. My departure was a leave taking. As I stepped out into Bow Street the Royal Opera House became as inaccessible and remote as it had been before I had met Tim. I said, 'Goodbye'.

The rest of the day saw a gradual diminishing of numbers ending with myself and Sylvie in the sitting room at home. Before going to bed she lingered a while. Tears welled in her eyes as she delivered the eulogy of the day, 'I think of Tim often but I always remember him with tears'. The day ended as it began - I put Pasha out into the garden and made a cup of tea. I was proud of my boisterous East End labrador who had been so rightfully and nobly honoured that day. Tim always needed space, even now - the flame in the temple-lantern flickered on into the night extinguishing itself alone, unobserved.

I'd hoped for a thunder and lightning moment. Tim had been mourned but something was wanting, missing; and consequently I was still in mourning. Bewildered thoughts clouded the tangible proof I needed to liberate me from my mourning robes. The next day I returned to St Paul's hoping to find the answer. This time I was alone. It was late, the gates were locked but that didn't matter. I peered through the grilles into the still gardens. The answer was there if only I could remember, if only I could 'see'. I didn't know what I was looking for, an object, a thought, a memory? I retraced my path across the cobbles to The Royal Opera House. Maybe there something would jolt my blind mind to 'see'. A poster advertised Wagner's opera 'Siegfried' which had been significant to Tim and me; we had first made love following the opening night of the Welsh National Opera's production six years before. The Royal Opera's opening performance of 'Siegfried' had been the last opera we had shared together the previous year. Siegfried's story ended with death as did Tim's.

Meaningful memories but no answers, I returned home on the faithful No. 6 bus. Still I mourned. The next morning I received this letter:

13.9.91
Shaftesbury, Dorset
Dear Rob,

Thank you for the service of thanksgiving for Tim yesterday. I found it most thoughtfully compiled and sensitively carried out.

I apologise for not staying to be social as I have happy and joyful memories of Tim which I would have been pleased to share. However, I found the combination of organ, voices and church thoroughly overwhelming and just could not cope, I'm sorry.

Roger joins in sending our very best wishes to you and hope things are going well for you.

Love, Jenny

The one word 'overwhelming' helped solve the puzzle, but not completely. Tim's funeral had been a tearless cold affair. Again at the scattering of Tim's ashes his family reined in their emotions. Andy's presence had allowed for me to express my grief, but due to his family's inclement attitude I could only cry dry tears of restraint. A few days before the memorial service his sister said, 'I hope nobody will get upset as it would spoil it.' I'd thought her statement as ludicrous as saying one shouldn't show emotion and laugh at a party. Didn't they know how readily and frequently tears had been shed, that tears had been as much part of Tim's life (and mine) as opera, motorbikes and Pasha. There had to be unfettered tears for Tim to be mourned. That Jenny hadn't been intimidated and had cried free tears for Tim his mourning was complete, but not quite mine.

I sat on the motorbikes in the garage. I played Berlioz. I felt compelled to return to Covent Garden each night. I kicked the cornerstones of The Royal Opera House, as if the mighty temple of music would wake and divulge the secret. I peered through the grille gates of St. Paul's at the lantern lit gardens and the silent church; that maybe there held the locked answer. I sat on Tim's bed. I went to counselling and therapy. I was restless and driven; obsessed to discover something that seemed determined to outwit me, or didn't exist at all. My eyes were wide open but my mind was blank. The sun had passed over Abu-Simbel and the gods were wrapped in their shrouds of darkness again. If only my mind would let me see.

Post memorial life took on new hues of colour. Shirley said it was a time to be, to reflect, to readjust. In some ways it felt again as it had following Tim's death when in a state of numbness I was just 'being' not 'doing'. Reawakenings ceased. A rubber band of anticipation stretched out over the nine months since Tim's death went twang releasing a roller ball of emotion that left me limp and exhausted.

Finding myself the leeward side of the final partners group and memorial service was like going through a door from summer into autumn. Without these hurdles there was nothing to check my momentum; it was a down slope to Christmas and the first anniversary of Tim's death.

In the natural anti-climax that followed slowly the importance of the memorial dawned on me as a true watershed between Tim and myself. A few days after Tim died Ken's wife Jo had said, 'Tim will know when to leave you'. I was horrified at the thought of there being an emotional separation and resisted the thought steadfastly. But her words were wise and true - Tim's emotional death had been held in abeyance. I had only said goodbye to his body the night he died. I had known all along he wasn't coming home but I'd kidded myself he was working away in Cardiff, Antwerp, Belgium etc. At some point towards the end of the memorial service we had been given back to one another, to say goodbye, to cast one another free. The separation had begun. I began to think of Epping Forest, and some tears flowed free. A few months prior I had told his sister I had no desire to go to the beech tree around which we had scattered Tim's ashes. She had replied, 'One day you will'. She was right. Now I wanted to go there.

I went through all the motions of carrying on but my mind was sagging. I was all over the place; I coped and functioned well, and I equally had days, hours and moments of complete dysfunction. I planted the irises. I marked out the site of the proposed circular pond with old sash cord rope. A man came to fix a security gate in the porch. I answered a second wave of sympathy letters prompted by the memorial service. Alongside Angela's signature I co-signed more papers for the solicitor. I dressed in my blue suit again and attended a formal meeting at The Royal London Hospital to discuss HIV inpatient care with the Deputy Director of Inpatient Services. I went as Tim's representative. I invited Angela to represent his family, she declined the invitation. I would have liked her company. I was quietly confident and spoke without anxiety or emotion and with a courteous resolve that would not be countered. Despite the time lapse of nine months since my letter of complaint, their positive response and policy changes to benefit the HIV patient showed the value of writing a balanced critical letter of complaint. Impudently I took it upon myself to be the voice against 'those who dare' (show unkindness to anyone HIV or with AIDS, their partners, friends or families.) For if you dare then tremble; feel the ground shake beneath you. You are my enemy. I am your foe. Do not underestimate me. I could not change the past and undo the taxi driver's great injustice to Tim, but I'd achieved something for those that followed him. I surprised myself, I didn't recognise myself. This new me was unfamiliar to me. Max gave me a beautiful book about his region Lombardy and a poster of dolphins which he had made my logo. Despite these varying positives and growth points colouring September's pattern I slipped, struggled and failed spectacularly too. I had had some crises in my life, we all do, but bereavement was proving the hardest ever to recover from.

In the worst moments it seemed that all the progress I had made since Tim's death was for nothing and I was back to square one. But this wasn't so. Setbacks are as an important and integral part of the forward march of bereavement as are the markers and hallmarks of progress, normality and growth.

I don't believe it was any coincidence that a couple of weeks after the memorial service I again succumbed to a virus of high temperatures, sweats and debility. Again I thought of HIV. Again I wasn't ready to face the test. This was not because the result might be positive, but negative! 'Good News' would mean I could look ahead. I wasn't ready to raise my horizons. Uncertainty allowed me to plod on emotionally contained. I could still only live a life within narrow boundaries. When I could fulfill and explore extended boundaries that would be the time to be tested.

My emotional pendulum dramatically swung to the downside. The depression I began to experience in the following weeks and months was what I had expected immediately after Tim's death. Shirley told me that bereavement brings back previous bereavement(s); I discovered that depression brings back previous depression(s). I was time warped back to my vulnerable teenage years when I had grappled with my homosexuality which had produced a teenage breakdown. Then I hadn't understood or been in touch with my emotions, hadn't known how to express my feelings and innermost thoughts, had never seen a counsellor and would have rebuffed any such suggestion. I had only been able to express my inner confusion in desperate statements. Now suddenly at the age of 34 I regressed.

Ten months into bereavement I was in the midst of a personality and identity crisis attempting to re-establish myself sexually, professionally, intellectually, emotionally, and socially. I was questioning and re-evaluating everything as in my late teenage years. A few instances already I had experienced phases of anger; but this was different - the violence was focused inwards. I felt almost mad; the only language I possessed was of desperation. Unfortunately a petty squabble with Max proved the trigger, and I rammed a fork into my hand cutting my finger. I hold no grudge against Max because if it hadn't been an argument it would have been something else to act as emotional detonator, and the outcome could have been a lot worse. It seemed there had to be an outer representation of my inner reflection; and that there had to be a balancing of the inner and outer selves to bring relief. I didn't fully understand this until I received a letter from Goran's partner Patrik, He ended his letter, 'I recently had a fall from one of my horses - I broke a rib, it was a nice bodily pain that for a while relieved the pain in the heart.'

Though I was beckoned back many times that autumn to the wretched naïve days of my youth, the counterweight of experience held in favour of 1991. Curse the text book psychiatrist who spoke of 'exaggerated grief' of the desperate behaviour of a parent mourning the loss of a child; the words of a 'professional' who clearly hadn't personally experienced the instability and mental fluctuations of bereavement to speak with such pompous flatulent arrogance.

One wants to cope magnificently. Sometimes one just gets by. Society tells us that anything but a state of well being is unacceptable, that happiness is our right - this is not so. At the age of eighteen I was naive and gullible. This time I was prepared. I recognised the symptoms. What I knew from my teenage experience is that depression is as natural a phenomenon as sunshine; more terrifying because it is a window into all that man does not fully possess or understand. For the first time I profited from that bitter experience of my youth, contrarily I might have been tempted towards the taking of psychotropic drugs. My doctor wanted to prescribe me antidepressants. Instead I went willingly to Gil and Shirley who validated my melancholy moods as a normal part of bereavement. Facing the unleashed depression and accepting it and not resisting it and bumbling along with it; I came to realise that it had a purpose and needed to have its rightful place for its time intended. I stabilised at a low level of functioning. Gil was very vocal in her opinion that it would have been more worrying if I hadn't become depressed at some point after Tim's death. I recognise the very serious nature of depression; it is such a horrible condition it can undermine the very desire to recover. Sometimes different approaches work for different people. But therapy worked for me, this was my way through.

And then quite unexpectedly came the light bulb moment. At the end of a therapy session with Gil I said my usual, 'Goodbye'. She usually stood framed in the neo-gothic doorway of The Little Tower hands folded with a gentle smile. This day she responded similarly, 'Goodbye'. In that second, in a flash of consciousness, of course, it was so clear now - Tim had never said 'Goodbye' to me. He didn't let me go. I hadn't wanted to leave him but I had said, 'Goodbye'. Unless I was to live in a state of perpetual morbid grief I had to do the leave-taking for us both. How? We hadn't wanted to separate or end our relationship; but Death overruled us without any appeal to its superior authority. But with this knowledge something was complete. My mourning period had ended.

I saw Gil on a more regular and intensive basis. I realised that there was a parallel process going on in my head that reflected my nine months reappraisal of the house and garden. But now instead of picking up, holding, moving, discarding, and acquiring old, existing and new objects; I had to do the same with my thoughts. In the last four years with Tim I didn't have the time to think about and process one trauma before the next one happened. There was a backlog of traumatic memory that was causing my depression. I had to prioritise space in my life to revisit and work through what had happened.

My new found comprehension of Tim's death finally released backlogged thoughts of what death had deprived him as if the memorial service allowed for me to remember: From March to August 1990 he had had no energy to do anything but laze on the sofa in front of the TV September he discovered superhuman strength defying his doctors and condition for a final creative outburst almost convincing me life was normal and would be again. He may have lived a little longer but 'Siegfried' destroyed him, voluntarily. Blessedly some of his partings were disguised as matters of habit such as his daily homecoming departing from his desk, office and colleagues as on November 19th. Never to return he had bid Covent Garden farewell. The next day after a routine appointment with his Consultant, he was so exhausted he was forced to abandon plans of continuing on to work and came home instead. 'This day is the zenith of my life,' he said of this poignant moment as I rolled the motorbike away into the garage. Irrevocably deprived of his work and independence that were fundamental to his existence he declined rapidly, so fast in fact that a routine week at home with Tim prior to a short visit to my parents in Wales proved to be our last time together at home. Again dreaded farewells that I had known would come, they passed disguised as ordinary happenings: the last supper I cooked of chicken and baked potatoes, the last films we watched 'Dumbo' and 'Batman', his goodbye to Pasha. We shared a cup of coffee together in the sitting room, Tim dressed in a white T-shirt and jogging bottoms. He sat at his desk doing his accounts where I have written this book. He looked so well! He smiled a dazzling smile. It was our last moment at home together. I kissed him goodbye. And without knowing the portent my words carried I said as I had so many times, 'Goodbye'.

In those final few days at home, with his mother in the garden room he listened to the last music he would play, Margaret Price singing Schumann and Schubert. In the few hours between his sister's unwilling departure and the nurse's arrival to take him to The Mildmay, always needing space, in that private time he bade farewell to his home and garden knowingly, unknowingly.

One of Tim's biker friends said he would have to live to be 200 to achieve what Tim had done in 39 years, but kind words didn't make his premature death any more acceptable. In fact through my belated awareness of what Tim had been forced to reluctantly relinquish I began to see what he had been prevented from doing;

the job he had not been able to accept in Berlin, the new home someone else would occupy there, the Berliners who would not know him, the roads of East Germany that would not throb to the sound of his Kawasaki, the pranks they would be spared, his perfect German they would not hear, etc. He was not there. He was not here. Begrudgingly he had died, been cremated and his ashes scattered on a forest floor. I needed the memorial service and Jenny's tears to fathom that Tim was dead. However grandiose or humble, formal or informal, conventional or unconventional, rites are important for those left behind to mourn - tears are egalitarian. In my ninth month of bereavement I was beginning to grasp I was solo.

It was an incredibly painful time but I gradually nudged forward. I had the double whammy of having to rework the traumas of my youth which were rekindled. But this time I avoided a breakdown. As a very experienced psychoanalyst in her mid seventies Gil shared her personal view that said she felt everyone had three difficult stages in life to negotiate; each time having to rework the previous stage or stages. At times I felt so skinless and raw I could hardly see the point of continuing.

Still like Jane Eyre who ran onto the heath to lie down and die, 'Hopeless of the future', in the morning she wakes up again, 'Life, however, was yet in my possession, with all its requirements, and pains, and responsibilities. The burden must be carried; the want provided for; the suffering endured; the responsibility fulfilled. I set out.'

CHAPTER 11

October

The nine months anticipating and organising Tim's memorial service had been like a long rehearsal period for a single climactic performance. The curtain had fallen. It was over.

> *'Coming out in the limelight*
> *Going home in the rain.*
> *Margot Fonteyn, Prima Ballerina'*

In her reminiscences Margot Fonteyn, Prima Ballerina said of her dancing partner Rudolf Nureyev (who died of an AIDS related illness). *'I worked with Rudolf and often went out with him. But I hardly ever saw him go home. He always walked off into the night, a lonely figure diminishing in perspective down a desolate street. There was something tragic in his departing step after the uproar of laughter and gaiety over supper. It is frequently so with stage people who pay for coming out in the limelight by going home in the rain.'*

A period of anticlimax followed. The long wait for the memorial service had provided a forward moving focus for my life after Tim's death. Now there was nothing. And this sense of nothingness was the beginning of the rest of my life without him. Whether my friends were just busy with their own lives and problems, or thought I should be 'over it', or found Max's new presence discomforting, or imagined I was alright now, whether I gave out signals saying 'keep your distance', or a bit of all - the sense of abandonment and isolation was still developing as I found myself in an emotional wilderness without a compass or a map. The autumn had a quality of solitariness unlike anything I had ever experienced. Or was it just the growing realisation of Tim's absence and the void he had left in my life?

Though mourning had ended, bereavement continued. Many people use the words grief, bereavement and mourning interchangeably. I discriminate between the words and the meaning they carry. For me bereavement is the total experience. Grief is the word for the blows, bruises and haemorrhages of psychic pain. Mourning is the primary phase of bereavement when the living of life is compromised; where death is the metronome and pulse of existence. Mourning is often culturally recognised and limited. It has fashions and colours, buttons and armbands, blacks and purples. It has rituals and ceremonies as in the setting of the headstone in the Jewish tradition on the 1st anniversary of the death. Neither is mourning restricted to the human kind. The noble elephant suffers comparably, with individual and collective outpourings and trumpetings of visceral grief. Mourning is usually delimited with a time boundary, such as the ending of court mourning after a year, by the change of garments and accessories, or by ceremony as in my case. We the bereaved continue to grieve but socially, environmentally the death is swiftly forgotten and relegated to the past. Other more recent deaths had displaced Tim from ongoing observance. There had been 4 funerals this month of acquaintances who had died of AIDS, not close friends, but friends of friends. I would have gone to the funerals and written meaningful letters. I did nothing. I was spent. I could only show my respect through guilt. Tim's death was no longer headlines. He was old news. Other men were the new fallen. Friends were tired and bored of it all; people wanted me to be ok. They were sorrow-fatigued and I could feel were becoming weary of me. Gil, Shirley and Maria were the main exceptions and continued to endorse my entitlement.

I completed the metamorphosis of Tim's filofax address book from his to mine. I had already destroyed my blue plastic one transferring all entries to his better quality black leather bound book so ours would be together. Now it seemed the right time to remove Tim's loose-leaf pages which I locked away with all the other precious mementos of his life stored in my wardrobe. But looking through my entries that remained, the majority was now obsolete belonging to my former life with him. I am not saying the previous friendships were fickle but that they had only been sustained on a social basis in Tim's lifetime. A death changes life so decisively that metaphorically speaking the difference is as great as moving from a civilised city to frontier territory - the physical, social and emotional criteria by which one has lived no longer apply. The thought of providing or attending a normal social event such as a party or sport weekend with friends was both impossible and meaningless.

Whether bereavement carries an automatic sentence of loneliness or whether I had put myself out of reach only a few people followed my trail. Both Gil and Shirley were keepers of the key that opened the gateway to the landscape of my bereavement; they were both frequently alongside the path I trod. Only Max, my witness, had a pass to cross either way through that gateway; to share either my remote existence, or to tread in the world of those not compromised by loss. It was only my immediate family and a few friends who bothered to keep in touch by phone and letter enough to know the details of my emotional wanderings.

Pioneer territory enabled me to reflect on my 'former life'.

I didn't know if I even wanted to go back if I could. But we don't have that choice. I couldn't go back to what I'd known. I could only go forward into the unwalked unknown. Questioning and re-evaluating everything, I even changed and experimented with familiar routines I had lived by for years. We all, each one of us have our own individual set ways. Before Tim's death the regime of routine had helped hold me together; now it didn't matter. I had always made my bed soon after getting up; now I made it as I got up or alternately left it unmade. I used to shave every day sometimes in the evening as well; now I shaved every other day. I used to wash or shower after Pasha's first walk; now before. There were no rules, existing habits died easily and new habits were established. Long hot baths became a necessity, my only chance for time-out, a time each day for myself, whereby I could temporarily leave all my problems above the waterline, nobody could get at me, and the warmth helped annul the hoar-frost of death that cast its dark sparkle over my life. It was my only predictable source of daily pleasure and comfort.

I had hoped that with the ending of mourning I would have been free to replan my life. But both the question of my HIV status and duties of executorship curtailed any major decision making. I was not ready to find out whether my future was compromised by HIV or not. Though the solicitors were just doing a job, their directives laid down by the law society, the boundaries of my executorship were not so well defined and impersonal. Only with a clearance certificate obtained from the Inland Revenue, the final distribution of Tim's estate completed; only then with the dismantling of this bridge between Tim's death and my life would he be truly free from life's trappings, and would I be free to take stock of life without him. This ongoing aftermath phase undoubtedly contributed to my continuing sense of bereavement.

The ebbing of the memorial revealed the issue of my

relationship with the house. I loved the house and had done my best to bring it alive again. But Tim had chosen the house for criteria that did not apply to me - its close proximity to the road to Sussex where his parents lived; and easy access to theatreland. I didn't have to move for financial or legal reasons as do some partners whose relationships are not recognised where the absence of a will leaves the bereft survivor unprotected. Both Gil and Shirley independently advised me that a decision to stay or move shouldn't be made until at least a full year cycle has passed. But change may prove as unavoidable as if it were compulsory for reason of career, emotion or relationship. Will I ultimately be able to re-establish myself in my right in what was once Tim's house? I will not know until the residues of bereavement disperse. I liked the large space of the house and its close proximity to Victoria Park. The transport links to central London were good and I was lucky to have a good sized inner city garden. All those factors were static and remained the same. Yet already it all seemed different to the day Tim died. Would there be a day that I would recognise as judgement day? I'd committed no crime but I felt I was on trial for my life. Would the defense counsel for life successfully challenge the prosecution counsel for death? Would I be liberated from bereavement? Or be sentenced to life without appeal? Again I had no answers. But whatever the outcome I was getting savvy and understanding that the changing face of bereavement was having a direct impact on how I perceived the world; and I knew I would feel different yet again about the house.

Ultimately I wanted to work within the sphere of AIDS but again was advised that a minimum of one year, preferably two should pass; that if I didn't give myself time to work things through I could hinder my regeneration; and produce problems for those already working within this sphere. It's natural to want to give but bereavement is a 'self'-ish time; one must give to ones 'self' first to be able to give to others. Occupation is important. Everyone in society is encouraged towards employment though in bereavement it is not always applicable; as in the case of one member of the partners group who relinquished his well paid city job and suit for life as a skinhead on the dole. Nor should work be used as a vehicle to try and outrun and deny ones' grief as in the experience of one friend; though brilliantly successful outwardly his attempts to displace the natural process within culminated in a nervous breakdown two years after his loss. The occupations of my friends from the partners group ranged from fashion to sea-pilot navigation, from insurance to toy manufacture from unemployed to pantomime. A few months before I'd requested an application pack for the counselling training at The Westminster Pastoral Foundation that I had put off embarking on again and again. The envelope lay unopened at the back of my desk. The deadline for the autumn entry had passed. I threw it away. I was so dispirited; I'd lost my foothold in the real world. I had no idea how to get back. I was frightened. I lived under a spell I had not cast. I was frightened I might not shake its hold.

'The Fighting Temeraire' became my short term occupation while the first and second year cycles of bereavement passed. So private was this work that few people knew of it. Some thought I was just 'a drop-out at home with the dog'. I didn't care. I didn't have to justify or explain myself. It was right for me. It was something I needed to complete before doing anything else. I would get up at 4am and write feverishly until 9am. Through the day I would roughly plan my next day's writing. I would brief myself from diaries and memories, poems and music, and walks around Covent Garden. During the evening my thoughts would tumble, shriek, recede, quieten, agitate. I would go to bed and sleep deeply; but was aware when I woke in darkness, that though I had slept my mind had not.

Yet before I could settle down into a regular writing routine my grandmother's decline and death unfurled as the prominent theme of the month. By October it was clear that time was not on her side. She was dying.

To be waiting for and attending the deathbed of a loved one brings back previous pre-bereavement experience. The emotions of the previous autumn were invoked. Waiting for Gran to die the leaves were falling again. Autumn '91 gave way to autumn '90. I was sitting on the back step contemplating Tim's inevitable death looking at the sycamore tree and its leaves that had begun to fall, 'when, how?' I asked myself, 'I am not ready; I will never be ready, please a little longer'.

A death brings back previous bereavements. With Gran's demise on the 18th again I was relieved, the suffering, the waiting, the uncertainty over. But there were differences between Tim's foreshortened life of 39 years and my grandmother's extended life of 92 years. 'A time to live, a time to die' as quoted philosophically by my aunt was appropriate for Gran but not for Tim. Tim would 'always remain young and would not know old age' was appropriate for Tim but not for Gran.

My sister and I accompanied our father to view her body in the funeral home. Looking small and white in her shroud in her coffin I was glad I had asked for Tim to be dressed in his blue pyjamas; funeral clothes seemed right for Gran; but not for Tim. But this part was missing in my experience with Tim - I didn't visit him in the chapel of rest. Seeing my grandmother laid out I thought of Tim in his coffin with only the long stemmed freesias within from his mother and narcissi atop from me for company. The long dormant memory of the body bag issue raised its ugly head. I pushed away the prehistoric DHSS ruling that a person dying of AIDS must be sealed after death in a body bag; and whether or not Shirley had been able to circumnavigate this degrading outdated decree. I never asked her. I couldn't bear to know.

The following day my grandmother's final journey began

from my parents' home which had once been hers. As her cortege set out for her funeral at the crematorium; my thoughts retreated to Tim's lonely unaccompanied journey across London from Dalston to Golders Green. I regretted not accompanying his body on his last journey which should have started from his home and not from an impersonal funeral parlour. I began to feel faint and nauseous. We all began to feel faint and nauseous. My uncle's face turned cherry red. We were overcome - but not by emotion, by fumes! Unbeknown to us a severe petrol leak in the boot of the limousine had exposed us to risk of asphyxiation and explosion. 'Six mourners gassed in funeral procession', I imagined a headline as we stumbled from the car. This element of black comedy would have appealed to Tim; I had not encountered such black humour since Tim used to play dead. Intoxicated with memory and petrol I felt unexpectedly close to Tim as we made our comedic drunken entrance into the crematorium.

However this comforting sensation was short lived. Although the funeral service well invoked my grandmother, memories of Tim's funeral nine months before freshened. That cold ritual devoid of anything to do with Tim contrasted harshly with the ceremony underway. Tim slipped away from me again. As the funeral progressed a number of things heightened my sense of bereavement. With all the written and unwritten rules of British society like so many gay men my progress through life has not been without a sense of loneliness and exclusion. This was now highlighted and reconfirmed again by the family gathering. Of my grandmother's four grandchildren only I, the homosexual, had been bereaved; the partnerships of the three heterosexual grandchildren including my sister, alive and sustaining. Not that for a moment I wished any unhappiness on any of them; not that they hadn't been sympathetic, in fact my cousin's husband sympathised, 'Twice for you in one year'; yet why Tim? Why me? It was hard not to feel envious of what I too had held - and lost.

I was quietly angry too. Out of all the formal invitations dispatched for Tim's memorial it was only some of my more elderly relatives who did not reply or attend. I felt rebuffed by their cool disregard of me. I felt their prejudice by their aloofness and avoidance of me and lack of acknowledgement about Tim's death and his memorial service. The thought of my parents shunning the memorial service of one of my cousin's partners if equally tragic circumstances prevailed would have been unthinkable.

As my grandmother's coffin was encircled by a red curtain 'she died' and I saw my mother elevated to position of family matriarch. When the shutter fell across the end of Tim's coffin at Golders Green I'd had no sense of 'he died'; that had happened only the month before at St Paul's. Being reminded of Tim's funeral further aggravated my sense of solitariness of how I'd felt that day; the unbearable isolation in the chapel pew before Angela's compassionate gesture of leaving her parents to join me. Tim should have been with me. He was everywhere. He was nowhere.

Some members of the extended family encountered difficulties with certain aspects of my grandmother's death - viewing the body, even attending the funeral itself. This left me feeling not unsympathetic but a little cynical. It had once been said, 'Rob needs a protected environment'. For all the problems I'd had in making sense of a life as a gay man in a provincial narrow minded community; I was certainly viewed by 'the family' as an oddball. Yet AIDS had exposed me to every rough and raw edge life can produce. Only eleven months before I had taken Tim a cup of tea in the middle of the night for his cough. I sat on the edge of his bed holding his hand. He wanted me to assist his suicide. He couldn't bear to go on. The explosions of Kaposi Sarcoma over his body were terrifying and their hardness made mobility more and more difficult. He wasn't just dying but becoming increasingly disabled. He couldn't bear it. He wanted it to stop. We debated and planned his death. If that had been his wish I would have gladly participated. But it was the risk of my prosecution or his not succeeding, his fear of dying alone because he didn't want me to witness his death, and the cruelty of leaving me to find his body that ended Tim's considerations of euthanasia. But I nevertheless did feel some strange sense of superiority over these amateur mourners.

To have survived the teenage confusions of being somehow different to my contemporaries, the consequent feelings of separateness, of coming to terms with being gay, to finding great happiness, just to lose it horribly, that I had survived and lived through an experience quite beyond the comprehension of those whose sensitivities present had been shielded to once more feel a sense of solitariness, and now subtle but effective prejudice of being different - gay, I further excluded myself from 'the family'.

After returning to London I didn't cope well at all for a few days. For a week I couldn't even answer the phone. One day I cried a lot and was able to tell Max how much I had loved Tim; that we had been so happy; and then slowly HIV started to destroy everything, little by little; I had so feared Tim's death would be my undoing, drive me mad even - Max came to my rescue and said I wasn't mad, never had been, just sensitive. How he strengthened our friendship, being there, shoring me up when I threatened to crumple.

Towards the end of the month I began to produce symptoms of high temperatures, fevers, chills, and exhaustion again which had occurred intermittently throughout the year. One afternoon overcome with a profound tiredness I cut short Pasha's walk. Reluctantly I went to bed. I felt as if life was ebbing from my body. There was no sensation of pain or fear, just a sense my body was about to abort life. I seemed to float in and out of myself, gradually the mixed sensation of absolute relaxation and exhaustion passed. With such an emotional quality I knew this experience was not virus, bacteria or organically generated; but the consequence of a tumult of emotion impressing its effect in physical terms, that my mind couldn't hold and was somatised into my body.

Nevertheless my doctor conducted some routine blood tests. Ten months of bereavement found me the most overweight and unfit I had ever been as a consequence of the strains and stresses which had forced me increasingly to the succour of comfort foods and escape in alcohol. I thought that the liver function test might have revealed some damage from excessive drinking of late. Surprisingly all the tests were normal. Though the liver test result was well in hand I now limited my intake of alcohol. These simple tests proved the remedy to arrest my plunge towards obesity and alcoholism; and so began the slow process of fighting back to the fit healthy individual I had been, a battle not without it setbacks. Long walks, sensible eating and moderate drinking brought swift results. I never went back to the gym, I so associated it with Tim's final illness. But I did buy sets of weights and religiously built up an exercise routine. But for every pound of weight lost, for every extra millimeter in the girth of my biceps brought a memory of AIDS attack on his body and imagery of his advancing physical decrepitude.

Two potential reawakenings unexpectedly added to the tally of October's disappointment. I set aside an evening to bring the kitchen back to life. Only by looking at every utensil, touching every gadget, opening and rummaging through every drawer could I negate the spell of Tim's death which had invalidated everything; only then would I be free to use, enjoy again, replace, displace, and augment. But a storage jar of pudding rice, one of Tim's favourite desserts, with label askew where he had stuck it, stopped me dead in my tracks. I wasn't ready and closed the cupboard door on still raw memories I could not yet face.

A few years prior I had stopped using The Body Shop in Covent Garden. With the spreading of the Kaposi Sarcoma over Tim's body it would have been cruel for him to be faced with products promoted in the name of health and beauty. But now Tim was dead; it was time to release and find again my sense of personal pride that bereavement had benumbed. I returned to The Body Shop to buy some toiletries. This time it was a small bottle of massage oil that foiled this reawakening - I had used such a bottle to attempt to massage mobility into Tim's stiff swollen ankles and legs only days before he died. I could smell the acrid decay of his blackened flesh. Instead of flattering my vanity I found myself again mourning Tim's physical disintegration and destruction. I left empty handed.

In one of the Partner Group sessions earlier that year Annie had suggested it might be helpful for one of the participants to write a letter to the deceased partner. I had thought at the time the idea was denying, unrealistic, a little sick. Now I understood and wrote a letter of my own to Tim. Using the present tense than the past tense - it allowed me to 'be' again in the time of our relationship. Knowing there would be no answer didn't matter but I sent it in fire across the chasm separating life and death scattering the ash in the garden. I told him I still loved him and missed him, that Pasha and I were surviving, that life was hard without him, but we would cope somehow. With so few stabilising points around me, to look over my shoulder, to glimpse and grasp the sense of Tim in his lifetime allowed for me to go on again, without him, strengthened.

Tantamount to how we function generally, both negatively and positively, excessively so in bereavement, October spun its usual weaves including the productive and beneficial kind. On the very first day of the month Max brought his things to the house, our commitment growing; a respectful length of time had passed and it was right for him to have his own things around him in his room. Max moved his few things remaining from one of my bedside cabinets to his room, his rightful space. Tim had always kept files in a chest in my bedroom, other business papers and boxes of mementos clogged my wardrobe - I moved them to the bottom drawer of the chest of drawers in the spare bedroom which I designated as Tim's space. For the first time ever I had my own bedroom in my own home. On the 2nd I had a carpet laid in the spare bedroom and finally the house was carpeted. On the 3rd I wrote in my notebook 'I cleaned the black filth from the skirting boards, not cleaned for over a year, removing dust and dirt from Tim's time - I felt as if I was spring cleaning myself'. On the 8th I completed security improvements to front porch with addition of a security post box. The most creative transformation of the month was my purchase of ten beautiful Cypress trees to make a hedge at the bottom of the garden. Considering that ten months before I couldn't even enter the garden the sense of achievement was quite beyond what any neighbour might have observed as routine weekend activity with a trip to a garden centre. There was now a wall of growing green where there had been an empty void and an ugly chain fence.

With the conclusion of the partners group it was a film 'Truly, Madly, Deeply' that provided a measure of how well, badly and normally I was faring ten months into bereavement. An old friend Frank was an actor and played one of the ghost's in the film. He left me a message saying I should go and see it. As the sighting of landing lights by a disorientated pilot allows for him to check his course and fly on confidently; so the film became and remains an important and comforting touchstone mid journey through the long autumn.

The film detailed a young widow's bereavement experience. I was able to identify with Juliet Stevenson's performance; so authentic was her portrayal this cinema experience proved as valuable as any session of the partners group:

Her tears with her counsellor reminded me of mine with Gil the last time I saw her before Tim died.

Her need for space, that when pressurized by the 'ghosts' who had returned to help her through bereavement she threw them all out. I had never particularly liked or needed my own company until after Tim died. I would feel great anxiety, intolerance and irritability if I felt my space threatened or invaded at those very private times during bereavement when it is imperative to be alone.

I well identified with her sense of hurt and anger when her sister asked her if she would part with her husband's cello. She clung to the musical instrument as if the embodiment of her dead mate. In the same way I detained Tim's motorbikes and felt acutely sensitive to remarks people made when they pointed out I would be better off selling them.

Incredibly her words to her new potential partner that she had 'loved someone who had died' were almost identical to my recent words to Max.

The ultimate message was one I was in the midst of experiencing, that I would only fully comprehend on the anniversary of Tim's death - the ghost of her husband wanted to get rid of a mildew covered carpet. However reasonable his offer of help, however illogical her decision to keep it she had found her voice to make executive decisions good or bad. She had submitted to her man in life but would not be dominated by a ghost; the moral being she was finding her sense of self again; her wishes prevailed uncompromisingly so in bereavement.

The developing emotional theme of October was the progression of grieving for what Tim had lost to lamenting what I had lost. Through my conversations with Gil in the Little Tower I recognised that my depression far from being an illness was a godsend; something that would help me make the transition from life with Tim to life without. It was a no man's land; he was dead, I was single. But was he still my partner? Was I still his partner? I did not know.

Slowly it was dawning on me we would never share any

more special moments on the long haul motorbike trips we had made across Europe. The idea appalled me that there would be no more picnics amongst the lavender hills of Provence, stopovers alongside the deep green lakes of Austria, the revitalising cups of coffee at roadside bars, moments of respite in the time that we rested in a pear orchard on the shore of Lake Constance watching Wagnerian swans gliding out of the summer mist, greasy bratwurst and sauerkraut, looking at relics of the Hindenburg in Friedrichshafen, the home of Count von Zeppelin creator of the Graf Zeppelin and Hindenburg airships - there would be no more mundane and magical moments of being a pillion passenger. I was not a blood biker but with that history of shared experience on the Kawasaki GPZ 1100 I had earned my 'wings'. But with Tim's death my days of riding pillion were over. I'd ridden the red Kawa illegally in France but if I was to become a biker and learn to properly ride the motorbikes, this was the time I would have begun. I thought about it. I would not make this part of his life mine. I knew I never would. I looked at my crash helmet. It was as dead as Tim's.

I had never taken the opportunity to go to the Royal Opera House with Tim for granted. Before we met I remember reading a scathing review of 'Aida' at The Royal Opera House and thinking, 'I don't care whether it's good or not, I just wish I had a chance to go'. Nor have I forgotten my excitement the first time Tim took me there to see Carol Vaness and Jon Vickers in Handel's 'Samson'. Yet one roasting hot summer night in 1987 I almost declined two good seats for 'La Bohème'. I didn't want to go. It was not the night to be in an airless theatre. But I changed my mind at the last moment as if knowing one day such ready access would be gone, as it is. I wasn't transported into the theatrical experience. Snow fell on stage but I remained rooted in reality as summer sweat ran down my neck. Mimi's death was convincing but make-believe; Tim's death would be convincing but for real, he wouldn't get up to take his curtain calls. In the sitting room Tim always kept handy records of whatever productions he was working on, often giving me records as presents; but his death brought an end to the organic growth of our music collection, and the changeover of recordings propped against the sofa. Having better concentration than Tim he would give me books and different subject matters to read, to feed him with thoughts, ideas and background information. Over the years I developed a wealth of useful information; now with his death it is useless information; and the bookcase is no longer that of a helpmate but an opera buff that I never wanted to be. If Tim had lived he, we would have moved to Berlin. There would have been a new opera house and productions to experience, CD's of whatever he was working on in his new sitting room, new books and magazines to read for him - there are none. For Tim music was synonymous with work and life. For me music is synonymous with Tim. There is a music orientated absence to my life.

No less my nickname he used to call. Like any relationship regardless of orientation one partner is often more dominant, the other more passive i.e. leader and follower. I was always a good follower. I was not born to be leader of the pack, I recognise this. Yet bereavement has forced me into the position of being the boss unwillingly; but already I would not relinquish the battle-won anchor points of my future. Already ten months into bereavement I miss my nickname. It wasn't just a pet name, it was the 'me' I had been in his time. But I will keep forever the photograph Tim took in a remote clearing in Canada where he traced out my nickname in ferns on the forest floor.

I miss the farm, his mother's cooking especially her cakes and homemade jam, walks with Pasha in the meadows, the bedroom where Tim and I had slept - 'his' bed and 'my' bed as we called them, the environs of the farm that had become familiar during those too few years I had known him, reading copies of Farmers Weekly and talks with his father about the collective paprika fields of Hungary, the dogfights over the farm and the huge losses of shipping in the minefields off Margate in WWII. There were good times on the farm and I miss the agricultural aspect of our union which had always been a welcome antidote to city life; and no less for Pasha who can no longer exchange his town house/city dog identity for farm dog chasing cats in the barn and searching for hedgehogs amongst the farm buildings at night. My maternal grandfather was a farmer at Rhyd Lafar Farm in Wales and my paternal great-grandfather at Old Rhoose Farmhouse. Being with Tim on his family farm gave me some glimpses into the daily life of my family past that I had not known; all were now lost again to history. The rumble of his motorbike announcing his homecomings, caring for him, his pranks - when the wind billows one of the curtains I still imagine him hiding - but most of all I miss Tim.

This developing phase of self-pity was one I felt ashamed to carry; that I should conquer it quickly. Phases of numbness, denial, loneliness, anger, guilt, depression all seemed permissible; not so with self-pity. The adjective 'selfish' is always used in a derogatory way, similarly with self-pity - yet bereavement is an inner experience of the 'self'. Shirley said it was not only important but natural to feel sorry for oneself, and what one has lost; and that I had to give this phase its head; and more so that it could last months, years even. This self-pity phase was relatively short lived; and in fact was a diving board that gave me a huge and decisive impetus and shove propelling me through the bereavement phenomenon.

In as much as observing the blackened forest floor after a forest fire one doesn't see the microscopic green shoots rejuvenating; so I only aware of my self-pity failed to perceive the kindling of a new spirit within. The other side of self-pity is a slowly developing awareness of what is left; but this can only be appreciated by recognising what one has lost. And from what is left grows ones new self-identity.

What I was left with wasn't what I wanted, but it was what I had - a house, possessions, a garden, dog, a questionable amount of money, all the responsibilities and decision making, and most of all the dawning sense of myself and a future which would not include Tim. Although I wrestled and baulked with the weight of responsibilities that I was still adapting too, I had in fact a greater freedom and independence than ever before; if anyone had threatened to deprive me of my ability to make absolute decisions within the new extended boundaries of bereavement I would have defended my position vigorously. I thirsted for self-expression; even if I made mistakes it didn't matter. Already I was no longer who I had been. Who was I? What was I? I didn't yet know. I wanted to find out.

The loft had been Tim's space full of business papers, files of opera production notes, accounts, boxes and boxes of theatre memorabilia, old cushions, empty bottles for the beer and wine he had planned to make, picture frames, Christmas decorations and carpet cut offs and luggage. In early 1988 anticipating his days of health were numbered Tim began the task of putting his affairs in order. He spent a few hours one Saturday afternoon sorting through all the old programmes and music magazines he had amassed in the loft. Crashes of sound reverberated through the house as he dropped every pile through the loft hatch onto the landing below. 'It was like junking myself', he said on return from the refuse tip. The beginnings of his illness a year later with a high fever forced him to abandon the assembly of an internal loft aerial. Soon overwhelmed by illness the loft and its partially assembled aerial were forgotten, and we got used to the blurred TV pictures. After Tim's death I gathered those papers required by the solicitor; and slowly in my own time worked through the remaining things - I disposed of some, returned oddments to his family, displacing other things to the main body of the house.

The T.V reception had worsened considerably with the completion of the tower at Canary Wharf distorting signals from the South London transmitter so on the last day of October I had an external ghost aerial fitted. Later that day I dismantled the now redundant loft aerial; I had no use envisaged for the loft but I had completed the 3-year transition from it being Tim's space to mine, albeit empty. As I plugged in the aerial to the back of the new TV I completed something which he had begun.

Yet this very last day of the month while I was confronting practical and emotional consequences of bereavement through the medium of aerial sockets and transmitter cabling; through the medium of grey paper the solicitor dictated the following letter representing the impassive business face of bereavement.

Dear Mr. Lewis
Re: The Estate of

  I enclose a copy of the Insurance Policy Schedule issued by Sun Alliance. I have placed the original with the deeds to the property.

  As you are aware, we have paid the Insurers premium, though this is strictly your responsibility. I would propose dealing with this when I am in a position to make a final distribution of the Estate, which will not be until tax affairs are agreed with the Revenue. As yet I have no indication as to when this is likely to be.

  I have heard nothing from the Capital Taxes Office regarding the District Valuer's Assessment of the property. Did the gentleman in fact call?

  I will be in touch with you again as soon as I have anything further to report.

  Yours sincerely,

The practical, emotional and business matters of bereavement are inextricably entwined. Always there are business letters to be received and written. Somehow I always managed to deal with them whether on the crest of a little creation or reawakening, or in the trough of a passing failure.

At about 6.30pm on Wednesday October 31st I switched on the new TV for the first time. The first undistorted picture cleared of a weather report about a ferocious storm, The Halloween Blizzard crippling the Midwest. In the transition from the small fuzzy picture of Tim's black and white portable TV to the large clear colour screen of the new Sony; my electronic reconnection to the world was immediate and startlingly strong and better than it had ever been.

CHAPTER 12

November

Fireworks! Bombs! Noise! Destruction! November 5th - Bonfire Night! Rockets exploded overhead and Bangers rocked the road and neighbourhood. I could avoid Gulf War reports but not the air of apprehension and danger on the street. The IRA was mounting a mainland bombing campaign against the capital. We were told to carry on as normal and we did but there would be more damage and death. Yet despite my best attempts to isolate and protect myself against the harsh forces of the world the biggest offensive of the year was waiting to ambush me at home on November 15th; and I was foolishly complicit. As November began I had no idea that this was going to be the good, the bad and the ugly month of the year.

Entering the eleventh month of bereavement I found myself in the first period where there were no ceremonies to plan or attend, few matters of correspondence, no executor duties to perform or emotional hurdles to face, and few aftermath responsibilities to distract my thoughts or consume my energies. And mid distance between the memorial service and the approaching anniversary of Tim's death, there was a dearth of orientating references. With this slackening of activity I had time at last to take stock of Tim's death, my mind uncluttered. In the reading of my diaries I was getting a clearer panoramic overview of the last five years. Each day had been like a piece of a jigsaw; only now was I completing the 1500 piece puzzle and getting a picture of what had happened to Tim - and to me.

Dear Rob,

My name is Ruby Milton. I wanted to introduce myself to you at the tea party in the Royal Opera House after dear Tim's service, but there were so many people waiting to talk to you. I only had minor walk on parts but he made me feel very special. Tim was always as respectful and deferential to me as the divas. During rehearsals we shared many sandwiches and coffees in the awful Italian Café in Floral Street. He talked about you and Pasha a lot. When we knew something was very wrong we wanted to help but we had to pretend we didn't know. It broke my heart when I last saw dear Tim in the cafeteria, he looked so unwell, I wanted to put my arms around him and take him home and look after him, but we had to pretend everything was fine. I cried so much that day for you both. Many years ago when I was very young a man I loved very much died and I don't think I ever got over it. It was worse because he was married and nobody knew. I couldn't talk about him. I think that's why I never recovered. So I'm going to be a bit bossy here. I want to know how you really are. I want you to eat lots of 'yellows' - bananas, grapefruit, peppers. Please ring me on this number xxx.

With affection, Ruby Milton.

And so with the arrival of this letter on the sixth day of the month my Fairy Godmother entered my life. I remembered Tim pointing her out on stage one night saying, 'that's Ruby'. Apparently she was a character and had had quite a racy youth and been painted in the nude by a famous artist. But for me she was just kindness personified. I did ring her and a telephone friendship developed. She rang often, usually late at night, like an unearthly supernatural presence. We never met. She asked deeply personal and direct questions; yet I never experienced her as intrusive. I was always able to say it as it was, and she would hear it so. Ruby was a theatre person; she knew how the theatre-world and gay people work. She gave me a lot of outrageous and unsolicited advice - to have lots of sex and boyfriends but not to commit to anyone for a long time. I wasn't sure she realised how dangerous sex was now, but I knew her motivations came from a good place. The Royal Opera House had been good to her when her husband died, paid bills and given her money until she recovered, and could return to work. She hoped it had looked after me. Upon Tim's death I was acknowledged by formal letter from all departments, was given widow's rights, was offered financial help and felt very cared for. The Royal Opera House was constantly in the news and heavily criticized for its enormous Arts Council funding; but when I walk by that massive white stoned building I just think of its benevolence. With Gil and Shirley I was usually more serious and earnest because I felt my psychological survival depended on them; but with Ruby I was more carefree and I learned to laugh again.

It is natural as the anniversary of the death of ones partner approaches to relive the last days of the relationship. Memories rekindled impinging as freshly as if the day before, my thoughts dwelling on what had been Tim's last full month of life; his transition period from living with AIDS to dying from AIDS. The following extracts from my last diary show the quality of our final November together:

November 3rd: 'I felt alarmed - Tim gave me my Christmas present in advance of 'The Legend of Siegfried' in four American style comic books. 'Look after me, protect me,' he said when I put him to bed.'

November 10th: 'Slept in Timmy's bed (for last time). Felt very

271

emotional when he said 'This is the last lap, it's the end of Timmy.'

November 11ᵗʰ: 'I managed with Tim's encouragement to break out of the routine and went to 'The London Apprentice' (gay bar), found it quite nerve-wracking - what has come over me? I used to like such places, I used to feel excited. There was a collie dog wandering around sniffing everyone - I left and hurried home, Tim already asleep, Pasha slept on my bed.'

November 12ᵗʰ: 'I rubbed down the kitchen ceiling ready for painting. As long as I keep the house alive and growing everything (Tim) will be alright.'

November 19ᵗʰ: 'Tim dragged himself off to 'Fidelio' dress rehearsal, home early afternoon to bed exhausted for rest of day (Tim's last day at work).'

November 20ᵗʰ: 'We went to Ken and Jo's for tea, we stayed for two hours, I was amazed Tim was able to mobilise himself (our last outing).'

November 22ⁿᵈ: 'I felt very depressed while out with Pasha. When I got home to find Mrs. Thatcher had resigned I felt even more depressed - despite my misgivings about her tenure, any external change seems to threaten and exacerbate my already crumbling world.'

November 25ᵗʰ: 'We played backgammon (for the last time).'

November 26th: 'An explosion of cherry red Kaposi Sarcoma lesions have appeared over Tim's shoulders and back in the matter of a couple of days. Interferon isn't working.'

November 27ᵗʰ: 'Tim now needs continuous care; I can't leave him even to walk Pasha. Ralph a volunteer came from The Mildmay to look after Tim while I drove Pasha to the farm. Tim hugged and kissed Pasha Goodbye (as if he knew it was his leave-taking of his beloved dog). I was so upset as I drove Pasha away I avoided crashing into the side of the Blackwall Tunnel by a hairsbreadth.'

And now one year later my heart cried as readily as my eyes had one year before. Only with the rear window view of hindsight could I appreciate the chain of events that led to his death. At the time we just lived each day as a total life; I'd known he was very ill, but I'd had no idea he had only weeks to live.

I navigated November on a day to day basis just determined to get through; I had been forced to forsake one identity, yet not found a new one. This emotional nudity found me at the age of 34 in the greatest transition of my life since leaving childhood for youth. Unsure of myself I sheltered behind the security gate, less a fortification of the house's vulnerability than mine; and I delayed the installation of a new doorbell further adding to my inaccessibility - I well understand how the Irish folk singer Mary O'Hara retreated into a convent after the death of her poet husband. My world only accommodated Max, Maria and Pasha within my home; Gil and Shirley outside. Though I went regularly to 'The Falcon & Firkin' I did not, could not, talk to anyone. I was managing but it was on a rudimentary and minimal level.

Unexpectedly it was against this reclusive background of retrospective reflection that I experienced the worst and greatest after-blast affect of bereavement; as if The Perfect Storm that had just devastated America had changed course, infiltrated my defenses determined to wreak havoc within my mind and home.

One week into November I found a message on the answer phone from Tim's sister; she intended a surprise visit. This left me feeling a little uneasy. In Tim's time she had only visited once in the years we had been together. Following the memorial service two months before there had been no contact either way but for one business letter from her beginning with the words 'the service was beautiful', no thanks, and no criticisms, just written with quiet impartial neutrality.

A few days later I returned from an early walk with Pasha to find another message; she had come to the house, and unable to get a reply she had telephoned from a nearby phone box. I was beginning to feel aggravated, something didn't feel right, and to travel such a long distance on the off chance of finding me at home when a simple phone call before could establish a meeting. Why no forewarning?

Gil said I had a right to set a time and date convenient for me; that Angela too had a moral right to visit what had been her brother's home of which we were both co-trustees. Interestingly both Gil and Shirley said independently of one another, 'maybe she doesn't know herself why she wants to come, it's just an instinctive need perhaps.' I tempered aroused feelings of paranoia with, 'well maybe she just wants to fill the gaps that must exist for her about Tim's life and illness; maybe she wants to share how she feels eleven months into her bereavement; and maybe she wants to find out how I am faring.'

I found another message that she would visit a few days hence. I was starting to feel harassed. Why the urgency to see me? I rang her to ask the nature of her visit but her assuaging almost sensuous voice completely put me at ease that her visit could only be of creative purpose. We agreed a time and date when she would come four days later.

Two nights later however I was overtaken by a premonition and awful attack of nerves in regard of her visit. It was a pure gut reaction, an instinct rankled; there was nothing logical or tangible but the sense of foreboding was overwhelming - it seemed all my emotional scars were peeling and raw again.

As often was my late evening habit I went to 'The Falcon & Firkin' trying to forget; but the sense of vulnerability and consequent self-protectiveness only increased; I didn't want anyone invading my sanctuary exacerbating my grief; I was holding my own but it was a sensitively balanced equilibrium. It was a struggle to see anyone, even old friends who were unequivocally on my side, let alone someone who I felt might not be.

I left the pub to ring Angela. It was late but I knew I would not sleep with the anxiety her intended visit was causing me. She was very accommodating on being woken and seemed magnanimously concerned for me. As often is the case with a conversation one has rehearsed, it took on a different hue altogether. I failed to ask, 'Why Angela do you want to come so earnestly?'

The dynamics of our ensuing conversation demonstrated the multiplicity of our relationship. Her initial concern was born from the first level of our underdeveloped friendship where we were each genuinely kind and sympathetic to the others' loss; she of my partner; me of her sibling.

She asked what had been going on in my life since we last talked (at memorial). When I told her most of the intervening weeks had been taken up with my grandmother's decline and death a cold chill took the warmth out of her voice. She said of Gran's death only three weeks before, neither kindly nor unkindly, 'well life goes on'.

I couldn't blame her for she was in fact experiencing what Tim had rehearsed the night a few months after his HIV diagnosis - he came to me and burst into tears saying, 'My father has just rung, Stefan has just died playing squash. What's happening to my family?' I couldn't console him. His elder sister having died a number of years before, he saw his brother-in-law's death for what it was; a precursor to his own.

Steering the conversation to the business level of our relationship where as joint executors and co-trustees there had never been a problem; this restored harmony to the conversation. There was little to discuss. We were just waiting for matters to be settled with Inspectors of Tax for Inland Revenue. She just commented, 'the solicitors tend to sit on things, it's a pity Timothy didn't complete his outstanding tax returns'. She had absolutely no idea of the depression, overwhelming anxiety and anger that had beleaguered his last four years.

Around the subject of her young son the conversation shifted and became increasingly strained, 'he must never know what Timothy died from, he has to be protected.' This exposed a colossal difference between us - I was progressively entering a life of truth; she a conspiracy of silence and fabrication. I knew the personal cost of maintaining a deception; how much harder it is the second, third and fourth years; the isolation, the sense of separateness, the feelings of unreality caught between fact and fiction. If Tim hadn't released me I would have released myself. When reality is tampered with honesty is compromised, openness is renounced, all truth is sullied, and all untruths are privileged - integrity is violated.

And the irony of this was that it was only a month ago in the last week of her life that my grandmother talked of her brother who died in an institution in the early 1920's. Choosing my mother to be her life's witness, she unlocked her heart and broke her 70 year silence. She wanted to die unburdened. I was left with many questions unanswered about my great-uncle Eric. What was he like? Was he handsome, average looking or ugly? Was he gay or straight? Was his life defined by his illness? What was his illness? What were his likes and wants and needs? Did he have friends and lovers? Was he intelligent? Did he err towards the sciences or arts? His death ended his earthly life; but my grandmother's silence erased all sign of his footsteps upon the earth - she effectively annihilated him. I hope he had someone who cared for him - a doctor, nurse, and friend or lover, who could remember him as he was in his entirety and so grant him his legitimate place in the planetary system as someone who was born, lived, died, was remembered and so passed into history. My grandmother's shame of her brother's mental health issues was born out of ignorance; and her silence only strengthened and perpetuated her shame and meant that because part of him wasn't acceptable to be remembered and known that all of him was to be unknown and forgotten. But all it achieved was a silencing of something within her that waited 70 years to be known. It is only openness, truth and honesty that counteract prejudice and discrimination. It isn't always easy to be open to counteract stigmas and myths that surround AIDS but I am. I live by the value that 'if other people can't handle the reality of Tim's death it's their problem not mine.' I tried to communicate this to Angela, but failed.

Our conversation ended on the level where there had always been problems; me as spokesman for my partnership with Tim versus she as family spokeswoman. I naively confided in her the proposed fundraiser I had in mind for The Royal London Hospital. There the conversation soured, 'It is not our wish, we forbid you, and we will use all our powers to prevent you.' I was so furious I terminated the conversation.

I thought that would be the end of her intended visit. But no, the next morning she rang and said we had to talk. We found a shaky compromise that suited neither of us; she not wanting to be drawn out to confront facts; me not wanting to be drawn into any collusion. I had my experience of 'Tim', she of 'Timothy'; her visit was unknowingly to bring 'Tim' and 'Timothy' together for the first time; they were not compatible; an experiment akin to mixing sodium with water, both inert substances but explosive when mixed.

I awaited her visit the next day with a sense of trepidation. All my dark instincts proved right the moment I opened the door. 'Toilet first, cup of coffee second', she ordered with an imperious cold glacial smile. 'What third?', I thought ominously. I asked her if she wanted to see Pasha who was shut in the kitchen, she didn't. She knew he had been very important to Tim, more than a dog - but OK it didn't mean she had to like dogs. 'Maybe she is just a little or very nervous coming here', I thought to myself. She had last visited the day we scattered Tim's ashes. And we were approaching the anniversary of Tim's last day at home which had been her sad privilege to share. 'It must be hard for you to come here', I volunteered, attempting to open the conversation deferentially. 'Not at all', she countermanded with a backhand worthy of Wimbledon. She was not at ease and did not want to be put at ease. I was starting to feel uncomfortable.

We then had the most unpleasant and artificial small talk ever - she began by belittling Hackney, 'this ghastly place, we (the family) never could bear it.' I bristled. 'Tim loved it here and so do I', I silently defended. She then complained about the price of the black cab fare from Mile End, a miserly sum she could easily afford. 'Why didn't you get the 277 bus and walk through the park', I wanted to say. 'Have you done anything to the garden', she asked disinterestedly. 'No', I said not wanting my efforts diminished. Where was the warm kind Angela? It was very clear she had not come to ask about Tim or to share her bereavement feelings; and she certainly hadn't come to see how I was. She was angry. I did not need this. Worse still I knew I didn't have the capacity to manage this situation if it became anymore difficult.

I made a bid to restore stability guiding the conversation to the business level where we had always been in accord. 'The district valuer came a couple of days before the memorial', I said. 'He did come - good', she replied authoritatively. 'And now of the fundraiser, we may be able to come to some agreement', she said haughtily. I wished that Gil or Shirley was there to umpire things.

It's like fighting a battle for four years, a much loved comrade falls, a family visit the front line, mourn and depart saying 'we forbid you to erect a monument in our son/brother's name - he did not fall in this battle, there was no battle'; yet I remain in the trenches where he fell.

A dark force was starting to grow inside me; larger than anything I had experienced so far since Tim's death. What frightened me was that I felt I was becoming Tim; I didn't understand the dynamics then and I don't now, I just experienced it. In the garden room where Angela and I now sat facing one another Tim had had one of his worst AIDS related rages.

We had been en route to have lunch with his boss and had stopped at Columbia Road flower market to buy a tray of polyanthus. While waiting for Tim the police moved me on; this was enough to unhinge Tim's precarious emotional balance. I drove him home, quite mad and beyond all reason. Tim sat in the same place where his sister now sat. I thought he would kill me; he ranted and raged, never have I seen such black anger in anyone's eyes. Suddenly something made me grab him. I shook him. Our eyes connected. 'Where is your anger coming from?' I yelled into his soul - I knew the answer but he had to connect with himself. In a moment of realisation he did - HIV. He burst into tears and said, 'I can see that you really love me.' 'Of course I love you, you stupid thing', I replied and then it was my turn to cry.

All this flashed through my mind while Angela waited for a reply about the fundraiser. 'I too have a point of view that needs to be addressed, understood and respected', was all I said. I wasn't going to be subjected to this patronising crap from her or anyone.

Hindsight is a great thing. At this point I should have politely asked her if there was a reason for her visit and if not that it was best she curtailed her visit. But I did not. What upset me far more than her manner was the 'proof' under test and duress that I had lost all my emotional robustness. I had none. I felt skinless. I'd backed myself into an isolated corner so I wouldn't be exposed to my vulnerability; and now in my own home prompted by his sister, I had been.

By now we were in absolute opposition; her anger was ballooning in parallel to mine. Whatever thoughts went through her mind I have no idea, but mine kept returning to the past. She knew nothing of the last years. Didn't she have any interest or curiosity? All she seemed to bring was an air of superiority, criticism and censorship. It was I who sat on Tim's bed late into the November night not quite one year before discussing active euthanasia with him. I sound like a martyr but I wasn't - as Maria replied to one doctor who challenged her devotion to Roger and asked her if she saw herself as a martyr, she replied, 'Don't you dare speak to me like that, if you love someone you just do it and it is bloody hard.'

The only card I had up my sleeve left to play was The Mildmay. It was the only ally I had to hand of what it had come to stand for, in its care for Tim and afterwards now for me. Whether I go to the chapel, or to see Shirley, to the gift shop, to see the nurses, it is always a joyful pilgrimage, a concrete focus for Tim's HIV experience, and my experience; both of which climaxed there. 'I go to the Mildmay often', I said hoping this would shock her into reality and some meaningful connection. It did not. Far from restoring peaceful sobriety, this allowed her to vent her deepest feelings. 'Well I did go to The Mildmay you remember, I have sat with those people but you could tell from their backgrounds they were the sort of people who would get this sort of thing. It must be so depressing for you to keep going there.'

I was so livid I couldn't speak. I think if she'd been male I would have assaulted her. Things went from bad to worse. I made one futile attempt to confront her with the last four years of her brother's life. She responded dismissively, 'Well if it was as you say, which frankly I doubt, why did you stay? I wouldn't have, I would have given him an ultimatum'. I was too angry to condense those battle years into meaningful sentences, and she was too angry to listen and had absolutely no desire to know. I wanted to force feed her with truth, the sadness, the awfulness, the tears and the triumphs she could not possibly imagine.

Despite her weighty bereavement experiences she revealed her total ignorance and compounded her insult, 'You are just feeling sorry for yourself, you are just full of self-pity,' she correctly diagnosed. Absolutely bull's-eyeing my vulnerability my bubbling rage came to a head, my heart pounded, my mouth went dry, and I began to shake. I was having a panic attack. She knew things were unredeemable and grandly ordered me to call her a taxi. I stormed out of the room like Terminator I, II and III; unlike Tim's rage in the same room which I had defused, she detonated mine. I wanted to physically throw her out of the house. Instead I grabbed a bottle of bleach propping open the shower room door and I flung it down the hall exploding over the front door, the whole hallway needing redecorating. But that didn't matter I deflected a massive potentially violent rage. I yelled and cursed myself hoarse telling her to get out. The dead don't rage, only the living.

Hindsight is a great thing. I should have listened to my instincts. I did not. Shirley said of November 15th: 'I am not surprised. I've often wondered if it can be otherwise; but death always leaves mess, especially gay/AIDS death. It's not just people on the outside but inside too who are prejudiced, unsympathetic and ignorant. We try but sometimes we can't make it OK; and it can not be OK. Tim left you a multiple legacy - a house to live in, money and his unresolved problems of his homosexuality and HIV status with himself and his family.'

She told me that our highly charged quarrel was not untypical; that a number of physical fights had taken place in her office while refereeing meetings between usually the surviving gay partner and a brother of the deceased; people who but for the death would never have met; matters of the will bringing people uncomfortably together; the vulnerabilities of the bereaved partner who has lost his anchor-buoy and will be feeling acutely oversensitive; and the angers and guilt of an often excluded and perhaps prejudiced family equally grief stricken who will be feeling acutely vulnerable and over alert too - such equal and opposite chemistry of emotion bringing about an inevitable clash of world views.

But one thing is absolute. The only way to successfully

negotiate bereavement is the gradual coming to terms with the death; and this happens through acceptance. One can only accept truth, not in half measures, not only the nice acceptable bits, but all of it including the most unsavoury aspects. One can not accept deletions, or corruptions of the truth; that only leads to stone-frozen grief of denial and delusion. In the few visits his family made to The Mildmay they rose to the occasion within the boundaries of the hospital; but once they had lost their Timothy they wanted to leave behind at least two of those truths - GAY and AIDS. But Pandora's Box had been opened. The truths had been spoken. I was his family's stumbling block. Thank God Tim had me in full glorious 3D Technicolor substantiating that his life, his truth was that he lived his life both personally and professionally as a gay man and died from AIDS. I was his witness. I was the writing on the wall. If Tim had been single they most likely would have sold the house, dispersed his possessions and rewritten his history as Stalin did of Russia's, omitting, erasing, falsifying, misleading, dishonouring truth if the way they chose to represent his life through his obituary is anything to go by.

There was a difference between Tim and myself. I chose to come out to my family. I was only confirming what they already knew; but a spoken truth is very different to an unspoken knowledge. My family was equally conservative and though they were only confronted with homosexuality they were shocked and horrified. My father never really wanted to address it or think about it. He couldn't talk about anything emotional anyway; he just didn't have the capacity or language to do so. He took a relatively neutral position and probably remained quite homophobic; but was never actively rejecting. I thought my mother would be fine; but she was a nightmare and cruel. I had never seen my mother look at me with hatred before; it was hard to bear and our relationship never fully recovered. But she did slowly come to terms with having a gay son and this extended to include my relationship with Tim; and they were supportive at the time of his death. But importantly my parents had time; and at least as they moved through their adjusting and accepting experience they had me alive.

Though Tim and I lived openly as a gay couple he hadn't 'come out' to his family. If he hadn't developed AIDS I can not imagine he would ever have come out to his family; Tim was outed by AIDS. The reality is more often than not that AIDS, perhaps more than any other serious illness, does force peoples hands as it did Tim's unwillingly; families do gather at death beds; they are confronted as Tim's family was with in the last weeks of his life with the horrific triumvirate of AIDS, GAY, DEATH. This would have been a trauma for the most liberal family; and indigestible given the time available. In these circumstances families have to prioritise; and this usually means dealing with the imminent death. Necessary open conversations weren't possible; they did not have the language or resources; did not believe in help so could only try and keep things as they were. I said to Shirley, 'I wish he'd sorted his stuff out'. She replied, 'We don't do psychotherapy, there isn't time'.

The Deadly Dance: Tim seemed very comfortable with himself as gay man until it came to his family. It was a different matter then altogether. When we met he didn't want to introduce me to his family. I was quietly political then. I just said I'm not and our relationship isn't going to be a hidden secret. He acquiesced reluctantly. I was very familiar with conservative provincial middle class convention. In the years before his illness his sister and father visited only once, his mother more often and we made a few visits to the farm each year. Things were kept on a very superficial social level. He was always moody, awkward and uncomfortable itching to get away. He seemed to get on better with his three aunts. His family seemed to put him in to a state of seething anxiety, guilt and anger. Other than in irritable closing down statements he refused to talk about his family. But they were nice enough and genuine enough as long as I played along with their convention. Paradoxically Tim said 'the trouble is my parents seem to quite like you'. I didn't make waves, why would I? There was no need for any greater interface and it would have remained like this until they died but for the advent of HIV.

Once he became ill with his first major opportunistic infection everything changed. The dance began. We were separated at the time. I was living in Chelsea. I went back to look after him but I had to go back to my job, so he went to the farm to convalesce. His mother left him for hours. He was distressed and furious. Did she know? Couldn't she bear it? I drove to the farm to collect him. Extraordinarily she gave us her bedroom to sleep in instead of the spare bedroom we usually occupied; this felt like a validation.

His sister had guessed he had AIDS. She misinterpreted his 'old man look' for AIDS, it was in fact the side affect of the anaesthetic, but she wasn't far wrong. He got better. Far later she told me she thought she had got it wrong, yet it was at this point he was diagnosed with AIDS with the first KS (Kaposi Sarcoma Lesion) on his upper pallet. Later that year, over the New Year of 1989, Tim was hospitalised for blood clots on the lungs. He shut down on the world completely. I was fielding messages constantly from the Royal Opera House and his mother. I was put on the spot by Judy Mackerass, the Conductor's daughter. Tim was supposed to be doing a translation for her of Iphigenie en Tauride. Without telling her he had AIDS I told her confidentially that he was in hospital. She was kind and said she wouldn't say anything or bother me again. His mother was so desperate I openly lied to her that Tim had gone to Hamburg at short notice. I was now complicit in the dance.

I would support him, look after him and do all I could to help, but I refused to be the messenger of death. It was his illness, his responsibility.

Peter Day wanted to go to the farm to confront them. I

begged him not to. Maybe I was wrong? I feared he would break down completely, shun his family and maybe disappear to Germany to die alone as he had threatened.

On a visit to the farm whilst he was quite well, after his father and Tim had gone to bed, I was in the kitchen with his mother and Pasha. She said, 'after Henry I asked Timothy if he wanted to talk about it, he didn't.' She was letting me know in her own way she knew Tim was gay, he'd had one other relationship with a man called Henry and it was an acknowledgement of me. She had tried, Tim had closed her down and here whilst she was acknowledging me she gave me a strong message not to respond.

During the long period of debility between January to September of 1990, Tim's last year, he lay on the sofa every day. In the summer he asked me to go to the farm to tell his mother he was ill. This was my chance for the opportunity I had wanted for things to be open. But this time I held back. Again I refused to be the messenger of death. They could be forgiven for thinking I wanted to control everything. I didn't. I wanted inclusion. I said I would tell his mother he had cancer (KS) which was true, but only half the truth. I drove down. She provided lunch and small talk. She was in a rush to go to a charity event. She was very dignified and just said, 'thank you for telling me, I wish Timothy could have told me himself.' That was it. She asked no more. I was silenced.

Tim seemed relieved. He now wanted to go to the farm almost every weekend in a way he had never done before. Friday after Friday I drove him down through storms, fog and endless roadworks, always listening to Strauss, Berlioz or Wagner. He was ready to tell his parents. At dinner one evening looking deathly unwell he said he was seeing a psychoanalyst, Gil Parker. His father laughed, he thought it funny. His mother was aghast he couldn't sort out his own problems. He fell silent. He looked defeated. He had tried. They had closed him down. I think in that moment I realised it really was going to be me who was going to see him through this. I didn't feel unsympathetic to them, it was agony for everyone, they had already lost a child. This was a breakpoint in the dance. It was Tim going to be Tim and me from now on.

In his last few days at home, when his condition spiraled, his mother and sister came to London to look after him he wouldn't allow his illness to be mentioned. He at last wanted to talk to his mother about his homosexuality and our relationship. She didn't, only wanting to refer to the new Docklands development. He'd left it too late.

Shortly after this I did confirm to Angela that he had AIDS; my hand was finally forced. She said that it would have been easier all round if we had known all along as if she had not been one of the participants in this deadly dance.

Tim's life and my life were framed by homosexuality and AIDS; his family's wasn't. Tim was the pivot between the participants. He couldn't manage this position between us all. This is why I believe he tied Angela and I together to sort it out what he couldn't. But his family certainly wasn't going to start doing upon his death what they hadn't done in his life. I wasn't sure if he or they or both or I were responsible; everyone wants someone to blame; but the endpoint was he left a mess - like the AIDS virus itself, what was left was neither solvable or understandable and ultimately destructive. The fact that it so reflected the killer disease felt like insult to fatal injury.

The Fundraiser. 'It is not our wish, we forbid you, and we will use all our powers to prevent you.' Who were these people? Tim had already organised the Margaret Price concert at St. John's Smith Square for Crusaid, The National AIDS Charity. Tim was very well respected and connected within his profession and was able to mobilise powerful forces for fundraising; and though in angry denial I believe brought him some solace and germinal acceptance of his HIV status and destiny. Did Angela know anything about this and that I was continuing what he had begun? I'd had talks with the Director of Crusaid, about mounting another concert in Tim's memory and he'd agreed. The London Borough of Tower Hamlets would match the money raised and the large sum of £50,000 would have been made available for donation. I requested this be donated to the development of the new specialist HIV clinic, The Graham Hatton Centre at The Royal London Hospital.

The AIDS epidemic and the response to it had taken place entirely under Tory government. Already there were cutbacks in many areas of specialism and excellence. There wasn't even a basic foundation yet for HIV and AIDS care. Funding was essential and the NHS provision needed substantial charitable supplement. The Terrence Higgins Trust, The London Lighthouse, The Mildmay, The Ian Charleston Centre at The Royal Free Hospital, to name a few of the HIV charity's, hospitals and specialist clinics, they relied on charitable donation. Tim and I had spent hours and hours at The Ambrose King Centre, the sexual health clinic at The Royal London Hospital. I had made a promise to Tim to continue to help Dr. Greta Forster his consultant who had looked after him at The Royal London Hospital. She gave me a tour of the basement designated to be The Graham Hatton Centre. Only a pleasant reception area and few basic consulting rooms had been built. Behind a plastic wall was a large derelict area waiting to be developed. In tandem with gay men themselves, sisters' and girlfriends' had helped spearhead the response to AIDS and the provision of services for the care of people with HIV and AIDS. His family didn't attend one clinic appointment with him over the four years of his diagnosis. I had invited Angela to represent Tim's family at the meeting with the Deputy Director of Inpatient Services in September but she had declined. What a tragedy that Tim's sister actively wanted to sabotage and limit help and add to the suffering than help to alleviate. Whether I was infected or affected or both, how dare anyone try and censor my lived experience of AIDS and how I chose to respond to it. Tim loved his family but he didn't like them particularly and he loathed their Middle England values. He didn't give his family much of a chance to prove he was wrong about them. I did. I'm not sure he was.

I will probably never know why Angela wanted to come to Hackney so resolutely. But I do know sadly the great alliance Tim had hoped for between Angela and me will end with our co-signatures on a document for the solicitor in our role as co-executors. Our 'relationship' will remain primordial, a cold war with no contact, never to meet yet never forgetting; our positions diametrically polarised like two moons orbiting the memory of Tim.

Initially it seemed the argument between Angela and I was wholly destructive; and I felt angry with Tim for linking us together in perpetuity through his will. Yet as time went by it proved to be far from a totally negative experience; it was regrettable and ugly but it obliged me to go to the foundations of my beliefs and to define my convictions. In fact her position gave me a very clear reflection of myself. I had to acquire an unquestionable standpoint of my war won opinions, re-evaluating and redefining my self-image; for only an inviolately defined image of myself as both a homosexual and a bereaved gay man could inure me against such malevolent ignorance as I experienced on November 15th. There was a two fold consequence to November 15th. Regretfully I gave up the fundraiser, she probably couldn't have done anything to stop me but I didn't have the fight in me; but the consequence of this was my life as a political gay man began. Homosexuality and AIDS are political issues. I'd lived and was living these issues, and they would inform the rest of my life. When I'd first gone onto the gay scene in Cardiff in the early 1980's I didn't find the 'brotherhood' I had hoped for. It was a shallow, promiscuous, unstable and bitchy world. Just over a decade since decriminalisation, the grubbiness of the basement and attic bars and the transient uncaring attitudes reflected the unsound and unacceptable face of homosexuality from inside and outside. At the time my family reinforced this. Meeting Tim gave me the soundest, most stable and secure loving base of my life. Though Tim had gone and I now lived quite separately to my family I carried forward with me the essence of what he'd given me; and the reasons for his loss was the basis of my solo status; and consequently my political identity would gradually replace my bereavement identity. The gay world had changed irrevocably in ten years; gay men were now a much more responsible, caring, thinking and considerate group. So in a strange way the clash with his sister forced me to take up arms; this was born from and within bereavement but will outrun it and last as long as I do.

I needed to escape from home, Hackney, London and November 15th to begin to get things in perspective again. The morning of November 27th I was standing with Max looking over the wake of the 'Quiberon' en route to Santander in Spain. The ship was navigating the Atlantic islands off the Brest Peninsula, the sea was green, a gentle swell rolled the ship, and waves broke over rocks and isles around us. Lighthouses punctuated the horizon. It was invigorating to embrace the wind and breathe the cool clean air.

A flurry of activity off the portside caught our attention; a mêlée of dolphins were accompanying the ship. In unison a pair leapt gracefully. My heart leapt too. It was good to be alive, so good to be alive again in my time; not just surviving with hope but living - bereavement annulled for the first time. The dolphins disappeared and the thoughts of my reason for leaving England returned. The ship chugged on, and though the spell of bereavement wrapped me in its mantle again; it wasn't the same as before. The second hand of my life clock had started to move again.

The early evening of December 19th 1986 I had walked across the Piazza in Covent Garden with Tim's Christmas present, excited about Christmas, confident and secure Tim nearby at The Royal Opera House rehearsing 'Lucia di Lammermoor', my heart singing. Yet the next morning at approximately 10am Tim told me he was HIV positive. My heart stopped singing, my life clock too. Now on the high seas in a living world of metaphors; for the first time in five years I could feel the tick-tock of my heart once more.

Though bereavement proper began with Tim's physical death, anticipatory grief had begun on December 20th 1986. What I had learned from 'The Quiberon Dolphins' was a glimpse, an anticipatory glimpse; that in time if a new sense of aliveness and wellness could prevail; where if at the same time I could hold the fact that Tim is not physically with me anymore, and at the same time my heart can sing - then that will be when the enveloping aura of bereavement like a cloak will finally slip from my shoulders. As I didn't know when Tim would die, I knew he would; as I don't know when I will be freed from bereavement, I know the day will come.

CHAPTER 13

December

The moment I turned the leaf of the kitchen calendar to December, the first anniversary of Tim's death came into view all my thoughts focusing on December 30th; and on a converging collision course were my memories and unconscious thoughts of the previous December, Tim's ultimate and incomplete month of life.

The racehorse jockey has to plan his approach to clear the fence in steeplechase; so I too had to think carefully if I was to successfully hurdle December 30th. But immediately beforehand Christmas had to be vaulted; surely this double jump would bring my downfall. The clock ticked on, the gap was closing fast.

Life seemed to take on a chronological feel again, perhaps because of the emotional undertow of the previous December; for the first time since the year began there were no running parallel responsibilities to be managed together; further reawakenings would have to wait until the second year cycle. I protected myself ruthlessly from any further setbacks this solemn month; as Christmas released the spirit of merrymaking, I responded by becoming increasingly private.

Appropriately the month began with World AIDS Day. Vanessa Redgrave said of her ex-husband who had just died of

AIDS, 'He wasn't ashamed of anything and nor are we'. I empathised with the actress and her daughters. Her words echoed the previous World AIDS Day December 1st 1990, the day Tim had been admitted to The Mildmay for a blood transfusion and been visited by a health minister. That night I had watched a programme of people talking of their personal stories of loss. With no idea it was only 30 days to the beginning of my bereavement I cried for each story with no idea they were my tears of anticipatory grief. Perhaps on some deep level I knew how grave things were, perhaps I didn't; but I rang The Mildmay late just to reassure myself Tim was still alive.

Now a year later I had my own story of loss too. December 2nd I picked up a 'Hello' magazine in the Indian Takeaway. A famous woman spoke of recurring suicidal thoughts following the death of her husband emulating thoughts similar that I had harboured too - but she hadn't, I hadn't. 'We' were survivors. Though the last month of prebereavement almost claimed me, it did not; however hard bereavement had proved it would not claim me either though I tumbled frequently. I wanted to survive and live again, but I was still compromised.

I wrote in my notebook, 'I feel OK, I feel good, I feel at peace, I feel great - I want to write all of these things again sometime honestly; to feel them. The spell of bereavement still weighs heavily. It's not OK. I have to make it OK. Only I can make it OK. I have to make the essential step. I've had to pick myself up a few times in my life; bereavement is proving the hardest trial ever; like brushing off a dusting of snow just to be engulfed in an avalanche. Keep going.'

December 4th: Just by making a simple cup of coffee in one of Tim's favourite mugs and drinking it in the sitting room I paid my own private observance that one whole year had passed since our last precious moment at home together:

December 4th: I made us a cup of coffee each which we drank together in the sitting room the most commonplace thing partners could do; but for us our supreme moment of domesticity. Tim worked quietly at his accounts. I left for a few days to visit my parents. Tim gave me a dazzling smile, he looked so well. I kissed him goodbye oblivious we would never be at home together ever again.

December 7th: Tim admitted to Mildmay for respite care.

December 8th: Long talk with Angela. After much contemplation I rang Angela to tell her of Tim's whereabouts. Following my departure for Wales firstly his mother and then sister had shared the responsibility of looking after him; though bizarrely he allowed no possibility of AIDS being mentioned. Cruelly he forced Angela to leave before the homecare nurse collected him to take to Mildmay; even the day he left his home forever he could not admit to being HIV to his family. And Angela having no idea of his destination it was a lesser evil for me to betray Tim's whereabouts than keeping silent. It was I who spoke the fated truth for the first time confirming her worst doubts of eighteen months! 'Yes Angela, we are talking of AIDS.' 'I am grateful for this conversation', she said with harrowed relief in her voice.

I turned my back increasingly on the modern world, not watching T.V. or news, nor listening to the radio. The Gulf War appalled me. Only music seemed permissible. I turned to Mother Nature for succour - for all 'her' wondrous creations HIV was of 'her' genesis too. HIV which had claimed Tim and held him transfigured on the forest floor was something that seemed to belong more to medieval days than our world of computer technology. It was to the ancient elements I turned - earth, water, air, fire - always asking why? Long contemplative walks with Pasha along the canals I asked 'Why?' Winter gardening I asked 'Why?' Feeding the ducks, geese and squirrels in Victoria Park I asked 'Why?' There were no answers; but I discovered I had acquired a greater affinity and kinship with nature than I had before.

December 9th: I must return to London. Something is wrong. I need Tim and Tim needs me. He has been in hospital many times but something weighs heavily on my heart. Arriving at The Mildmay Tim looked better than I had expected but very weak and breathless. I am alarmed at the severe degree of fluid retention - his swollen arms, his limbs, stomach and genitals bloated and misshapen, carrying about a stone of excess fluid (kidney failure).

There were Christmas trees in Regent Street and festive window displays but I shied away from them. Walking into the expansive Christmas Department of Peter Jones in Chelsea was an unwelcome harbinger of the approaching festival that I could not sidestep. I had to talk to Gil to discuss tactics of how to successfully negotiate a festival I wanted no part of.

I decided in respect and in memoriam for Tim that I would do some things we always did the same - strings for cards in the kitchen; the little painted glass Danish decorations that Marianne had given us five years before would again hang over the kitchen table. No longer possible to make the glass bauble tree decoration for the card table on the top landing (it had been returned to Tim's parents); to reflect change I would dangle the two dozen clear spheres from the magnolia at the bottom of the garden.

Tim's last reference that I know of to the house was to Kate, 'Has Rob done the glass bauble tree?' 'Yes', she replied. 'Good', he said settling back into his pillows. Kate felt that with that given knowledge he bid adieu to his home.

To reflect life on-going I decided to have a real tree that I would adorn with new ornaments; though the little Christmas teddy bear Tim had once given me, that I had taken to The Mildmay to cheer his room the year before; it would crown the new tree this year.

Painfully I determined to burn the little paper snowman Tim had given me our first Christmas together and to scatter the ash in the garden; also to destroy the outrageous artificial pink Christmas tree and its worn silver baubles that belonged singularly to Tim's era. Dismembering the tree and smashing the baubles and firing the snowman I felt like a vandal; but they were necessary sacrifices.

December 10th: Tim has been in hospital many times; he always gets better and comes home; I carry on much as usual visiting him two or three times a day. I went to the gym in the afternoon; but something seemed wrong, wrong, wrong. I left and went straight to Mildmay not even changing from my sweaty gym gear. Tim very negative and depressed; quite unlike him. He doesn't want to see anyone but me. He gave me a little wave that struck my heart like a blow. Tim is dying.

I dreaded the arrival of the first Christmas card; yet ironically it was the one card, from Gil, that provided me with a solid foothold on Christmas. Her card sold in aid of Russian Christians featured an ornate domed orthodox church in a snowstorm; and instead of the usual now meaningless printed message 'Happy Christmas' were three simple words 'Grace and Peace.' These meaningful words gave me a concept of this first Christmas post-Tim that allowed for grief; I appropriated these words as a bridge between the happy Christmas it could not be, and the empty Christmas it now did not need to be. The consequence of receiving Gil's 'enabling' card was to choose cards of my own. Naturally I wanted to support The Mildmay so I selected their charity card - incredibly it featured a Christmas snow scene of St. Paul's, Covent Garden the very church where Tim's memorial had taken place. 'It could have been designed especially for you', said Julia.

December 11th: Liz Smith from the home care team was the first to vocalise my worst nightmare; that Tim was unlikely to recover from this bout of illness, 'He is so tired now.' I thought I would die of grief. I had bargained and bartered, lied and deceived, colluded and betrayed, prayed and cried in vain attempt to stave off this inevitable moment. And now it was going to happen and there was nothing I could do to stop it.

Later that day at The Mildmay the dynamics of the situation plus the great care and comfort given to Tim, and to me, allowed for our moment of total reconciliation. We were each other's confessor; secure in our love for one another we confided all our past misdemeanours. I told Tim about Sean my lover during our months of separation; that I had gone onto autodestruct as if trying to obtain HIV, and maybe had; that I had tried to fall out of love with him, he having given me every good reason to do so prior to separating; yet I had never been able to stop loving him. 'That's nice', he said. Tim absolved me from the guilt I had long carried when I confessed I had betrayed his secret to a number of people. He was remorseful for burdening me with such a responsibility. He apologised for his promiscuity and getting ill and causing us both such heartache. I absolved him from his pangs of conscience. He knew that Sean had been more than just a friend, and of the few friends I had told of his condition - 'they tried so hard to behave as if they didn't know, but I could see the fear in their eyes of being found out'. I'd always been very aware of his separate sex life. There had been no secrets between us after all.

Once again we made love as only a healthy man can do with a very sick man; through hugs, kisses, tears, holding hands and gentle words. We were so in love again as at the beginning of our relationship before HIV upset and spoiled everything. All our HIV related inter relational difficulties since December 20th 1986 were purged. We were in absolute harmony; a closeness existing between us that we had not known before. Our love had finally conquered HIV and we rested on death's pillow.

Tim was increasingly tired. I played Richard Strauss' 'Four Last Songs' throughout December; the words of the last song capturing Tim's merciful transition from tiredness to death:

At Dusk

Here both in need and gladness
We wandered hand in hand;
Now let us pause at last
Above the silent land. Dusk comes the vales exploring,
The darkling air grows still,
Alone two skylarks soaring
In song their dreams fulfil. Draw close and leave then singing,
Soon will be time to sleep,
How lost our way's beginning!
This solitude, how deep
O rest so long desired!
We sense the night's soft breath
Now we are tired, how tired!
Can this perhaps be death?

I had a vivid dream about Tim. I walked into a dark room that I did not recognise. Tim was propped up on pillows on a bed looking frail but not ill. He was tiny, dressed in his teddy bears dressing gown. I broke my heart in the dream. He took my huge hand in his tiny hand, smiled at me, and told me reassuringly, 'Everything is OK.'

December 12th: I brought home a wheelchair from The Mildmay ready for Tim's planned discharge two days later for his final decline at home. I hated it. Tim was a biker; his two wheels were one in front of the other, not side by side. 'The tide has turned and he is on the up now', I wrote deludingly in my diary.

December 13th: Tim weepy, hopeful, not hopeful.

Glen rang; she wanted to meet for a Christmas drink at 'The Falcon & Firkin' with her husband Andy. I accepted. But the next day I gave my apologies; approaching the first anniversary of Tim's death I felt too vulnerable to disturb the balance of friends around me - Max and Maria - even to see important old friends like Glen and Andy who I cared about deeply.

A whole host of Christmas phone calls intruded on my secluded life; yet left me feeling mean and ungenerous because people were only being kind. I talked to Gil to try to find a comfortable perspective. She said that being the time of the year friends would want to meet; that they need us too, that they so want to see us 'over it', back to our old selves; but of course this can not be within only one year.

December 14th: I changed Tim's bed and went to Tesco to stock up on provisions; it would be difficult to go out shopping once Tim came home that evening. Late that morning I accompanied him to The Royal London Hospital for tests that could not be done at The Mildmay. Late afternoon we were supposed to return to The Mildmay from where I would take him home. Instead Tim was admitted to The Royal London Hospital. I was told in the nicest possible way that Tim would remain there and be transferred back to The Mildmay for terminal care once a bed became available. TIM WAS NOT COMING HOME AGAIN.

I waited with Tim in a consulting room in The Ambrose King Centre while a bed was found for him in the hospital. Over the four years that Tim had been treated at the clinic from his HIV diagnosis until the decline in his health necessitated the specialist care of The Mildmay, he had become popular with the staff. They now showed their appreciation by presenting him with a poinsettia. He became very emotional and said he had always wanted one for himself having given so many as presents. He held it like a baby, half asleep due to morphine, with a patch over his left eye following radiation to a Kaposi Sarcoma on his eyelid. My tough biker boyfriend was as vulnerable as a butterfly; I could not protect him enough. I had to be strong for him; but when he looked up at one of the high consulting room windows and whispered, 'blue sky' the grief was too hard to bear; I had to leave him for a few minutes to weep alone.

Returning home unaccompanied was not unusual. I had spent hours, days, and weeks there by myself before and after Tim's HIV diagnosis; but this day that should have seen his homecoming, instead only mine was the definition of loneliness itself. Tim was yet alive, but this was it; this was what it was going to be like. It was a thunderbolt moment of what my life would be like after he had died. From that moment I abandoned the top floor of the house. I gave up sleeping in my bedroom moving to the sofa in the sitting room. Tim insisted I brought the plant home 'to wait for him'. Immediately it began to drop its leaves, a dark foreshadow of the days ahead.

December 18th: I received an unexpected Christmas card from Tim's mother. After the quarrel with Angela I didn't expect to hear from any of his family ever again. I guessed she hadn't shared the awfulness of that day with her mother.

December 19th: But for '10.50' that I would write on December 30th I wrote the penultimate entry in my diary - 'Tim'. From that moment Tim's decline seemed precipitous. We were as close as two pieces of polished marble touching; there was nothing between us, not even words - we had said it all. For the little time Tim had left he marshalled his waning forces to admit his family and as many friends as possible into his reality. Yet he hadn't lost the ability to reprimand anyone who displeased him; me included. Overwhelmed with anxiety for himself he could not be pleased. I began to function like an automaton at times; the weight of grief I carried could not support any additional pain.

December 20th 1986 had been the day Tim had told me he was HIV five years before; Tim and I made an early start. We were going Christmas shopping. He wanted to buy some Waterford Crystal wine glasses for his mother. I was excited - this was going to be the best Christmas we'd ever had. It had been a hard year. I'd been ill and in only the last days fully won back my health and was planning the return to my studies. Tim had been with The Welsh National Opera for 8 years and it was time for a career move. He was very clear that if he'd been single he would have gone to Germany. But he wanted us to have a more settled domestic life. This meant a job in London at The Royal Opera House. For all its kudos it was not the best career step; but the only possibility of us having a proper life together. A job became available. It was a nail biting time for him and for me whether he would get it; our future depended on it. After months of uncertainty he got the job. He was enjoying it and we'd had a few months now of being quite the old couple. And only three days before he'd had the result of his HIV test. It was negative. To celebrate the good news I flamboyantly decorated the sitting room for Christmas. AIDS was no longer remote, happening somewhere else to other people. Edward had died the year before in New York and people were talking of gay friends falling ill with strange infections. I'd tested negative earlier that year in hospital. We assumed therefore that Tim would be negative. How could one partner be negative and the other positive if full sexual relations had been practised? Nevertheless Tim was extremely anxious before his test result and convinced himself he had it - someone he'd had a relationship with before me had recently developed Kaposi Sarcoma lesions on his feet. 'If you had it Tim, then I would surely as well', I reassured him logically. I wasn't in the least surprised with his negative result and I thought no more about it. We were safe.

'Give me twenty minutes by myself', Tim said unusually as he climbed into the bath. I complied and went downstairs to have a shower. Stepping under the hot spray I was oblivious that life as I knew it, happiness as I'd known was about to end, and life would never be the same ever again as when I'd woken that morning. My head was filled with the frippery of Christmas. I wanted to buy a new shirt for a party that night. My Godfather was coming around later to borrow extra plates and glasses for a party he and his wife were holding the next evening. In addition to Christmas Shopping we had to go to Tesco to buy food to prepare for Sunday Lunch the next day - Tim's mother and aunt were coming. It was going to be a busy day. I went upstairs and started to dress. I put my Jeans and vest on. Before pulling on my shirt something made me spontaneously pop my head around the bathroom door and ask, 'Are you sure you are ok?' Tim had just stepped out of the bath and was wrapped in a large towel. Always the practical joker he bowed his head and pretended to cry. 'Oh come on Tim, there's no time for this; we've got far too much to do'. Something clawed at my heart. Time stopped. Real tears ran down his face. I knew what he was going to say before he said it, 'They found antibodies in my blood, I didn't want to tell you, I didn't want to spoil your Christmas'.

Each successive anniversary of that day I had chalked up another year of Tim's survival; now it was I who had survived one year posthumously. The Mildmay had been instrumental in my survival. To show my appreciation I wanted to make a gesture to the staff of The Elizabeth Ward; Max from his eyewitness position also wanted to add his salute, so this 20th day of December we collected two chocolate logs his boss had made for the hospital. But despite being a shared experience there was friction between us; for the first time since meeting Max I felt I was in a triangle relationship with him and Tim; the uncomfortableness persisting - until we paid our respects in the chapel.

Teresita one of the nurses who had looked after Tim was sitting quietly at the back of the Chapel, I asked her if she minded our intrusion into her solitude. She welcomed us and in fact seemed glad to be able to share her burden of grief with two sympathetic mortals - one of her favourite patients Michael Paton had died that morning. We admired the beautiful dove tapestry he had just completed that now hung above The Book of Remembrance. We held not just hands but the fact that the tragedy befalling Tim and his loved ones; the sad reality being that one cycle of life and death would follow another. Teresita was a nun who had taken religious vows; though I did not have her faith I experienced her unquestionable belief; almost palpable, her faith and serenity vanquished all pain, grief, suffering and uncomfortableness. That precious moment in The Mildmay chapel with Max and Teresita became the core-experience of my first Christmas post-Tim. Already Christmas was evolving as a new experience; it had a greater spiritual quality than any I had known.

December 22nd: I wrote in my notebook 'I am approaching Christmas as a very different person to the one I was a year ago.'

I departed London for Wales on Christmas Eve with Max and Pasha. Following the extraordinary shared experience with Teresita the essential sustenance for my survival were not the former jollities of Christmas I had previously been accustomed too; but quieter moments of theological thought. The year before wild horses wouldn't have dragged me into any holy place; I remember ringing Francis and Kirsten to ask them to pray for Tim; to do the praying that I could not. For the first time in many years I wanted to go to Christmas Mass. Now with Max and my sister I went to All Saints Church, my home church where I had been baptised and confirmed. I believed Jesus lived according to the scriptures as a historical character; yet he did not save Tim from anything that I could see, or me. Whether I satisfied the criteria to qualify as a practising Christian I do not know; yet I could go honestly to church and be comforted. In the sermon were the words 'wonderful counsellor' for Gil and Shirley; and the words 'those departed' encompassing Tim - I had bridged the penultimate hurdle of the year.

Christmas Day itself my thoughts focused tenaciously on the day; an emotional portcullis blocking off recall; yet a sense of underlying anxiety troubled my unconscious all day long. That evening I went for a long soul searching walk to the beach. The sea was running high, it was choppy and cold. A biting wind touched the flesh. I walked down the slipway. I dared Mother Nature who had claimed Tim to claim me too, to overwhelm me - or free me; but not to leave me carrying Tim's death around with me. This was where I had come as a boy, in happy and troubled times; now I turned to the touchstone of my childhood, boyhood and youth for solace. Of course a freak wave didn't sweep me to my death, nor was I freed from bereavement. I learned grief is a possession of the personality; only by giving it its head and allowing it to run its inevitable course will it gradually relinquish its clutch; fighting, resisting only makes its hold more tenacious. Easily adopted bereavement is not so easily disposed of; it is a wearisome encumbrance. But it felt right to be standing alone hidden in the darkness, with big frothy waves for company, separate from the yacht club nearby, its inviting lights beckoning, but refused.

December 27th: I wrote in my notebook, 'I will follow you Tim into eternity, wait for me but I am not ready yet to follow; I have things to do.'

December 28th: Nightmares. I woke soaked in sweat, but I could not remember. It was while I had slept my dreams battered against the unconscious barricade that stopped me remembering - it wasn't just my diary writing that gave out on December 19th the previous year, but my memory as well. From that day there is nothing in my diary and little in my memory banks of those last days of ours. In the approach to his death I began to shut down; and now a year later I had little clarity of mind from that time. I would visit him early each morning about 7.30am before his assigned nurse washed him and attended to his medical needs and readied him for the day. I would return in the afternoon and again in the evening; but had no idea how I spent my time away from him. I asked two of Tim's closest friends Kate and Julia if they could fill in some of the gaps for me. Here are their recollections.

December

Kate's Story

December 17th 1990: Monday evening. Today was the start of the last week at work. The festive season is very much in evidence with little urgent work to do but much planning of 'end of term' parties and celebrations.

Our team has only been together for six weeks and staff team building - and socialising - is still considered very important. When I get home that evening several ideas are dominating my thoughts. Mark's broken arm and dislocated wrist - my husband had had an accident at work just over a fortnight ago and was still encased in plaster to his shoulder and was waiting for me to come home. Our forthcoming trip to Australia - we were leaving on New Years Eve and would be away for a month - would Mark's arm be out of plaster then? My boss' party - a very smart occasion - I had to find my long taffeta skirt, press it and decide what I could wear with it. I didn't get home until quite late - normal for me, so it was nearly 11pm when I finally hung my pressed taffeta skirt and blouse on the bannister rail near the door so I wouldn't forget them in the morning. I put the finishing touches to the food I had prepared for the party and packed a basket of extra cutlery and items which had been requested. All ready for the morning.

Time to go to bed. The phone rings - it's Rob. It was nice to hear from him. Perhaps we can arrange to meet him and Tim sometime between Christmas and New Year. So much to tell them both. My new job - the trip to Japan - plans for Australia - Christmas presents to exchange and the souvenirs from Japan. There's something wrong. Rob seems distant and vague. I know that Rob has been through some very bad patches in the past - but that's all long ago. I ask what is the matter. Pause. Tim's ill - very ill. What's wrong? He's in hospital. What's wrong? Tim's very ill. What's wrong? He's very ill. What's wrong? He seems to be talking in riddles. There are silences that I am supposed to fill. My mouth is dry and my heart is thumping. Say the worst I can think of, because it is never as bad as that. Has Tim got AIDS? Yes. Another silence. What to say? How do you make it not be true. How long have you known? Four years. Four years!! That can only mean that Tim hasn't just been diagnosed. Tim is very ill after four years of knowing. How can I say, is Tim dying? The rest of the conversation proceeds with each new bit of information like a blow to the head. Tim probably contracted the HIV virus ten years ago. He found out about it four years ago. Rob was sworn to secrecy. Their life has been one bound up in deception, so successful that it is clear that Rob is losing touch with reality. He feels he is betraying Tim by telling me but has not the courage or the heart to tell me only when it is over, when Tim is dead. Rob knows that the pain of telling me like that would be indescribable. The vow of silence laid on him has hurt him more than he can tell me but Rob being Rob can not bring himself to be an instrument for inflicting pain on me. There are others who should know - Barbara and Julia. Special friends. I spare Rob the anguish of another betrayal - I will tell them. Rob has a desperate need for human warmth. I promise to be there as soon as possible.

We talk of trivial things which have become important too. Rob is distraught because he has dropped Tim's electric shaver and has been banned from buying another. Tim exerts his will over Rob - he has to show his strength in small details, I will bring Mark's shaver - say he borrowed it, but not from us. I mustn't know. Tim must not know of Rob's betrayal. This time I'm going to London for Rob - it is unlikely that Tim will know I'm there or that my love for him means that I cannot rest unless I am near.

When I put the phone down I have to tell Mark. Fill in the gaps from the half-heard conversation. Going through my head like a Greek chorus punctuating every other thought is 'Not Tim - surely not Tim.' Other people get AIDS, not someone as intelligent as Tim - he couldn't be so stupid. Gradually I realise that ten years ago, when Tim supposedly contracted HIV we knew nothing about AIDS. In our ignorance we had sat around the television listening to documentaries about the spread of this mysterious new illness. We had discussed it and wondered whether it would lead to a hysterical reaction towards gay people. Tim was our lodger, our friend. It's a cliché, but he felt like family - a sort of brother.

A fitful restless night. I woke up and I was crying - it was early but I had work to do. I rang Vanessa - I was supposed to be taking her to work. I'll be late - something dreadful's happened. Tell her later. I had to see Barbara. How early can you wake someone up? It was eight o'clock. Barbara in her dressing gown knew it must be bad news - there's no other reason for me to be there so early. I wanted her husband to be there too, get him out of bed. What if Barbara cannot bear to hear what I have to tell her? She has known Tim longer than any of us. I tell her but I cry more than her. I'm so sorry to have to be the one to tell her but it must be done. Barbara is upset but she had heard a rumour. She had dismissed the rumour but it had at least planted a seed of possibility in her mind. Upset but not in shock. I had not recognised my shock at that stage - I just felt an overwhelming shadow. Up until that time I don't think I have ever encountered any situation which I didn't believe I could change either by stubbornness, hard work or persuasion. Now everything seemed beyond my control. Barbara promised that she would tell Julia - but only her. Tim's need for secrecy was to be respected - also to protect Rob. It was clear that Tim did not want to slip easily away but hung onto life with tenacity. Telling people was admitting defeat and we knew that if Tim found out that Rob had told us, then he would punish him with every means he had left to him. My love for Tim did not blind me to the fact that he could be a tyrant and I knew that Rob - the best friend he could have - was simply falling apart with fatigue, grief and loneliness.

I took Vanessa to work and told her why I had to sort

things out and go to London. People at work chat about Christmas presents and parties. They think I have a cold. No, I stammer, my best friend is dying. I've got to go to London. They understand but they do it simply and without display. I would have found too much sympathy unbearable - I just want to clear and go to London. What I really mean is I want to leave work today and not come back until February, because after this week it is Christmas and after that I'm going to Australia. Nobody raises any obstacles. Nobody says anything about docking my pay or working time in lieu. We don't say anything but we all know that this is the beginning of an era where AIDS will affect us all. First people we have heard of, then people we have met, but vaguely. Finally people we know - people we really care about. Our friends, our family perhaps ourselves. I am the first of our group to feel the pain directly but we know we all will eventually. We know that people within our sphere, the arts, are being affected seemingly before anyone else. I tidy my desk, hastily make arrangements for my absence and drive to my boss' house, where she is preparing her party. On the way I nearly run out of petrol. I simply forgot to check I had any. It is overcast, raining and foggy. I remember O' Level English lessons where they spoke about the microcosmic/macrocosmic relation. The world and its weather reflecting the situation in the drama. A bleak and grey day which perfectly mirrored the numbness and helplessness I felt.

Tuesday 18th December: It was around midday when I arrived at my manager's house. She had taken the day off to prepare for a grand Christmas party in the evening. I was clutching some food I had prepared and other articles I had offered to lend her. She was surprised to see me - I probably looked in a bit of a state - dishevelled with red eyes. I explained that I wasn't attending the party, that I had to go to London, that I wouldn't be back until after I had returned from Australia. I told her that I had discovered that my best friend was dying from AIDS.

It had not occurred to me to ask permission for time off and I was lucky that my blunt statements were greeted with sympathy and understanding. With tears in her eyes she told me of friends and relatives that she was worried about. We worked in the Arts - we all knew of people that had contracted AIDS, but so far it had not affected anybody to whom we were really close. He had been my friend, not hers but she recognised that sooner or later we would all be touched by the grief that goes hand-in-hand with AIDS. I had just been the first in our group to have felt the pain.

I went home, there were things to do before I could go to London. I kept calling Rob, needing to be reassured that he was OK. I was desperately concerned that the agony of the past months was making him lose his reason.

Wednesday 19th December - Sunday 23rd: I caught the train to Paddington. I kept having to buy drinks because my mouth felt so dry. Strangely, this is something I now always associate with shock and grief. The proffered cups of tea to the bereaved probably do help, after all.

When I met Rob at home we just hugged each other. I could feel Rob's aching need for physical comfort. It seemed impossible that I could say anything which would make either of us feel better but I knew that my arms around him made him feel less vulnerable and alone. We both loved Tim and we were both shaken by our inability to do anything to stop the inevitable outcome of the disease.

Rob spoke with the sort of croaky voice that you get when you don't speak to anyone except the shopkeeper or bus conductor. It seemed as if all his energy had been drained by the effort of getting through the days - a constant round of going to the hospital, sorting things out for Tim, back to the hospital. This itinerary didn't seem to include any time to look after himself. He hadn't been sleeping, the house was devoid of food, his biological clock was totally unsynchronised and he didn't really seem to have any idea of the time - other than hospital routine. He said that he had been drinking too much at night after visiting Tim, but the drink didn't even seem to bring him the oblivion he was seeking.

It became clear that I was unlikely to see Tim - for Rob's sake the deception had to be maintained. If Tim had known that Rob had told me of his illness, he would have given him a hard time. It seemed that in his illness, Tim who had always been a strong and dominating character, was now attempting to exert his will with an almost manic force. Looking back, I can admire this - he was trying to cheat death by holding on to life with all his strength - that meant being 'in control' and most of these efforts were concentrated on Rob. It made life very hard for Rob, who seemed unable to please Tim, however hard he tried. Tim made no allowances for Rob's grief and his harsh words often made Rob more nervous and clumsy, displeasing Tim all the more.

Tim had often directed death-bed scenes but he wasn't going to conform to the standard image. He had no time for tender words or soppy scenes. Rob's deep love for Tim was all-forgiving but he was very hurt by his distant manner.

I felt that the best thing I could do would be to remind Rob that he was alive and had better start to align himself with the living. I made him laugh at some of Tim's more preposterous requests - requests lovingly fulfilled, but not because he was an automaton. I made him take me to the pub and we bought a take-away. I managed to make him eat at least twice a day.

One morning I brought him a cup of tea in bed. I sat down beside him as he poured out the horrors of the last few weeks. It was cold, so I asked him to shove up and got in beside him. As he told me all that had happened he laughed at the ludicrous situation he was in - a gay man in bed with a married woman. The days still revolved around hospital visits but at least he did not feel so isolated. By helping Rob be strong, I was helping Tim - he needed Rob's support and continued presence.

After months of secrecy, a few of Tim's friends gradually became aware of his serious illness. One day Tim mentioned that he had a book he wished to give to Francis - whether this was a deliberate move to inform Francis of his predicament or merely a slip-up, I wasn't sure. However, by inviting Francis and his girlfriend Kirsten to The Mildmay, then Tim's illness would be obvious.

The visit was a farce. Francis and Kirsten did not realise the urgency of their visit and arrived late at Rob's house. By the time he had taken them to the hospital, Tim was refusing to seen them. Was it cold feet or was Tim angry? Later I learnt of the supreme efforts Tim made to get through the day - every action had an optimum time - if his timetable got out of synchronisation, he couldn't cope. Their moment had come and they had missed it. That evening Rob prepared about five meals for Tim each one at his request and then rejected. Rob could have cried, instead I made him laugh about it.

Somehow, we got so caught up in the daily routine that we forgot about the 'real world' outside. Thats how we came to go shopping in Tesco on the Saturday - a totally crazy thing to do on the Saturday before Christmas. Rob's lack of food in the house was causing him problems but we managed to choose the busiest place in the world to shop. We queued for a whole hour to pay our bill. It seemed like madness when Tim was so ill - it was the longest Rob had been away from the hospital or a phone for weeks. Finally we got into the car, and another nightmare began. The car ignition made a terrible noise which continued after the key was removed. An awful smoky smell seeped from the engine. I called the RAC and said the car was about to explode. It took them a mere 10 minutes to arrive and tell me that it was the oil from the starter motor burning off - and that it was not serious. More farce.

Whenever we found ourselves in the other 'real' world it

was a strange experience. Life goes on unaffected by your own personal problems or griefs. It make you feel alienated - a feeling that was heightened by the celebrations for Christmas. Those days with Rob before Tim died were the time for office parties and we constantly came across loud and lurching revellers. It was like being on another planet a million miles away from the hushed and intense atmosphere of a hospice.

Gradually Rob and I introduced a sub-plot. On one occasion Rob told Tim that I had telephoned to say that I would be visiting Mark's aunt - I normally would arrange to see Tim and Rob at the same time. On a subsequent visit, Rob said that I had arrived at Aunty Flora's house and was coming to visit them. After several more visits where the plot thickened we came up with the final story - I had called in to see Rob and demanded to know where Tim was. I was not fooled by Rob's excuses and had come to see Tim. Rob could now tell him that I was waiting in the Day Room.

I had never expected to see Tim - it was his right to choose how he orchestrated his illness and I had not intended invading his privacy. I was not the only one waiting in the Day Room. Barbara had kept a vigil one night as well, so had Francis and Kirsten. Tim had eventually seen Francis and Kirsten and now he would see me.

Tim looked frail and sickly but seemed pleased to see me. It has always been a joke between us that he would shrink from physical contact - but now he clutched my hand as I kissed his cheek. He asked about Mark and his accident, then Mark's sister, Melanie and the family. The usual small talk which avoids the real issues - but then Tim was always interested in the news of his friends. When he asked how long I had been with Mark's aunt, I couldn't lie to him. I told him I'd been staying with Rob for five days, that I'd been outside in the Day Room waiting for the right moment. His eyes misted over 'Good old Kate', he said and grasped my hand more firmly. I made some flippant comment about how he'd managed to fool us all - I still couldn't forgive myself for not having guessed the truth. Like a jigsaw coming together - all the individual pieces had suggested that he had contracted AIDS but I had been too blind or stupid to recognise the picture.

'It wasn't a game', he said suddenly intense and urgent. 'It was deadly serious. If anyone had found out - if the news had got back to people - I couldn't have worked. I'd have been without a job. I couldn't afford it.' The truth of that statement hit me. However sympathetic his friends might have been the deadly reality was there - people would have panicked, he would have suffered even more. I admitted that, had I known, I would inevitably have fussed over him - it would have driven him mad.

We were interrupted by the doctor, so I withdrew into the Day Room. I was shaking with the emotion of having seen him after all the hours of waiting. The Day Room was populated with other people's tragedies. The respectable looking proud woman who tended her emaciated and scared son, who in his illness had reverted to childishness. The father and mother bringing their son back after a day out - his mind wasn't really there, but he had seemed to enjoy his visit. The two Brians - Brian the Scot who had been around, travelled a bit - probably contracting the deadly virus from a fatal needle. Brian - the lad, cheeky and personable with the Bohemian life style. He'd been married fifteen years, he told Barbara and me but if you counted the times when they had been together between bouts of separation it was about seven years, he grinned. He looked haunted and scared. 'Do you think my kids will see me on Christmas Day? I've sent them a card.' I said that I hoped that they would. We shared a pot of tea and the two Brians told me of their various bouts of illnesses, of their fear of persecution when they were back home. They were scared of illness but it brought the relief of hospital and security from the yobs that taunted them in their flats. The illness brought poverty in its wake - the trap that

Tim had striven so hard to avoid - so hard that he had created the lies that had formed his daily life. I certainly understood why he had done it - I just wished that it hadn't placed such an enormous strain on Rob. It had been Tim's decision but Rob had been sucked into the deception.

I was told I could go back into Tim's room, but they should have asked him first - he was slightly embarrassed that he was still peeing into a bottle. Normally The Mildmay was so good about maintaining the dignity of the patients - it didn't matter. Tim talked about my forthcoming visit to Australia. His voice was tired and every so often he would be overcome by a flood of emotion which brought tears to his eyes and his voice would crack. He wanted to be strong, so we only discussed things without emotional content. The effort was exhausting him so I said I was leaving him to get some rest. He told me that I had to look up one of Rob's friends Menna when I was in Melbourne and I said I would. 'Send me a postcard', he said. 'I'll send you lots', I promised. 'And I'll see you when I get back and tell you all about it.' 'I'll look forward to that - give my love to Mark and Melanie.' He kissed me and I left. We both knew that he would not live to receive any postcards and that my proposed visit to tell him of my holiday was a final bit of fiction. I knew I would never see him again.

Postscript: Tim was always the best of friends - always the most obliging. When he died on the eve of my trip to Australia I almost believed that he had chosen that time for my convenience - so that I could travel without the pain of leaving him dying. For the next few weeks I struggled to make myself believe that it had really happened. Much of my holiday passed in a blur. At night I was haunted by complicated dreams that undid the reality - by strange and devious means Tim's death had only been a sham. I used to wake up and cry as the true situation dawned on me - Tim really was dead.

By a strange twist of fate we spent an evening in Cairns,

on the other side of the world, watching an Australian Arts TV programme - it was a recording of a production of Elektra that Tim had worked on recently. It was almost as if I expected him to pop up at any moment - it was very unnerving.

About three months after Tim's death I had a vivid and memorable dream. We were in the Apollo Theatre, Oxford and I was drinking at the crowded bar - I had just finished a half pint of beer.

'Let me get you another', he said.

'You look so much better than when I last saw you', I said.

'That's because I was dying', he replied. 'Then you are dead, after all', I said.' And you weren't much help', he mocked. 'You're really useless at death bed scenes - Barbara was much better - but, there again, she's had much more experience', he was laughing at me. 'If you are dead then can anyone else see you', I asked?

He shook his head. 'Then everybody thinks I'm standing here talking to myself and I look an idiot.'

He grinned at me - it was a typical Tim-type joke.

The barman appeared and I ordered another drink. I wanted to pay but Tim kept insisting that he did - a scene that we had re-enacted countless times before. He tried to pick up my money to thrust it back at me - but he couldn't. He had no substance, he was a ghost. I had won - I paid and we laughed together. I was still laughing when I woke up.

After that I had no more distressing dreams trying to explain away Tim's death. I miss him enormously but I know he is dead and I know he is happy. I really felt that I had been visited.

Julia's Story
Seeds of Doubt

Lunch with Alison. 'There's a rumour going around the Royal Opera House that Tim has got AIDS.' Me: 'What nonsense.' 'Well, he has been ill a lot lately.' Me: 'Yes, but you know what he's like, he hated working with 'Z', it's probably just a political illness, you know Tim.' 'Well you should know if anyone does.' Subject closed.

Late night drinking session with Peter, who is staying in my house.

'I've heard a rumour that Tim has got AIDS - you must know, has he?' Peter reluctantly says he thinks it is possible. I am horrified that he could be so careless but Peter points out that it could have happened years ago, before anyone had even heard of AIDS. He is right. Like a coward, I push this information to the back of my mind - the thought that one of my best friends is going to die I am not prepared to face, yet.

Confirmation: The small tour, Port Talbot - an awful place, no dimmers on the houselights. I am hot in my nylon boilersuit. Ian Jones, Lighting Designer and Deputy Chief Electrician calls me to the phone. It is Barbara - am I going home this evening (stay in Port Talbot, hah!). She would like to come round and see me. We make a time. She sounds very serious. When I break the connection I get this mad idea that she is going to accuse me of having an affair with her husband. Against this crazy notion comes the thought that another obvious link between us is Tim. She is going to come and tell me he is dead. I spend the rest of the day in a daze.

At home, a knock on the door - I let Barbara and Tony, her husband, in. To put off the moment I make Lemon Verbena tea. My hand shakes as I fill their mugs. They tell me that Tim is very sick with AIDS in The Mildmay, and that Rob, his partner, sworn to secrecy for all these years has broken the silence to appeal to his friends as he can't help him alone anymore. Kate has already gone to London and is waiting to see if Tim will see her.

As I had written a letter saying I wanted to come and see Rob and Tim on the 23rd December and wasn't supposed to know anything was wrong, could I go and try and see if Tim would see me.

When a friend or someone you love dies one of the worst parts is not being able to say goodbye - when my father died my brother and I were watching boys flying kites on Wormwood Scrubs, although anyway he had been unconscious for several days. My friend, Mother Hilary died in Ireland far away from me, and although later I made a kind of pilgrimage to her grave I never really forgave myself for not seeing her at the end - here at least was the chance to say goodbye.

The next day I receive a Christmas Card - the last ever in Tim's inimitable and beautiful script saying he will be away so I can't visit. I ignore this and phone Rob. 'It's all right, Rob, I know.' Rob is still worried that he has done the wrong thing, but he needs our support now at what is probably the end - it is the most sick Tim has been. I say I will come on the 23rd as arranged and hope to be seen.

23rd December: By now Kate has been allowed to see Tim. I'm due to arrive I think at six, but Rob and Kate have already left the house. In desperation I phone Mark, Kate's husband at home in Wales. He doesn't know where the hospital is, but thinks they have gone early so Kate can get the train straight home. I do not want to see Kate - her kind of compassion I would find impossible to cope with at this moment. I buy 20 Marlboro and wait in my car outside Tim and Rob's house, smoking and listening to Handels Messiah on the radio. Just after the Hallelujah Chorus Rob comes back. I am relieved he is alone. I ask if I can stay the night and visit Tim in the morning. Rob goes and gets us an Indian Takeaway - we drink, eat and talk but I can't remember what about, except that he warns me Tim has refused to see some close friends. He shows me all the Christmas Cards for Tim from all over the world - people who love him who have no idea that anything is wrong: as Tim wished. At least I am lucky enough to be prepared, even if he will not see me. Surprisingly I sleep well.

Christmas Eve: We set off early, me following Rob in his car - with one of those grim ironies of life he nearly knocks down a lunatic in a wheelchair who suddenly shoots across the road in front of him. We park outside The Mildmay.

I am terrified - not because I dislike hospitals, although I do, or because I'm afraid of my reaction to the physical effects of AIDS but I am terrified that Tim will refuse to see me. To be rejected by a friend like Tim at this stage would be unbearable. I wait in the pleasant sitting area and smile at the nurses while Rob goes to see Tim and find out if Tim will let me visit him. When he returns it is alright: the nurses are with Tim but when they go he will see me. I feel so incredibly privileged. I still feel apprehensive in case I do the wrong thing, but I tell myself there are no right or wrong things to do in the face of death: he is still Tim, I am still I. The love between us is this strange warm emotion engendered from what? - Association - liking chocolate - liking Opera - liking swimming - liking each other - it's untouchable and inexplicable, our friendship. Rob takes me in, but he leaves us alone.

'Give us a kiss then' says Tim - it is a greeting and a challenge except it is the most natural thing in the world to kiss him and as I look at him weak in the bed such waves of pity and love come over me I would have climbed into bed with him if he had asked me. He is covered only with a sheet - his legs are very swollen with retained water and he has skin cancer but it is still Tim: his eyes are bright with determination to cling to life.

He apologises to me for having to wait outside the house the night before - I say it was OK as I had the Messiah. He asks who was singing. I didn't know as I hadn't heard the end. He directs me to the Radio Times 'virgin copy, as you see I haven't even opened it.' I come back with 'well you've done better than me, I haven't even bought one.' The singers include Anthony Rolfe Johnston. 'Oh, you know him.' 'No, Tim I don't.' 'You must do, you've worked with him.' Tim is getting angry. I think dramatically 'Oh God, I've come to see Tim on his deathbed and we are having an argument.' I am tempted to agree with him, but then realise that I would never give in if he were well, so battle on. 'Honestly Tim, I haven't.' He backs down, I'm glad I didn't give in. I sit on the bed and he asks me to hold his hand. How did he know how much I needed that contact - perhaps because he wanted it too. With some difficulty I find his hand under the sheets and hold it tightly. He says he is sorry that he kept it secret that he had AIDS but he was afraid he would lose his job at the Royal Opera House if word got out - he is glad it is out in the open now - 'No more deception anymore.' I realise he knows he is dying, he knows that I know he is dying: this is the most final goodbye we will ever make, but we are not going to say this. Instead we talk of Opera Productions and how he would have loved to have gone and worked with Friedrich in Berlin but couldn't and couldn't explain why and I tell him about Tokyo and how peculiar I felt there and wonder how I dare talk about feeling peculiar to him in his state. He gets tired and drinks some water and says I must talk for a while - I tell him about the small tour, and about Yol's successful kidney transplant and about Karin and Martin's baby - not due till January but they already know it will be a girl and her name will be

Sophie. I tell him these stories of hope in life not to emphasise his own condition but to try and give him some extra will to come through again. The doctors arrive and I have to go out while they talk to him - I find Rob and he takes me to the conservatory where I can have a cup of coffee and a cigarette. All I can say, unhelpfully is 'Oh God, Rob', and try not to cry. Rob tells me how wonderful Kate was with all the other patients while she waited for days to be allowed to see Tim but I am careless of the others; all my compassion is focused on Tim. I am allowed back. Tim tells me they are going to try some treatment for his legs; I nod and ask questions but we both know there is little point in this. I tell him Peter is staying in my house now as X had the decorators in and then decided she didn't want to share her house anymore. 'That bloody woman', he tries to shout, and croaks - 'I warned him about her.' Rob comes back - Barbara is here, my time is up. I say 'If I don't come back, Tim, it's because I'm stuck in the depths of bloody Wales.' I can hardly look at him now that I have to leave. 'Keep in touch through Rob', he asks. I promise I will. 'Take care' I look at him - how can he take care, but what can I say? I kiss him goodbye and leave.

On my way home I visit my lover and try to explain what it was like but I can't. We make love but the image of Tim lying on his bed comes between me and him. With sexual release come floods of tears also. My lover understands and lets me cry. I also visit the nuns and ask them to pray for a young friend of mine who is dying of cancer - a cowardly compromise.

Christmas Day and Following Days: I can't tell my family, it would only ruin their Christmas too. The image of Tim comes between me and all the festivities. I am glad I'm at home for only two days and back on the small tour Boxing Day in Brecon. I can't tell anyone on the tour either of course, although some of them know Tim well. I phone Rob from the callbox by the church in the pouring rain - I want to come and see Tim again as we have time off again after Brecon. Rob doesn't think it is a good idea - I get the impression Tim is deteriorating fast. The following day the shops are open and I am able to send Red Roses to Tim with a message 'Thinking of you all the time.' It is true, I can think of nothing and no-one else.

December 31st: At home with my mother again I phone Rob in the morning. His mother answers; haven't I heard. No. Tim died yesterday night. I put down the phone and seek solace with my mother - I now tell her about visiting Tim before Christmas. She always asked after him because he once wrote her a letter in praise of her Christmas cake. She shares my distress. Our cleaning lady is naturally curious that I am so upset - again cowardly I say a friend of mine has died of cancer. I tell my mother it was AIDS though.

Aftermath: Small tour - Aberdare. I still haven't been able to tell anyone on the small tour of Tim's death. I still feel sworn to secrecy although it must be in the public domain by now. I meet X in one of the dressing rooms - she has come to see the show. 'Julia, have you heard, our poor Tim.' 'Yes, I know.' I manage to escape - I cannot be comforted by someone he almost cursed in dying.

Small tour - Druidstone: A weekend in this wonderful place by the wild sea while we play Haverford-west. Getting drunk in the bar. The conversation turns to Staff Producers. I say Tim was one of the best ever. Ian Jones is sitting opposite me, he looks straight at me and says, very deliberately, 'Shame about Tim, isn't it?' They have all known for some time - Ian Douglas (Barbara's assistant) had come to Aberdare to tell them all and also to ask them to treat me with care. I am so relieved it is out in the open at last. The drink too helps release more pent up emotion - I am in floods of tears again. Y says 'was it your first AIDS victim.' I recoil from her - what difference does that make: I have lost one of my best friends - Ian Jones holds my hands to comfort me, and lets me talk it out. I am lucky to have such a friend with me.

Driving in my car I try to analyse why Tim and I were friends and wonder what happens to the love generated in such a friendship when one of the friends dies. I reason that the love goes on and thus we hold our friends in our hearts till <u>our</u> dying day. I keep my promise to keep in touch through Rob and so a deeper friendship builds with him.

Treorchy: Kate comes backstage - the first time we have seen each other since Tim's death. We just look at each other and our eyes fill with tears. 'We must talk', she says, but I know with her I will never be able to.

John Street: Back to the office to collect something I get this crazy notion that I must look in all Tim's old scores - afraid to find all his notation erased as permanently as he himself, but it is all there written as bold and strong as he himself was in life.

Spring: The golden rod that Tim gave me for my garden (and which he believed I had killed off) grows back strong and healthy as ever - a living memorial to a still enduring friendship.

December 29th: I returned to London in readiness to pay homage
to Tim. Within an hour of arriving home I spontaneously
decided to make my first visit to Epping Forest since the day
Tim's ashes were scattered. I asked Max to accompany me as I
was nervous of venturing alone into a dark remote forest; but
also of my reaction to the emotions I might find that I had
scattered along with Tim's remains nine months before. Over
the years Tim had collected seeds from the garden. There were
dozens and dozens of envelopes in a bag in the garage; I
emptied all the seeds and seed heads into a black rubbish sack
to take to High Beech. Sensitively Max brought the tape of Kiri
Te Kanawa singing 'Sanctus' with which The Royal Opera
Chorus had closed Tim's memorial service. Arriving in the
isolated car park we discovered that at night time it was the
local lovers' lane. Parking amidst the steamed up cars we set off
into the shadows. I led the way by torchlight, Max following
with Pasha. I couldn't recognise any feature; the leafless night
forest of winter bore no resemblance to the burgeoning forest of
the spring day when I had last walked these paths. After
walking for about ten minutes I knew we had to be close to the
spot. Always hiding, I had an image of Tim in substanceless
form watching us, darting unseen between the trees. Maybe we
should turn back and leave his forest home undisturbed; he
would hold the discovery of his resting place from us if he
didn't want to be found. A motorbike roared in the distance
comfortingly.

Chancing upon a track I followed it hopefully. Sure enough it
led to the clearing in the centre of which stood the beech tree,
the soil around holding Tim's ashes. I felt as I did the day I
brought Tim's things home from The Mildmay; I had truly come
home. Again as in the chapel with Sister Teresita I experienced
the effect of her faith, a faith I could still not say was mine; here
there was no pain, no grief, no suffering - only serenity. Talking
in whispers I didn't want to disturb the stillness. Max stood
aside respectfully with Pasha who seemed determined to
dispense profanity upon the Midwinter's Night play in

performance; pulling at his lead determined to try and urinate over the beech tree if given half a chance.

'Chaste goddess, who dost bathe in silver light
These ancient, hallowed trees,
Turn thy fair face upon us,
Unveiled and unclouded… Temper though the burning hearts,
The excessive zeal of thy people. Enfold the earth in that sweet peace
Which, through thee, reigns in heaven…'

Suzanne Murphy had already sung of this moment. Norma, the druid priestess enters a forest clearing in the centre of which is the sacrosanct Oak of Irminsul. As the moon rises she cuts the sacred mistletoe and then sings her prayer 'Casta Diva.'

Now I performed my own pagan ritual. I scattered seeds of the summer - sunflowers, mallows, cornflowers, poppies and many others around the beech tree. It wasn't just in The Mildmay's consecrated chapel but in a heathen clearing too that I could feel the blessing of Teresita's faith warming me as much as if it had been a hot summer's night instead of a cold night of winter. When we had gone Tim would leave the shadows and see the flowers grow; and again be enchanted as that day many years before when we had stopped on the motorbike midst a sea of flowers in an alpine meadow; Tim had stood apart from me and been enchanted. This was joyful grief for Tim. With no shadows in my voice I called his name once, this was my prayer, and we left as quietly as we had come.

Returning to the car I was horrified to see a police car enter the parking lot and drive through the parked cars. With blue light revolving and headlamps on full it picked us out emerging from the forest. We must have looked very suspicious; two men in black leather jackets, with a large black Labrador, torch in hand and empty black sack. Epping Forest was hardly the place to take a dog for a late night walk! What would I say?

Menacingly, tyres crunching, it approached us very slowly blinding us with its lights. My heart was in my mouth. Were we to be questioned? I imagined having to ring Shirley the next day to get her to validate my story. Almost upon us the police car unexpectedly spun around and accelerated away. We breathed a sigh of relief. 'Sanctus' restored harmony during the drive home. I lit the candle in the temple lantern to burn through the twenty four hours of December 30th. I had reached the threshold of the ultimate hurdle of the year.

December 30th: The day had a quality similar to that of September 12th; but whereas the day of Tim's memorial service was formal and public, December 30th was a private affair. Unexpectedly I received two cards acknowledging the anniversary of Tim's death. The first I opened was from Vicky - 'Just writing this to say I'm thinking of you, and know that it must be a difficult time now.' I much appreciated her missive of support, she acknowledging my love for Tim had survived his physical death aptly choosing a card titled 'Embrace' featuring two lovers hugging. The second was from 'All at Mildmay' featuring a dove of peace, the card titled 'Onward, Ever Onward.' Some people may think the first anniversary is unimportant, just another day. In fact it completes all anticipations stretching throughout the first year of bereavement; I had successfully navigated the emotional minefields of 1991. It's an opportunity to revisit the day of death as ones own witness; memories concur with the events of the day, the day is the same, the death is the same. But I am changed.

Late morning I set off for The Mildmay. Only now did a few hazy memories of Tim's last day of life more like dreams drift from my unconscious into my conscious thoughts.

Tim came out of a deep sleep and said, 'you've got to do something (to make me live)'. I could do nothing except love him. They were the last coherent words he spoke to me.

Maria met me outside the hospital coming to lend moral support; shortly afterwards Kate arrived from Wales wanting to pay her respects too. I placed a little vase of scented flowers at the foot of the altar that my mother had picked from her garden

- winter jasmine and pink viburnum flowers. She had written a few words commemorating Tim and stuck it to the vase expressing what everyone felt - 'with loving thoughts for Tim.' Every morning the hospital chaplain turns the page of The Book of Remembrance to tally with the calendar; and prayers are said for the deceased and their loved ones. There on the page December 30th lay Tim's name, alone; tangibility that this wasn't the passing of any ordinary day; that he will not be forgotten but remembered in the exquisite writing of the calligrapher. But I was shocked to see his name. He did come to terms with his illness but he died unwillingly and resentfully. What suffering he had to endure and the ultimate sacrifice of life itself to gain reluctant entry in this book. All I could see in his name was his desperate bid to defy this salutation posthumously conferred upon him. When life is done all that remains is the name. This was his headstone.

It was a meaningful moment but not the quiet one I had hoped for; unfortunately workmen were drilling nearby, the noise was relentless and deafening. Although I well accepted life and living go on hand in hand with death and private reverences, the thumping noise prohibited gentle memories surfacing.

As invited by one of the nurses ten days prior we visited The Elizabeth Ward. It was an inopportune moment, nurses bustled about feverishly. I sensed someone else was dying or had just died. We left on an anticlimax.

Even a drink at 'The Conqueror' adjacent felt like a commiseration of an unfulfilled visit. Maria went home; I accompanied Kate to Liverpool Street Station to catch her train home. While we were talking at the barrier I started to get angry - not at her but with her. I had no idea why. I felt dreadful for my unmannerly behaviour; though she didn't seem to mind or notice. I hadn't been alone the day Tim died, but with Kate's departure I was. The loneliness washed over me in waves as I made my way home on the No.6 bus. But December 30th far from being either a rich or demolishing experience was proving to be a non event. What was I expecting; a divine visitation, a supernatural revelation, a moment of thunder, a religious experience, a fanfare of trumpets, a chorus of angels? I didn't know what would feel right. This didn't.

Another blurred memory surfaced - of being at home mid afternoon with Hywel collecting something for Tim? I think I quickly ironed his navy blue pyjamas so he would have a clean pair for the next day.

Max returned later that afternoon having paid his respects at The Mildmay. He gave me a sensitively chosen present of 'The Year Book of Nature'. Reminiscent of our recent ploddings with Pasha through the wild sand dunes of Merthyr Mawr; the book symbolised not just the wonders of nature but the cycles of nature - life and death. For death there has to be life, for life death. The fated product of Tim's death was my bereavement - the emotional continuum between Tim's physical death and my physical life.

Early evening Julia rang and thanked me for my help and support throughout the year; that I had given her a lot of help with her grief for Tim and a focus! I was astounded! I was well aware I was pathologically introspective and wrapped up in myself; but I had lost sight of the fact I had any capacity to give to others. Something freshened within me.

Then Vicky rang. With her I held my anniversary confession. Balancing all the credits and debits of the year; the positives against the negatives, it was an emotional stocktaking.

I had done my best to fulfil legal and moral duties of executorship. I had successfully brought the house back to life, and reawakened myself as much as is possible within the first year cycle. Maria, Shirley, Gil had largely taken the place of all former friends; permanently or temporarily I did not know. I could not give Max the attentions or the commitment I had given to Tim; yet he had become the singularly significant gay man in my life since Tim; whether we moved away or towards an ultimate partnership I was extremely grateful to him for his friendship and companionship.

The three motorbikes would not be sold this first year. Additional heirlooms and pieces of furniture that had been too bulky to return with the car awaited collection in the garage. Matters would not be resolved with The Inspectors of Tax in respect of Tim's will, nor with the acting solicitor. I did not know my HIV status. Of Tim's family and for what he had hoped, the year was ending with a heavy list to the debit side.

But the all-embracing balance was that I had changed irrevocably from the person I had been one year before. If Tim materialised he would not find the person he had known the day he died; I had outgrown the 'me' I had been in our relationship, though not my love for Tim. More so I wouldn't want to return to the 'me' I had been prior to Tim's death despite the millstone of bereavement I still hawked about with me. I went to 'The Falcon & Firkin' to pass through the moment of the anniversary; to seek the environment which had been my only surviving reference point to normal life one year before.

Now I started to remember. My parents arrived at The Mildmay to give me some moral support. My sister had come ahead of them; in fact she was with Tim, his last visitor. I escorted my family back to the house and immediately returned to The Mildmay. 'It's Rob', said Tim's mother. He stirred and garbled something I could not understand; his mouth and throat were so dry he needed artificial saliva. I placed my hand on his hand and willed him to go, 'It's OK Tim, you've fought enough.' I was too distressed to share my distress with his mother. I squeezed his hand. He responded. This was my last moment with Tim. I knew. I didn't know. His hand slipped from mine. I pulled away and left.

I drove home. I sped past the house and parked at the bottom of the road. I needed to be alone. No I didn't want to be alone. I drove to 'The Falcon & Firkin.' 'By yourself tonight', smiled the pretty barmaid Sue. No I didn't want to be there either. I didn't want to be anywhere. Nowhere felt right. Everywhere felt wrong. I downed my pint of lager in seconds and left for home to wait with my parents for the midnight hour when I was to ring Debbie for an update of Tim's condition.

10.50. 'Last orders', called the barmaid. 10.50. 'He's just gone', Debbie said.

It had taken the full cycle of one year for my unconscious to find compatibility with my conscious; for the anniversary to release frozen memory. This year I was one of the stragglers leaving 'The Falcon & Firkin.'

Astonishingly at home there was a message on the answerphone from Tim's mother. A night she had an unquestionable right to think only of her lost beloved son; her own grief; she reached out to me to say I was in her thoughts this night. Almost breaking down herself; it was Tim's mother, the least likely candidate of all, with this compassionate gesture that proved the releasing factor of this day for me to pay my final lament of the year.

With the unexpected release of a few backlogged tears that I had been unable to cry the night Tim died, I selected the Mildmay card 'Rainbow of Hope.' In this moment, it dawned on me that though I'd been waiting for something to be given to me or granted to me, it was in fact something forged from within me that would provide the completeness to this day.

December 30th 1991

Dear Timmy,

I know you had to leave me, I know you didn't want too; I worried for you as you worried for me; but our time together had come to a close; but I will always love you as I know you will always love me. I miss you tonight Timmy - Tim - Tim, life is hard and seemingly pointless without you, the sun shines, flowers blossom, Pasha plays but there is a stillness where you no longer live. I hope you find a motorbike to explore the ether; ride free; shadow me.

all my love forever

Bonky x x x

Five minutes before I'd had no thought of writing to Tim.

The impulse and the words sprang from some deep unchartered fathom. Only he called me by my name. I would never hear the call of my name again. In the year long silence of my uncalled name I heard his goodbye. And my call of his name would remain forever unanswered. For the last time ever, I signed my nickname, my signature sealing and ending our relationship within its time; renouncing the one I had been up until the last day of his life one year before. Bonky was extinct too and with his 'death' there came an amelioration of the spirit. I'd said, 'Goodbye', for us both. I could now go on into my life.

Midnight passed. Once again it was the early hours of New Years Eve. It was time to go to bed. I put Pasha out into the garden. The flame had gone out in the temple-lantern; but Hope, Grace and Peace illuminated my heart. It was the eve of a new year for me - the second year of my second life was beginning.

Metamorphosis

Some things are lost painfully
Some things are lost reluctantly
Some things are lost wilfully
Some things remain, changed
Some things remain, unchanged.
There is space for new things
From that space self-realisation
Discovery

Rob Lewis
March 1992

CHAPTER 14

Epilogue

A barbarous force entered Tim's body in the form of the HIV virus. With Tim's HIV diagnosis threat and despair entered our home shattering our self-protected world of cultured order. I read every book and article I could find about HIV hoping to find a story telling of the discovery of a control or cure to restore balance to our lives; anything other than face the awesome power of death. Though I had been blessed with a fair intelligence, had a lovely home and sound relationship I found myself foundering, completely ill-equipped to deal with the implications of HIV.

We are continuously told of our rights - to me there are none. I believed I had a right to happiness - I did not. We had both left behind unhappy relationships, I'd recovered from a long illness, Tim had a new exciting job at The Royal Opera House, we were deeply in love with one another - our future looked bright; but it was not destined to be so. We each had to learn to live with adversity - Tim with his condition, me with his increasing bouts of anger which physically damaged our home and emotionally damaged our relationship bringing about our separation. It seemed barbarism had won but my love was greater than his anger and we were reconciled when he fell ill. Adapting to live with and survive his anger attacks that opposed every principle of civilised life was a learning and growing process for me that Gil singularly guided me through; so helping me to live with and survive my anger phase following his death which at times put me in a mood to kill. Now the restoration of peace and order to my life and home is my ultimate goal; and not without setbacks and difficulties it will be a continuous on-going process that will only end with me. The temple-lantern in my garden sanctuary is my symbol of hope winning against all forces of trial and trouble.

I see the microcosm of our little world expressed in the great world beyond my blue front door - the same triumvirate of cultured order, barbarism and sanctuary exist side by side not two miles away in The City; a symbol of sovereignty and might, it has been threatened by devastating bomb attacks by barbarians yet possesses the sanctuaries of many centuries-old churches including The Little Tower - merciful and forgiving establishments counteragents to the evil powers of greed, corruption and destruction bearing down on their old walls.

Ambition, law and order are important but they should not blind one in coming to terms with this unfriendly world. HIV is a lesson for Society, as was Titanic for 1912, reminding us of Man's frailty and subservience to the wild ungenerous forces of Mother Nature. But many people, if not most, are blinkered and fail to see this. Programmed to maximise efficiency and proficiency Modern Man concentrates on technological achievements and advances such as Concorde, the microchip, expanding computerisation and bar-coding as overly important - and misinterprets for Man's evolutionary progress. Whereas in fact Man of today is as contradictory as Man of Ancient Greece - cultured and ordered yet cruel and destructive, intolerant and prejudiced yet vulnerable and capable of deep emotional feeling. To have evolved to the refined state we imagine we occupy we should with every successive generation have increasingly lost the capacity for hatred, killing and unkindness. We have not. In reality Man's physical and emotional arsenal for war and destruction against his own kind is greater now than at anytime in history; yet profound feelings of love and heartbreak remain as potent as in the time of Aphrodite. In essence we have remained the same.

Five months after Tim died I was travelling along Threadneedle Street on a No. 6 bus going towards The Stock Exchange and Bank of England. I couldn't help but overhear a conversation between two bankers sitting in front of me. By the value system of our Society - emphasizing the want of power and money they had achieved success, and a presumed smug sense of security. Midst the imposing stone edifices of The City they were at the hub of one of Europe's most influential banking centres in both deed and being. I was not. I was on my way to see Gil at The Little Tower, centre track on the lonely road of bereavement with no mistaken sense of security - there being no such thing. All the reserves of The Bank of England couldn't buy me out of bereavement; but I was not oblivious to the warm touch of the afternoon sun on my arm.

The militarisation of The City following the IRA's bombings at the heart of power is the government's reaction to defy modern barbarism of Man versus Man. There has never been a day throughout history since the Ancient Greeks annihilation of The City of Melos 416 B.C. without war, terrorism, brutality, murder, etc. Yet we don't need to destroy ourselves; Mother Nature is quite happy to do it for us, HIV being 'her' newest and most insidious weapon in her offensive against Modern Man who seems remarkably, and arrogantly, untroubled by this menace. Maybe politicians and scientists will find a cure-all for warfare and disease; but death itself will not be conquered by the technocrats.

Our modern society is still reluctant to face and accept the phenomenon of death, despite its daily substance, as a normal part of life; and consequently is even less prepared to accommodate and understand the estate of grief - crosscurrents in our increasingly rationalised and regularised society. And when there is a valuable relationship be it between man and man, mother and daughter, sister and sister where one is destined to die, the other to live, the unsound value system of our society is exposed; it is frustrated it can not provide a remedy; that the press of a computer button can not rectify; and finds it hard to acknowledge that sometimes nothing can take the place of loss - did wealth, fame, applause, beauty, success, jewels, servants, possessions appease the loneliness and grief in the life of the Greek opera singer Maria Callas on the death of her lover? No.

For those of us who have experienced great loss it is for us to find a new value system to live by that will not mislead us - not to seek security or happiness (for happiness only occurs); but to understand that attendant to great sorrow are gleams of joy and the comforts of new companionship. The quality of relationships - be it the legacy of a great love lost, love in the seeking, new love found and held - remains the most important thing in the world.

In his appreciation of 'Medea' written nearly 2500 years ago by the Greek playwright Euripides, the modern translator Philip Vellacott reminds us that,

'The universe is not on the side of civilisation; and that a life combining order with happiness is something men must win for themselves in continual struggle with an unsympathetic environment.'

Dr. Veronica Moss
Former Medical Director at Mildmay Mission Hospital

I am writing in support of the author and to add my voice to many others who would wish to see this manuscript published as soon as possible. It is a courageous and beautifully written account of one gay man's bereavement experience through AIDS. It deserves to be published, but even more important, it needs to be published in order to enlarge the understanding of all those who become involved in the care of someone with a terminal illness, or in the support of those who grieve. It will also enlighten those with little understanding of loving gay relationships and of the deep hurts that may be inflicted on gay partners through fear, prejudice or ignorance.

Doctors, nurses and health care professionals everywhere would benefit from reading it's moving testimony to a loving relationship, and to the unique inter-disciplinary care offered to people with AIDS in Mildmay Mission Hospital, Europe's first AIDS Hospice. It opened to AIDS in 1988 and is now internationally recognised as a centre of excellence in AIDS care and education.

AIDS is sadly still on the increase in the UK, and is spreading in epidemic proportions in parts of Europe, Africa, Asia and the Americas. It is not confined to gay men and drug users but is rapidly becoming a major killer of women and children as well as heterosexual men throughout the world. Understanding individual perspectives, such as the one offered in this manuscript, will undoubtedly contribute a great deal to improvement in care for all patients with AIDS. It will also contribute to the public at large understanding issues which are still a mystery to the majority.

I have been involved from the start of Mildmay's AIDS care in the planning, implementation and development of its work. Mildmay pioneered AIDS palliative care through its inter-disciplinary team approach. I am involved in international consultancy and training courses (e.g. run by British Council in East Africa) and have also visited America, India and East Africa on study tours or teaching programme.

I co-authored the first book on Palliative Care in AIDS published by Edward Arnold. A second edition is due to be published in December.

I would strongly recommend this book to you for publishing.

Frank Romany
Lecturer and Tutor in English Literature
St. John's College Oxford

Rob Lewis has recently shown me the MS of The Fighting Temeraire. I read books for a living, and I found this one unusually, compellingly, readable. I read it on holiday - straight through, in two sittings, completely absorbed and frequently moved to tears by the candour and tough humility with which it chronicles his first year's bereavement.

'Grief,' he writes at one point, 'is a possession of the personality'; and in this may be a key to the book's strength. I can think of no other which describes so powerfully the disorientations of bereavement, or which tells you so clearly what it's like to have your life taken over by death. Reading the account of the partners' group in Chapter 6, for instance, I felt the resurgence of delayed grief he describes with uncanny vividness. But the book is also about the recovery of his own identity. He writes about the slow process of 're-awakening' and repossessing his home with a stylistic integrity - even, in the best sense, homeliness - that is profoundly moving. So too is the tact and dignity with which he describes his dealings with his late boyfriend's family. You read about his relations with them with the kind of anxiety about the outcome more usually associated with reading Dickens. This man's grief, then, is a possession of his personality in a different sense: his book allows the reader into the distinct emotional world of another human being. This is writing of great honesty and force; to read it is to have the range of one's humanity extended.

The month-by-month narrative is exceptionally faithful to the times and seasons of grief. As you read it, you find you are reconstructing the author's relationship with his dead partner, gradually, at the same times as he recovers his own memories. The reader shares his experience, finding patterns as he finds them. This is a considerable technical achievement, which reaches its climax in the 'December' Chapter where the past and its recovery in the present are deftly inter-woven. There are few writers who give you so accurately the <u>feel</u> of memory.

I very much hope this remarkable book will not long remain unpublished. Though I am not qualified to speak of its value for bereavement counsellors or those working with AIDS, I believe it would be of immense value to people - especially, though not exclusively, gay people - who have suffered a bereavement. It is certainly one of the most extraordinarily moving human documents I have ever read.

Geoff Warburton, Dr. of Psychotherapy
Head of Counselling at The Terrence Higgins Trust, 1992-1998
The national voluntary organisation leading the fight against AIDS

I feel blessed and honoured to have been given the opportunity to read this marvellous book. I also feel pleased that I have been asked for my view as an openly gay counsellor of people affected by AIDS.

I would dearly like to see this manuscript published. It is such an eloquent and hones description of gay bereavement - there is no book like it in existence. It confirms and values the experience of the many gay men that have experienced AIDS related bereavement and so boldly contradicts their dismissal through fear and prejudice.

The book beautifully and delicately depicts the emotional landscape of gay bereavement. As such I believe the book would be invaluable to HIV workers in understanding gay bereavement. More importantly the book, if made widely available, would be an enormous comfort to gay men bereaved through AIDS.

I experienced a whole rollercoaster ride or powerful emotion in response to the book. It restimulated some of the unresolved endings I have been left with and at the same time reminded me how to heal them - I am very grateful.

Psychoanalytic Perspective
of the Fighting Temeraire
by Stevie Holland

*T*he 'Fighting Temeraire' looks backwards through the lens of time through the eyes of a gay man now 55 then 31, from late mid-life to youth - the time span of a generation. It is a generation changed for ever by the face of HIV and AIDS, some like Rob afflicted at far too young an age by the death of so many friends and lovers. However no-one has been immune from its impact or consequences, even though many may have tried to distance themselves from its meaning. Of course the full ravaging force of its impact is still being felt within many developing countries, where retroviral drugs are not available and where the stigma and denial of the illness remains high.

The grief associated with debilitating illness and death unites all of these experiences of HIV and AIDS over thirty years. However, the additional stigma of and prejudice to homosexuality, distinguished the experience of Rob and his contemporaries, adding to the complexity of the expression of loss and grief. The Fighting Temeraire pays homage to this complexity.

It is a mesmeric story of one man's response to the death of his lover over the first year of loss. It was a profound loss inextricably linked to the barbs of so many other losses. It describes the ebb and the flow of the process of grief, its seasonal shifts of volatility and stagnation. It is both a unique account and yet speaks of a universal experience. Even though some may not share an understanding of all of the lyrics, they may tune in to the 'music' of its emotional rhythms as well as the wrench of the occasional counterpoints of distortion.

Although poets have written of both the rhythms and distortions of grief since time immemorial, it took the birth of psycho-analysis to begin to conceptualise its purpose and meaning. Freud (1917) in 'Mourning and Melancholia' set the ground for the study of bereavement, during a decade when millions suffered from the loss of loved ones, atrocious wounds and disability, and the more subtle losses of their own sense of integrity and selfhood. The actual trauma of loss was everywhere, but Freud focused on how people might recover from loss, making the distinction between the mourning of 'normal' bereavement and melancholia or pathological bereavement.

Melancholia was characterised by a lack of interest in the outside world, dejection, the loss of the capacity to care and love, an encapsulation and severing from themselves. In melancholia there may be an unwavering focus on the lost person, often idealising them, setting them forever in a halo of sentimentality, or the opposite reactive position of denial or erasure of all signs of physical or emotional connection with what has been lost. However they cannot think about what has been lost within themselves about their disconnection and discontinuity from themselves, the loss of their inner life. Freud introduced the term 'the work of mourning' to describe how the ego can free itself to seek life through reality testing, self exploration and understanding, whilst withdrawing their libido and separating themselves from the lost object.

John Bowlby, (1969) (1973) (1980) although steeped in the

Freudian psycho-analytic tradition sought to elaborate these distinctions of loss through research based exploration of attachment systems and relationships, in contrast to Freud's emphasis on internal libidinous drives. His famous trilogy on attachment, separation anxiety and loss, places the disrupted security of the loss of a loved person at the centre stage of internal life, the most intensely painful experience anyone can suffer. For Bowlby the process or 'work' of mourning takes place in the context of an attachment relationship with all the paradoxes and contradictions of that relationship. The related studies of his colleague Colin Murray Parkes (1972), suggested that the work of mourning goes though a number of distinctive phases over time: numbing initially, followed by intensely painful and angry yearning and searching for the lost person, leading to disorganisation and despair when the permanence of the loss is realised and accepted, and eventually a period of healing and greater engagement with life. If the mourning is not successful, by becoming perpetually stuck or blocked, then reorganisation of both internal and external life is adversely affected. Although the process offers a broad brush stoke of pattern, there are blurred edges and oscillations within it, and both Bowlby and Parkes also emphasise that it is not just played out on the inner stage, but that other influential attachment figures help or hinder the bereavement process. This is particularly relevant for bereaved children but also for adults; the understanding and mind of another can help that of the bereaved, helping them to find feelings and words.

The Fighting Temeraire is a rich, sensitive and eloquent account of this man's own first year of mourning. It demonstrates how the intense pain and anger felt by Rob shifted in focus within the seasons of grief. For instance, his initial anger with his partner for being ill and leaving him, contrasts with his later anger at the humiliating and dismissive responses of his partner's family to him personally. Although clearly in pain and vulnerable, they appeared unable to cope with and accept the reality of their son's sexuality and love for another man. There is grief here about so many losses, in which the non-recognition and acceptance of the love of one man for another plays a significant part and adds another layer for the work of healing to do. The hugely important acceptance and understanding of his therapist, eventually provided a trusted secure base Bowlby (1988) for the beginning of an honest 'working through' to be achieved and resilience found.

It doesn't matter whether you are gay or straight when you read this book, although those who have been affected by the additional prejudice may feel additionally understood. To be human is to grieve - we love and have to lose that love and yet can both lose and retain all that the loved one meant to us in our hearts and minds. In so doing we can recover our ability to know and be ourselves in all our complexity, and love again.

Like bereavement itself the Fighting Temeraire is moving and painful. It also pulses with life-giving honesty.

Bowlby, J. (1969) *Attachment and Loss Vol 1 Attachment*, London, Hogarth Press.
Bowlby, J. (1973) *Attachment and Loss Vol 2 Separation, Anxiety and Anger*, London, Hogarth Press.
Bowlby, J. (1980) *Attachment and Loss Vol 3 Loss, Sadness and Depression*, London, Hogarth Press.
Bowlby, J. (1988) *A Secure Base*, Harmondsworth, Penguin
Freud S (1917) *Mourning and Melancholia*, Standard Edition 14 237-58, London, Hogarth Press.
Parkes CM (1972) *Bereavement*, London, Tavistock Publications

Stevie Holland Psychoanalytic Psychotherapist BPC Registered

About the author

ROB LEWIS was born in Cardiff in 1957. He was brought up in Penarth, South Wales. He moved to London in 1985 where he has lived since and maintains a strong connection with Wales. He began his counselling training at the Westminster Pastoral Foundation in 1995, and later went on to do a further training to become a Psychotherapist. He has a private practice in Holborn in Central London.

He was first published in the Guardian Newspaper in 1982 in a series of articles about Teenage Depression. He had his first short story 'The Singer & The Storm' published in 1987 in The International P.E.N. Magazine.

www.roblewis-publishing.com
info@ roblewis-publishing.com

2874960R00196

Printed in Great Britain
by Amazon.co.uk, Ltd.,
Marston Gate.